THE CHRISTIAN CHALLENGE
TO PHILOSOPHY

THE
CHRISTIAN CHALLENGE
TO PHILOSOPHY

By the late

W. H. V. READE
Sometime Fellow of Keble College, Oxford

With a preface by
CYRIL BAILEY

LONDON
S · P · C · K
1951

952

First published in 1951
by S·P·C·K
Northumberland Avenue, London, W.C.2

Printed in Great Britain by
Richard Clay and Company, Ltd., Bungay, Suffolk

PREFACE

IN every generation of University teachers there will always be some who are not widely known as writers or lecturers, and have yet had a deep influence on the institutions to which they belonged, on their personal friends and their pupils, and through them on a wider circle. The author of this book was one of these. No one who came across him could be unaware of his ability, his wit, and his sincerity. But a genuine self-depreciation and a certain natural shyness kept him very much within the walls of Keble College, and even in Oxford there were many who after his death wished that they had known him better. A similar self-limitation set bounds to his intellectual range; philosophy and the Christian tradition of the Church were the mainsprings of his thought and inspired his books and his teaching.

William Henry Vincent Reade was born on January 13, 1872. His father, the Rev. Henry St John Reade, a nephew of Charles Reade, the novelist, was a classical scholar of distinction and captained the Oxford cricket team in 1863. In 1875 he was appointed Head Master of Oundle School and quickly raised the numbers from about 30 to 250. The death of his elder brother in 1881 left him the possessor of a considerable estate at Ipsden in Oxfordshire. To this he retired in 1883, but died, still a young man, in 1884. He had married the grand-daughter of Dr. Vincent, Dean of Westminster and a distinguished geographer. There were four children, of whom " Billy ", as he was universally known to friends and pupils, was the second; his elder brother, Herbert, entered the Civil Service, and won a considerable reputation as a mountaineer and a pioneer of guideless climbing.

Billy thus inherited a tradition of scholarship, churchmanship, and cricket, and they all played a part in his life. He won a scholarship at Marlborough, but after a few terms was transferred at his own request to Oundle, after his father's death. He became the mainstay of the School cricket eleven as a medium-paced bowler and a useful bat, and was also the leading scholar of his time. In 1891 he came up to Balliol as a Classical Exhibitioner. It was a distinguished year, and among his intimate friends were Nugent ("Bumbo") Hicks, afterwards his colleague at Keble and subsequently Bishop of Gibraltar and later of Lincoln, and (Sir) Arthur Pickard-Cambridge, Fellow of Balliol and later Vice-Chancellor of Sheffield.   Among the scholars of the College his acute mind and whimsical humour found natural scope and widened interest.   His cricket, too, brought him friends in a wider circle, and almost in spite of himself, he blossomed into a recognized popularity. In due course he obtained his firsts in Classical Moderations and in Lit. Hum., and took his B.A. in 1895, a marked man in a brilliant year.

For a short time after his degree Reade was an assistant master at Malvern; it was characteristic that when he later became a Governor of the College, he took and maintained a deep interest in its affairs. But his life's work was at Keble, where he was Tutor in Philosophy from 1897 till his retirement in 1937.   He became one of the original Fellows of the College after it received its new constitution in 1931, was Sub-Warden in 1924 and acted also as Dean and Librarian.

In his earlier years at Keble, when he was near the undergraduates in age, he gave them a new conception of a don and acted as a link with the Senior Common Room.   One of his first pupils says:

> " We saw at once that Billy was different from the others.   He seemed to us more human than the rest of the rather bleak men who were entrusted with our education.   Of them all he was the least professional: there lay for us his greatest charm.   He was— or at least appeared to be—entirely casual, and in this respect also (being undergraduates) we hailed him as a man and a brother. He dealt with us as if he were of the same age as ourselves, and would sit quite happily at a ' squash ' of a dozen or fifteen of us in a room which would comfortably hold five or six, listening to ' The Song of Hybrias the Cretan ' or the drinking-song from ' The Rose of Persia ' and sipping college whisky, with no apparent physical or æsthetic discomfort.   With his colleagues he gradually won his way and got most of the things he wanted.   He could not bear breakfasting in Hall with the undergraduates, and it was he who was responsible for the dons taking the meal in their own Common Room.   Nor did he appreciate what seemed to him the quite unnecessary austerity of the High Table dinner in Hall.   He was fond of good food and wine, and it was not long after his arrival that there began to appear strange and succulent puddings on the High Table menu."

In the discharge of College offices he was always imperturbable and just.   As Dean he preferred a friendly remonstrance to an official rebuke.   His sound judgement, good humour, and ready wit helped many discussions in College to a satisfactory conclusion.   The same qualities showed themselves in the University during his Proctorship in 1913–14, and in the Diocese on many of its important Committees.

Later on Reade gradually withdrew into his shell, though there were still occasions when his gaiety asserted itself. In the Senior Common Room his conversation was always witty and cultured; he showed little interest in gossip or trivialities. Similarly, though few of his pupils became intimate with him, many will have happy recollections of him as their host in his rooms, of his little asides and amusing comments. Over a game of Bridge he could become "almost boyish". Still more would he unbend when each year in his younger days he would take a carefully selected cricket team to play against a Gloucestershire village, when he was perfectly at ease with the local side. Nor was he ever happier than in the Devonshire village of Brendon, where he spent many of his vacations, often alone.

As tutor he was always at his best with the abler men, who could appreciate his learning and his habit of approaching a subject from an unexpected angle. To others he sometimes appeared remote; his natural shyness was a bar, and he would receive an essay with a silent pause and then state his own views without much reference to what his pupil had said. He did not care for the thrust and cut of argument. But when his pupils got to know him, they began to listen and to realize that what he said was "good stuff". Imperceptibly he conveyed to them something of his own interest in philosophy, especially where it bordered on theology. His lectures seemed in the same way remote, but a course on political philosophy made a great impression on his hearers.

Reade was a great lover of music and an assiduous attendant at public concerts in the Sheldonian or the Town Hall, and at weekly meetings of the Oxford University Musical Society. But his chief devotion was to Church music, in which both the religious and æsthetic sides of his nature were satisfied. In his undergraduate days he would often be found at evensong in Magdalen Chapel, " sitting as far as possible from everybody, apparently quite impassive, whatever the music ". In later years, after his Keble friend, Henry Ley, became organist there, his loyalty was transferred to Christ Church, and " he was constantly to be seen in the darkened Latin Chapel, listening to the music as it penetrated through the forest of pillars from organ loft and choir stalls ". He formed a close acquaintance with the Cathedral Choir School, where he was always a welcome guest. For several years in the twenties he would write short plays, " intimate and imaginative works ", which the boys performed on the Hall steps at Keble, being afterwards regaled in the Senior Common Room. In this love of beautiful music Reade revealed himself, though always with characteristic restraint and absence of visible emotion.

After his retirement from Keble under the age-limit in 1937, he lived with his sister Mary at the Dower House in the village of Wytham, two miles out of Oxford—an unspoilt country village under the famous woods of Wytham Abbey. There with occasional visits to Oxford, usually to hear music, he enjoyed the country, read, and wrote and worked at the present volume. He died on December 16, 1943.

Reade's character, of which some indication has been given, is not easy to describe. All who knew him would agree in appreciating his learning, his wit and wisdom, the sparkle of his conversation, his personal charm, and his deeply religious nature. But equally they would describe him as retiring, shy, detached, even aloof and remote. One who knew him well for many years has attempted to sum it up, and some quotations from his account may serve to form a more definite picture.

" He was not easy to know. Even to his friends he seldom revealed himself at all intimately; to his acquaintances never. By nature reserved and in manner somewhat diffident and shy, he had an air of detachment that was frequently mistaken for deliberate indifference or casual aloofness by those who met him. . . . Yet his companionship was a delightful, engaging and unforgettable experience. . . . His appearance of impassivity barely disguised his deep love of beautiful music, and indeed of all lovely things, such as the grandeur of Exmoor, his second home; the cities and picture galleries of Italy, and in particular of Florence itself, naturally enough in so distinguished a Dante scholar. . . . He was completely master of himself; never at a loss, never surprised or agitated but always cool, patient and unusually clear and concise. His constancy towards his friends was steadfast; he never changed. His humour, wit and powers of objective criticism made all conversation with him a delight. He was eclectic, somewhat fastidious in his tastes, but entirely unobtrusively so. . . . He had strong emotions and deep feelings, but these he kept under an almost Stoic control throughout his life. Yet he somehow managed to convey, even if only to a few, the warmth and depth of those feelings. He carried diffidence almost to a fault, being wholly incapable of pushing himself or stressing his claims. If ever he were slighted, a shrug of the shoulders, a laconic and

perhaps caustic utterance, with a twinkle in his eye, would be his
sole rejoinder. He was most discerning and penetrating in his
judgement—probably because of the obvious integrity of his mind
and character. He was a most engaging, and, if he wished,
brilliant letter writer—always the exact word, the terse and telling
phrase, the subtle observation. . . . I never heard him say, even
under great provocation, anything unkind or ungenerous about
other people. I believe it was fundamentally his strong Christian
convictions that gave him this generous quality of character. He
seldom spoke of religion, though in some of his letters he wrote
impressively about it. But nobody who knew and understood
him could doubt the reality and strength of his faith and beliefs.
It was this above all which accounted for the remarkable and
profound influence that Reade held over colleagues, friends and
pupils during all his years at Keble.''

It is time to turn from the man to his writings. Soon after taking
his degree Reade began a series of visits to Italy, usually in the Easter
vacation. I had the good fortune to be his companion on one of these
and to realize his deep interest in the country and its civilization. He
came to know it well, its cities and towns and people, its language
and its literature. From the first he formed a special love for Dante
and learned to know him with a rare intimacy. This led to a close
study of S. Thomas Aquinas and the scholastic philosophy, which he
always related to the Plato and Aristotle, familiar to him in his
Oxford teaching. He joined the Oxford Dante Society, which
contained such eminent members as Paget Toynbee and Edmund
Moore, and was for many years its Hon. Secretary. He wrote many
papers on Dante and kindred subjects, which appeared in various
periodicals, and gave many distinguished lectures. A paper in the
Journal of Theological Studies in 1925 on '' Intellectual Toleration in
Dante '' revealed his intimate knowledge of Dante's views and their
sources, but probably his most important contributions in this field
came later in life. In 1926 he gave a lecture to the University of
Manchester on '' Dante's Preparation for the Divine Comedy '', in
which he demonstrated the reasons for the poet's choice of language—
the *Volgare mediocre*—metre and manner. '' Dante's Vision of
History '', the *Annual Italian Lecture* delivered to the British Academy
in 1929, shows an equally intimate acquaintance with medieval history
and with the view taken of it by Dante and his contemporaries. In
1929 he published *The Moral System of Dante's Inferno*, which at

once placed him among the most eminent of English Dante scholars. He based his account so closely on S. Thomas that one reviewer was led to say " Mr Reade is a Thomist first and a Dantist afterwards ", a description which he would not have been likely to accept himself. The book was hailed by others as " much the most important original contribution to the study of Dante that has appeared for many years ". His studies in this region were completed by a notable preface to an edition of the *De Monarchia* and a brilliant chapter on " Medieval Philosophy " in the *Cambridge Modern History*.

In a wider field Reade often contributed articles to Church papers, and particularly to *The Guardian*, on such subjects as " The Old-fashioned Christmas " or " The Genius of English Religion ".* An attack on the services in Cathedrals and Colleges and the expense of their upkeep provoked him in 1923 to a series of three articles on " The Choral Foundations in the Church of England ", in which he repeated the argument that such services had an æsthetic rather than a religious value, admitted their cost, but compared the alabaster box of ointment. *Church and State* in 1923 covered a good deal of historical ground traversed in his earlier writings, but is a clear-cut statement of the modern problem. In 1919 immediately after the First World War Reade published a small book called *The Revolt of Labour against Civilization*. It is in tone slightly pessimistic and perhaps ultra-conservative, but very remarkable in its clear perception that the real enemy of European Civilization was to be not Germany but Russia.

His one contribution apart from reviews to strictly philosophical literature was *The Problem of Inference* in 1938. Characteristically he bases his contentions on Plato and Aristotle, and a reviewer in *The Times Literary Supplement* held that this was " an inauspicious beginning ", but that " he overcomes his handicap . . . by his outstanding capacity for investing the obviously dry bones of Greek philosophy with modern garments ". A more sympathetic critic in the *Oxford Magazine* thought that just for the reason of his classical background " his work may have a wider appeal than the esoteric doctrines conveyed through the abstractions of symbol and formula; the book is at once so delightful and so wise ". Here is the secret of Reade's writings; they are wise, the result of long study and thought, and they are delightful, because of the clarity and beauty of his style and the wit and humour which are always bursting through.

---

* The Editor of those days says that he often received letters asking who was this brilliant writer whom he had discovered.

The present work, which was written after his retirement to
Wytham, is the outcome of a life spent on the problems of philosophy
and the Christian religion; it results in the definite conclusion that
philosophy alone is not a sufficient account of truth or an adequate
guide to life—Christianity at once makes clear and makes good its
deficiencies. The central chapters, which cover some of the ground
in Reade's previous works, deal with much learning with the history of
the relations of the two studies and of their conflict through the ages.
The general reader will be more attracted by the first chapter and the
last four, which are more directly relevant to the difficulties and
discussions of the modern world. I am neither a philosopher nor a
theologian, but as a Christian layman I have found the book full of
suggestion and of the kind of thought which a layman can readily
understand. It is learned and wise, but always attractive in its lucidity
and in the occasional outburst of a dry and quiet wit, completely
characteristic of the " Billy ", whom with many others I loved and
respected.

CYRIL BAILEY.

CONTENTS

1

The Death of Greek Philosophy

THE official demise of Greek philosophy, announced by order of Justinian in the year of grace 529, was an event of profound significance in the spiritual history of mankind. By the general public, indeed, it may have gone almost unremarked. We hear of no solemn ceremony, no dirge or funeral oration. Who delivered the last lecture within the venerable precincts of the Academy, what was his theme, or what manner of audience he addressed, are questions with no recorded answers. And when the inevitable straggler—the man who always lingers behind to pose the lecturer with some impertinent objection—had reluctantly vanished, in what style did the curtain fall? Once more history is silent, but somehow I picture to myself an atheistical charwoman, flicking the dust off the benches from sheer force of habit, locking the door for the last of a thousand times, and then, with one huge contemptuous yawn, drifting homewards to whatever was the Athenian substitute for tea. To some such profane accompaniment may the affronted shade of Plato have been driven from its familiar haunts.

What was it, thus, that perished? On what grounds may one reasonably assert that the closing of the Academy, after nine centuries of continuous activity, was at least symbolic of a great revolution? The Academy, as we know, had not consistently upheld the doctrines of its founder. It was captured and long occupied by professors of the " Academic or Sceptical Philosophy ", which might, perhaps, claim descent with bar sinister from the Socratic criticism, but was certainly far removed from the inspiration of the *Phædo*, the *Symposium*, or the *Republic*. In due time, however, the second great edition of Platonism was published, and under the influence of Plotinus and his disciples not only did the Academy revert at last to its old allegiance, but nearly all the enduring notes of Greek speculation were absorbed in the prevailing harmony, so that a ban on the teaching of Platonism amounted to nothing less than the formal prohibition of all the philosophy originating in the pagan world. Even with this enlargement of its immediate reference, the full significance of Justinian's act may easily be missed. There is clearly a sense in which the genius of Plato and Aristotle, of Zeno and Epicurus, could not be extinguished by any important decree; a sense, too, in which some of their doctrines may still be affirmed, or at least seriously examined. Every philosophical renascence has owed something to these ancient masters, and even when a new movement of thought has taken the form of rebellion against the authority of tradition, it has never been denied that the Greeks did, after all, invent philosophy, and did in a general way understand the nature of its business. Nevertheless, there was, I believe, in the fiat of Justinian a genuine intimation of finality, a sign that not merely the Academy of Plato, not merely the Neoplatonism which had so largely reconciled the tenets of rival schools, but philosophy itself, as conceived and practised in the ancient world, had passed away.

> Le quattro chiare stelle,
> Che vedevi staman, son di là basse,
> E queste son salite ov' eran quelle.

Thus does Virgil briefly and symbolically expound to Dante (Purg. VIII. 91–3) the nature of the revolution. The four stars, whose beams had sufficed to adorn the head of Cato (Purg. I. 37), are the four cardinal virtues, but when these had waned, with the rising of the more illustrious three, Greek philosophy, in its proper character, was doomed. Revivals there might and would be, but each in its turn has proved to be a transformation; and while we continue to recognize the existence of " philosophy ", we fail to perceive that what we honour with that designation would, in the eyes of Plato or Plotinus, be little more than the shadow of a name.

And here again, if we are disposed to pass judgement on the act of Justinian, we have to beware of misconception. That the emperor was moved by his regard for Christian orthodoxy is indubitable, and without injustice, therefore, the Greek philosophers may be described as victims of persecution. But if we proceed to deplore the extinction of independent philosophy, and if by " independent " we mean to denote a philosophy outside the influence of any theology or religion, we shall seriously misrepresent the facts. Not only shall we be antedating by many centuries the conscious attempt to distinguish the provinces of faith and reason, but in effect we shall be confessing our failure to understand the meaning and status of philosophy, as the Greeks had practised it for more than a thousand years. The vital point is that philosophy was *not*, in the sense implied, " independent ". On the contrary, it was inseparable from " theology ", and even (though for reasons that require separate consideration) from the pagan religion which most of the Greek philosophers had come to regard with indifference or disdain. Had philosophy been a thing entirely apart from religion, its suppression would have been merely a senseless act of despotism, wholly foreign to the character of Justinian. In fact, however, the imperial decree was equivalent to a declaration that of two religious systems demanding the allegiance of mankind there was only room within the Roman Empire for one. Moreover, there was a fine touch of irony in the situation, for who can doubt that the author of the *Republic* and the *Laws*, had he been armed with the powers of a Roman emperor, would promptly have destroyed or banished any system of philosophy incompatible with the religion authorized by the State ? It was Plato who invented persecution, and if that unhappy expedient, which for him was only utopian, got converted one day into an actual instrument of policy and directed against the Platonists, the Platonists, surely, were the last people who had a right to complain.

If this interpretation of a famous incident is to be justified, we must turn now to direct consideration of a preliminary question. To present the philosophy of Plato (or Plotinus) and the religion of Justinian as rival claimants to spiritual empire is to suggest that, in the sixth century at any rate, they could reasonably be compared, that however incompatible in their specific doctrines, they were not wholly disparate in kind. But this, of course, is to imply that Christianity (its creed, its theology, its way of life) can properly be described as a philosophy, and again, that Platonism can assume the character of a religion. Now either of these implications may be sharply disputed. In histories of philosophy the Christian religion (apart from occasional remarks about its " ethics ") finds no regular place; nor is Platonism commonly numbered with the religions. Yet the propriety or impropriety of comparing the two systems cannot clearly be determined until we examine more closely the meaning of " philosophy " itself.

By way of preface, I must formally reject the pretence of discovering the " correct " interpretation of this famous term by means of its etymology or by appealing to its original sense. There are cases, indeed, when etymological structure and original usage are so closely allied that the bare analysis of a name into its elements may seem to disclose its primary intention. Yet no sooner do we inspect one or two notable illustrations of this evident alliance than we perceive the complete futility of attempting thus to stabilize dogmatically the meaning of any term with a long and important history. Take the single example of " geometry ". The name has endured for some

B

twenty-five centuries, but during almost the whole of that time its patent etymological sense has been entirely obsolete. As soon as the Greeks converted into science some old Egyptian dodges for the measurement of land—as soon as " space " was substituted for " earth " —the original meaning was superseded; and now that space itself has almost to struggle for existence, the only reason, presumably, for the survival of " geometry " is that the invention of a new name would be more trouble than it is worth. The case of " philosophy " is rather less remarkable; for, though its etymology is simple, its earliest usage (not too easily determined) was probably untechnical, and therefore none of its subsequent variations has involved a complete revolution. Variety, however, there certainly has been, and here, as in so many similar cases, we have a perfect right to maintain that a term does mean whatever it has meant in the course of its history, and therefore to deny that the usage prevalent in any particular epoch is decisive. To discover the true conception of a science, or the true significance of a concept, may require the passage of many centuries, and long before they are exhausted it may well appear that the original name commemorates only a blunder or a primitive superstition. My excuse for this small digression is that I do in fact propose to understand " philosophy " in the sense most obviously suggested by its etymology; not, however, because it is original, but simply because I believe that all genuine philosophy is an attempt to answer that most searching question—" O where shall wisdom be found ? " It is not, of course, by any Greek author that the challenge is thus precisely expressed, but, because in effect the Greek philosophers always had it in mind, they did, I believe, always hold fast to the essential meaning of philosophy. Their final answer was that wisdom was to be found in something like the message of Plotinus. Justinian, on the other hand, could find it only in the Christian gospel, and this conviction he declared in the act of authority which closed the Academy and scattered its inhabitants abroad.

But here again we are confronted with the difficulty of a term that lacks authoritative definition. Before embarking upon the pursuit, or even the discussion, of " wisdom " we seem to require an intelligible notion of it, but at the same time we have to beware of too definite preconceptions. As contrasted with " geometry " and the like, " wisdom " has no obvious etymology or original sense. It has also little technical history, but there is just enough guidance in philosophical literature, supplemented by common opinion, to justify one or two preliminary reflections. First of all, it is well to note that wisdom cannot lightly be identified with knowledge, and certainly not with any one of the special branches of knowledge which in course of time have secured recognition. As it happens, a formal distinction between " wisdom " and " knowledge " is made by Aristotle in the *Nicomachean Ethics* (Bk VI), and, in so far as he restricts " knowledge " to the limited province of demonstrative science, his reasons for assigning a more comprehensive and more exalted sense to " wisdom " are evident. A full investigation of Aristotle's position would take us, however, too far afield, and in the end it would be impossible, without some equivocation, to express in his terminology a problem that could not acquire its full dimensions in the fourth century B.C. In naming wisdom, rather than knowledge, as the goal of philosophy I purpose to leave room for the criticism, the valuation, and conceivably the rejection of every kind of specialized knowledge; not, however, for the sake of mere scepticism, but because any science, no matter how valid and authentic within its own department, must take another great and hazardous step forward if it would claim to be identical with the supreme wisdom by which the value of all things is tested and the truth or falsity of every doctrine revealed. In thus providing for the liberty of criticism I do not exclude *a priori* the possibility that the last word may rest with some kind of " expert ", but what I do contend is that, in order to make good his claim, he will have to go beyond his professional competence. To maintain that any one kind of knowledge is the very sum of wisdom, is to argue that all others are not, and this means that the expert will have to pronounce many judgements beyond the scope of his proper authority.

To some extent this right of appraising various kinds of knowledge from a point of view other than the expert's has always been assumed by those calling themselves philosophers, and this is one reason for their unpopularity, especially in modern times. In the days of Aristotle, and still more in the Middle Ages, it was possible for a man of genius and energy to cover the whole field of knowledge. To-day that is utterly impossible, and the greater the multiplication of the sciences the more absurd does it seem to attempt a valuation of them from an outside point of view. But, while the contempt of the professional for the amateur is only natural, it is easy to show that the possession of expert knowledge is often a very poor qualification for estimating its worth. Leave the sciences for a moment and take an illustration of Socratic simplicity. Find a cobbler and a hatter, and inquire of them what instruction they can offer, and how their respective trades compare in relation to wisdom. Would you learn how to make a shoe or a hat ?

Here, beyond question, are the masters. Would you know whether your own hats and shoes are skilfully made? Again the experts will not fail you. Take next a finer point, and ask whether certain styles are fashionable. Once more you will get an answer, but if your trades-men chance to be of the humbler sort, it may be a shade less confident. Go one step farther, and pray them to decide whether the most fashion-able style is also the most beautiful, and will you then feel bound to accept the craftsmen's verdict? Finally, pit one against the other, and bid them estimate the relative importance of hats and shoes in the economy of human life, or the value of their respective forms of skill as aids to the possession of wisdom. By this time, surely, you will have reached a point at which the hatter and the cobbler will be getting a little out of breath. It may be objected, of course, that these are modest folk, not to be compared with men of loftier understanding who deal with things more excellent than leather and felt. But is there any difference in principle? The eminent mathematician will doubtless seem to have a better pretext than the fashionable shoemaker for counting his own kind of knowledge sufficient, but is it not also possible that he may be the more deeply deceived?

If the "wisdom" for which we are searching is not the property of any limited science, it is even more important to understand that "philosophy" is not to be identified with any of its own departments, as conventionally distinguished, nor even, perhaps, with all of them taken together. The history of these subdivisions is somewhat con-fusing; terminology has fluctuated, and one of the most famous names, "metaphysics", was not definitely established until many centuries after the general character of the problems thus eventually designated had been recognized in practice. For our present purpose, however, many of the details are unimportant. It is enough that terms like "logic", "metaphysics", "ethics", "politics" have become familiar, and that any modern student, about to embark on a course of philosophy at the university, or perhaps only with the help of a library catalogue, will find the subject neatly arranged under these different headings. It is true, again, that the boundaries of the several depart-ments have never been fixed; indeed, they have been almost as fluid as territorial domains in the Balkan peninsula. Logic, reduced at one time to a verbal exercise, at another has swallowed up metaphysics and posed as the immanent law of the cosmos; ethics has now been identified, now violently contrasted, with politics; while psychology may be anything from a dubious branch of physiology to a consummation of all intellectual disciplines and a panacea for all human ills. Despite this perpetual skirmishing, the main partitions continue to be recognized, as we may easily ascertain, if further evidence be needed, by consulting an index of books published under the head of " philosophy " within the last twenty or thirty years. Obviously, too, there are reasons for some such discrimination, for no one would propose to discuss in the same chapter the technique of syllogism and the meaning of right and wrong. Yet the result of this progressive specialization of departments has been to obscure the main question, to reduce philosophy to a collection of quasi-sciences, or perhaps to build up a hierarchy, in which the metaphysician speaks *ex cathedra* to a number of inferior ministers who hang about the doors of the temple. What I desire, therefore, to contend is that philosophy, as the pursuit of wisdom, must be as free to scrutinize, appraise, and, if need be, reject these reputed parts of itself as it is to deny that physics or biology can discover the secret of the universe and govern the whole conduct of life. Nor is this the whole of the matter. We shall not fully understand what is meant by the quest of wisdom until we envisage at least the possibility that " philosophy " itself, as the term has now come to be used, may be a spurious claimant to an inheritance not its own. And that is why Justinian's suppression of the Academy was so momentous, because it signified the death of something which has never, under the name of philosophy, been perfectly revived.

Whereas in the Græco-Roman world philosophy, no matter what its precise intellectual basis, was always considered a way of life, in the modern world it is only a " subject " which may or may not be " taken up ", as at certain universities it is taken up for examination by undergraduates with the prospect of thus getting a degree. Of these novices the majority, perhaps, are only bored and bewildered, but many are interested for a year or two, while a very few are moved to persevere in the study, and even to adopt it as their professional business. An adequate supply of teachers is thus maintained, and books about philosophy—often the work of exceedingly able men—continue to enjoy a modest circulation. Nowhere, however, is there anything that closely resembles the act of becoming a Platonist, a Stoic, or an Epicurean in the conditions of the ancient world. To find a rough parallel to membership of one of the Hellenic schools we must look rather to the experience of a convert to some religious sect. " You said of a man that he was a Stoic or an Epicurean, as you say of a man now that he is a Calvinist or a Wesleyan." Disraeli was not expert in the history of the subject, but in this statement (from his early novel, *Venetia*) he illustrates his curious knack of hitting the mark. Doubtless there are flaws in the analogy, nor must we imagine, of course, that all who professed and called themselves Stoics or Epicureans took their profession seriously. Idle curiosity, deference to intellectual fashion, solemn humbug are common in every age; but when due allowance is made for the foibles of human nature, it remains true that swearing allegiance to Zeno, or whichever master it might be, was more nearly analogous to the adoption of Methodism or Calvinism than to taking up philosophy, in the twentieth century, as a subject for examination, or even as a professional career. " On the study of Philosophy as an Instrument of living " is one of the headings in Dr Johnson's *Prayers and Meditations* ; and after the prayer is added the laconic note, " This subject was not pursued ". Johnson's own repute for wisdom is not thereby impaired, but when philosophy ceases to be an " instrument of living " and becomes a " subject ", its proper genius is dead.

From these preliminary considerations two points of importance emerge: first, that this pursuit of wisdom implies the power of human reason to gauge the worth of its own products, and thus in some sense to criticize itself; secondly, that other disciplines or ways of life may chance to be serious rivals to the " philosophy " of examination statutes and publishers' catalogues. Now as to the first point, there is a familiar type of criticism (sometimes directed against Kant) which is thought to be fatal, but in truth is singularly inane. How, it is asked, can metaphysics be approved or depreciated for metaphysical reasons ? Or, more generally (if also more ambiguously), how can reason discover its own limitations without transcending them ? How, in a word, can any such proceeding avoid self-contradiction or some kind of logical stultification ? Ever since Scepticism, with its denial of the very possibility of knowledge, was propounded (or even since Aristotle's defence of the law of contradiction) objections of this sort have been triumphantly advanced, but I doubt if they have ever won more than barren victories. Far be it from me to advocate Scepticism, but, if I did happen to embrace that gloomy creed, I should be little disturbed by the argument that I was thus affirming the truth of at least one proposition. Similarly, if I could bring myself to question the law of contradiction, my nerve would be quite unshaken by the retort that I was thus contradicting myself. Why not ? But in truth these are sports for contentious undergraduates, so let them pass. That reason is by nature self-reflective and self-critical is just a fact; to deny it is about as sensible as to deny that fire burns or that water flows downhill.

It is not, however, by appealing to an abstract right of self-criticism that we should justify the claim to challenge metaphysics or to deny the finality of any kind of expert knowledge. What prompts us to ask for more is dissatisfaction with what we have. No kind of authority, be it that of pope or dictator, of scientist or transcendental metaphysician, can exact more than formal obedience from those who at heart are unconvinced. On the other hand, when a man is satisfied that he has found the way of truth, you will not easily persuade him to look farther afield. Listen to Hume in his library, as he handles each suspect volume in turn and rehearses his deadly question: " Does it contain any abstract reasoning concerning quantity and number ? No. Does it contain any experimental reasoning concerning matter of fact and existence ? No. Commit it then to the flames, for it can contain nothing but sophistry and illusion." A similar philosophy, with a new label, is rather fashionable at the present hour; and as a useful comment on that intellectual attitude we may recall the agreeable passage in Plato's *Republic*, where Socrates, enlarging (ironically, no doubt) on the charms of primitive life and vegetarian diet, is interrupted by one of his audience with the blunt remark—" Why, Socrates, if you had been founding a city of pigs, how else would you have fattened them ? " Diet for an intellectual " city of pigs " will always find a market, and suitable customers will always protest that no other is wholesome. The first step, however, towards the acquisition of wisdom is to realize that nothing of much importance can be proved. Philosophy is a journey through a barely luminous darkness towards the unknown source of light. To stop at the point where the gas-lamps end is to imitate, in another dimension, the young man commemorated in the gospel, who had never in his life done anything wrong, but was far too prudent to take any risks. Among the Greeks it is Plato again (*Rep.* 504) who provides the traveller with the authentic signpost, in his first intimation of the nature of " the Good " as " that which every soul pursues, divining that it is something, but full of perplexity, with no sufficient grasp of its nature, and with none of the firm assurance there is about all the other things . . ." " We love we know not what," says Thomas Traherne in simpler style, " and therefore everything allures us." Inexhaustible curiosity and inexhaustible dissatisfaction are the perpetual motives of the search of wisdom, which is also the demand for perfection or, in the language of Greek tradition, the quest of " the Good ". And here, still more plainly, is revealed the deplorable result of converting philosophy into a " subject ". All ancient philosophy was, and, I make bold to add, all genuine philosophy is nothing else but a striving after the knowledge and realization of the Good; a project formally renounced by Kant, and by " philosophers "

of the present day usually treated with contempt. The explanation—
or rather, perhaps, the consequence—of this strange heresy is the invention of " ethics ", as a sealed compartment in which a number of
moral problems can be discussed and solved without reference to the
one essential question in which philosophy consists. Where shall
wisdom be found ? What is the Good ? What is it ultimately worth
while to get, to do, or to be ? Form and phraseology may vary in
different ages, but when this all-embracing question is ignored, dismissed as irrelevant, or even stigmatized as a mark of Hedonism, then
is philosophy at an end, and all the meticulous wrangling about " duty ",
" right ", and so forth becomes mere babble resounding in the empty
air.

But if, as I have so confidently asserted, the Greek philosophers did
hold fast to the true conception of philosophy, how shall we account
for their eventual collapse ? To reply that they were crushed by persecution is no real answer, for the mere act of authority would have been
impossible or ineffective if the Academy had not been spiritually
obsolete before its doors were closed. Nor was it simply that, after
Proclus, the supply of distinguished teachers came to an end. The
death of Proclus (in 485) took place less than fifty years before the final
event, and there is no great school or university that has not survived
a comparatively sterile period of greater duration than that. Neither
through a general misconception of its business nor for lack of men
capable at least of handing on the torch did Greek philosophy languish
and fade away, but because, with all its noble achievements, it had
failed in the end to reveal the Good; because something was amiss with
its doctrine and by reason of some defect in power it could not secure
and maintain its dominion; because, in fact, it came to be overshadowed by another philosophy, greater than any that Plotinus or his
master could invent. *Vicisti, Galilæe*; but the victory was not what
Julian supposed it to be, nor what Gibbon and Voltaire were long afterwards to insinuate. It was not the overthrow of reason by superstition; it was not even an exclusively popular revolution, a change of
religious allegiance by the illiterate multitude; it was also the defeat
of one intellectual system by another which Greek philosophers, nutured
in the Platonic tradition, were unable to comprehend. The emphasis,
however, must be carefully distributed. To represent the triumph of
the Christian philosophy as merely an affair of the schools would be even
wider of the mark than to pretend that it was only a wave of superstition or the stifling of reason by political authority. Beyond question
it was the failure of Greek philosophy to reach the common folk, its

inability to permeate and transform the pagan cults, that most clearly exposed its impotence to compete with the Christian gospel for the mastery of human life. But when the professed philosophers were content to shrug their shoulders and remark that the multitude, after all, had no appetite for reality but must be fed on shams, they failed to suspect that some part at least of the fault might lie with their own philosophy. No one had perceived more clearly than Plato, or confessed more openly, that between the philosophers and the general public was set a most formidable gulf, but neither he nor any of his successors had found a way to bridge it that did not involve the sacrifice of truth. Knowledge, indeed, could be presented in the form of " right opinion ", but, strictly speaking, all opinion was false.

Every soul, as Plato himself declares, pursues the unknown good, and thus far the intellectual aristocracy enjoys no privilege. But though all may have some dim notion of the truth, we cannot cross-examine mankind at large, and even if, without impertinence, we could stop a few hundred travellers and inquire of each what he took to be the clue to wisdom, the secret of happiness, or the final criterion of worth, the variety of the answers could only be bewildering. From the majority we should elicit nothing at all, and even in the more serious attempts to satisfy our curiosity there would be so much evidence of idiosyncrasy, of merely personal faith or fancy, that we should at least become aware of one dilemma from which there is no complete escape. To combine the inside and outside points of view is virtually impossible. No man can precisely estimate the character and value of an experience not his own. " I captured this rare specimen myself one very fine morning ", says the old entomologist in Conrad's Lord Jim," and I had a very big emotion. You don't know what it is for a collector to capture such a rare specimen. You can't." That is precisely the fact: we can't. Nor is it merely the " big emotion " that is incommunicable. Listen again to the old man as he gazes on the " rare specimen ", the gorgeous butterfly that he had caught with his hat when it settled on a little heap of mud. " This is nature—the balance of colossal forces. Every star is so, and every blade of grass stands so; and the mighty Kosmos in perfect equilibrium produces—this: this wonder, this masterpiece of Nature, the great artist." Assuredly it is not every collector who can achieve this vision of the mighty Kosmos in the miracle of a butterfly's wings, but to every enthusiast who steeps himself in the spirit of his work there may be given a revelation of something invisible to others, and that is why the result of any census of opinions about the ultimate good would seem to be merely chaotic.

There is nothing for it, then, but to fall back on our clumsy but serviceable way of dealing with infinitely variable human beings. We must sort them into companies and assume that all whose lives have any intelligible purpose will follow one or other of the conspicuous high-ways. Setting aside for the moment philosophy itself—or leaving its sense indeterminate—the probable alternatives, the most likely claim-ants, that is, to the possession of wisdom, are Science, Art, and Re-ligion. If, for instance, the aims and methods of natural science (as defined by Hume, perhaps) are all in all, then the way of science is undoubtedly the true philosophy. Similarly, if the supreme revelation is to be found in Art, then the great artists are the prophets and guides.

> The rest may reason—and welcome—
> 'Tis we musicians know.

Thus Abt Vogler at the end of his improvisation, and how near the poet, the painter, the musician may get to the heart of the mystery, I shall not presume to decide. At this first stage of the argument, however, and with reference to that considerable expanse of history in which Greek influence was predominant, it is not unreasonable to judge that neither science nor art would provide an adequate basis for discussion of the problem we have in view. I doubt indeed if at any time the greater artists have themselves put forward the extravagant claims associated with the chatter of students; and although the time was to come when science would assert its supremacy, along with its clear differentiation from " philosophy " in the modern sense of the word, a better opportunity for considering that position will be found in another place. No set of doctrines, no creed, no method or system of life has ever moulded the general form of society, or claimed unlimited allegiance, unless it was offered as a way of salvation; and it is scarcely too much to add that every system with that high pretension must in effect be described as either religion or philosophy. For reasons presently to be considered Greek philosophy could never quite be identified with religion, and for reasons equally cogent the Christian religion (at least in its official expression) did not set up to be philo-sophy. And yet, if the struggle officially terminated by Justinian's authority was inevitable, because it was in fact a contest of two rival aspirants to the same sovereignty, no absolute distinction in kind between the two can be allowed. Every philosophy that would rule the world must be also a religion, every religion that would rule the world must be also a philosophy. And if it be objected that religion is for all, philosophy only for the few, the answer is that, while the distinction between the learned and the simple can never be abolished, no ordered system of life, however named and classified, can ever prove its "catholicity" unless it provides for both. This is exactly where Christianity succeeded, and exactly where Platonism failed.

Even of religion, therefore, it cannot be said without qualification that it claims to possess the true wisdom and to follow the perfect way of life. Not only of primitive and savage religions would this be patently untrue, but even of the cults and pious usages which continued to be recognized by Greeks and Romans at the very height of their respective civilizations. Religion, in fact, does not reveal its peculiar mission until it ceases to be merely a function of the family, the tribe, or the nation; until it enjoins a distinctive way of life, which may often conflict with accepted laws and customs; until finally, it can hold its own intellectually and meet the sceptic on his own ground. By the official religions of Rome and Athens not one of these conditions was fulfilled. On the other hand, if we inspect the three religions, Judaism, Christianity, and Islam, which have most deeply affected our civilization, it is clear that each of them, by its very nature, must create a society demanding complete allegiance of heart and mind. Thus far they agree, but owing to certain intrinsic differences the consequent problems have not been the same for all. Both Judaism and Islam are avowedly theocracies, aspiring to establish themselves in that character everywhere, or at least somewhere, on the face of the earth. Christianity, on the contrary, was proclaimed as "a kingdom not of this world", and, though that proclamation may often seem to have been forgotten, it has never been formally revoked. In their political experience, therefore, and especially in their relation to the secular power of the State, these three religions could hardly fail to differ. The same is true of their respective intellectual positions, for in the apparently simpler theism of the Jew or the Moslem there is no such manifest challenge to the philosophers as in the Christian creed. By examining Buddhism and other religions of the remoter East we should discover further variations in character, but on the whole it is safe to affirm that no religion can be fully qualified to engage in the pursuit of wisdom unless it satisfies these two essential conditions: that it promises salvation to all who are ready to follow a certain "method" or way of life, and that it be capable of expression in an articulate "theology", which may, indeed, require exceptional gifts for its comprehension, yet not more so than any system that assumes the name of "philosophy".

Theology (except in a primitive sense to be noted later) is certainly an intellectual discipline, and therefore can never be identified with religion; for though it be true that all genuine theology arises out of reflection upon a certain kind of experience, the second stage no more follows automatically from the first than ability to make poems or pictures from lively appreciation of a beautiful landscape or a beautiful face. There will always be many to whom the beginning and end of religion is worship, who find in their deepest experience something beyond the reach of words and wholly untranslatable into doctrinal statements. Hence in accounting for the transition from primitive superstition (or even from such piety and ritual as satisfied the common people of Greece and Rome) to religion of the higher order we cannot begin with theology, but must look first for some mode of experience which could at least dispel the terrors of darkness, the blind fear of mysterious forces inherent in places and things; and then, at a later stage, could emancipate the devotee from the belief that divine beneficence was reserved for one particular tribe or people.

Now at a comparatively early age of Greek history we find side by side, but as yet with little or no contact, two bands of dissenters from ordinary religion, the philosophers and the mystics. In speaking of dissent we must, of course, beware of anachronisms. We must not think of churches and creeds, for at that time no such things existed. We need not even assume that, in order to become a philosopher, it was necessary to flout your neighbour's piety. The philosophers did, however, fall foul of some preposterous cosmogonies described in popular myths, and they did sometimes make caustic observations on gods made in human image; and thus they incurred the suspicion of atheism, which could be used against them on suitable occasions. Meanwhile the early mystics followed an entirely different path. With the details of their rites and practices, so far as modern research can throw any light on them, we are not concerned. The only two points of immediate interest are that they tended to form themselves into communities outside the ordinary political or social groups, and that abnormal experience, rather than the propagation of doctrine, was their aim. When membership of a society depends only on some kind of initiation, when ecstasy takes the place of formal piety, and when purity or holiness becomes an ideal, there is material enough for startling religious developments, even though nothing in the shape of intellectual theory has yet found expression.

The full significance, however, of the impending revolution in the spiritual life of Greece could not be revealed until contact had been established between two things as distinct in origin and as diverse in character as the dry light of Ionian philosophy and the enthusiasm—

inspired, perhaps, by legends of Orpheus or Dionysus—which appeared
to set reason entirely aside.   From our modern point of vantage it is
easy, of course, to recall such figures as Plotinus or S. John of the Cross,
and thus to understand that the combination of the mystical temper with
high gifts of intellect is far from impossible.   But even Plotinus lived
seven or eight centuries later than the historical era to which I am now
alluding, and at that early date not only were the mystics still living
almost next door to barbarism, but the philosophers were boldly
striking out a line which may have seemed to diverge from popular
religion, but by no means pointed in the direction of theology.   On
this subject more will be said in the next chapter, but it is not too soon
to emphasize the fact that the first great movement of Greek philosophy
was entirely devoid of any theological character or intention.   When
the philosophers found that some ridiculous theogony, embellished by
the poets, stood in the way of their own speculations, they were prepared to quarrel with the poets and, if need be, to mock at the gods.
But this was not because they aspired to reform religion, to refine the
conception of deity, or to do anything of the kind.   Least of all did it
appear, at first sight, that their own audacious hypotheses could have
even the smallest affinity with the initiations and " orgies " of ignorant
mystics.   Nevertheless, it was by the fusion or blending of these
ostensibly alien elements that the religion of the future—not in Greece
alone, but throughout the Græco-Roman world—was to be fashioned
and the supreme problem of " philosophy " disclosed.

2

A Glimpse of the First Philosophers

HAVING begun with the death of Greek philosophy, we shall now find it profitable to turn back to the period next, or next but one, to its birth.   According to an old tradition, the first man to style himself " philosopher " was Pythagoras.   This does not mean that his was actually the earliest name in the history of the subject (Thales, of course, was considerably earlier), nor must it tempt us to forget that the original application of a term may fall far short of revealing its full significance.   Nor, indeed, can we pretend to know exactly why (if the story be true) Pythagoras did select that title; for, in spite of much diligent research, most things about his personal history, including the dates of his birth and death, are still obscure.   Nevertheless, he does belong to history, not simply to the legends with which his strange personality was adorned, and there can be no doubt that in the Pythagoreans we have the first important example of a society attempting to secure for itself the autonomous conduct of a life based, not on the laws and customs of any people or state, but solely on the " method " which its members believed to be the only way of attaining to truth and salvation.   To this end Pythagoras himself, with a small company of the faithful, fled from his native Samos to Kroton in southern Italy, where the exiles made a rash attempt to impose their rule on the uninitiated with no enduring success.   But though the political experiment was a failure, the Pythagorean has been one of the most persistent of philosophical traditions.   Apart from its undeniable influence on Plato, we hear at various dates of Neo-Pythagoreanism, and even when the name of the school has been forgotten, there have been periodic revivals —some of them extremely modern—of the type of speculation, and likewise the type of superstition, originally associated with a band of enthusiasts who flourished in the latter part of the sixth century B.C.

Those who desire to study the Pythagorean system with as much accuracy as the fragmentary evidence allows I can only refer to the works of John Burnet and other authorities.   The most I can attempt here is to draw attention to the strange and almost startling incongruity of the elements somehow conjoined and harmonized in the original practice of the society, and even in its more sophisticated development never entirely dissolved.   At one extreme we have perfectly genuine mathematics, at the other a veneration of taboos which may interest anthropologists, but which seems to indicate the mental outlook of savages or very young children.   What Pythagoras himself or any of his mathematical disciples really did believe about beans, cocks' feathers, and so forth, we cannot say with certainty, but at least we are bound to assume that the reasons for admitting to fellowship in the society men who knew a vast deal more about old wives' tales than about geometry were felt to be sufficient.   And when we begin to cast about for explanations, it is necessary to take account of both extremes, to examine the superstition; for only thus shall we catch a glimpse of the future transformation by which the primitive alliance of apparently incompatible tendencies was shown to have been a distant forecast of the eventual union of theology and religion.

The study of number is itself full of various possibilities.   Were it necessary to argue that from mathematics to mysticism is only one step, and thence to superstition only one or two more, it would not be difficult to produce a great mass of evidence.   The bare history of the number Three would fill a volume, nor would every chapter in it be merely a record of human folly.   The search for quantity and measure in the structure of the universe may flourish side by side with faith in mystical figures and ominous numbers.   One of your neighbours, with or without the aid of a telescope, will be discovering a geometrizing God (an ancient figure lately revived) while another discourses gravely on the number of magpies it is expedient to meet or avoid.   In the most modern of American hotels the thirteenth floor will be missing, and even the boldest of mathematicians will scarcely dare to argue with the manager that the gap should be filled.   It is not, however, by this fascination of numbers for minds of every grade that the Pythagorean medley can be adequately explained.   We have to search rather for some intermediary, some influence that could act upon all alike, reconciling understanding with emotion, and thus providing a corporate bond of union.   One such instrument of mediation the Pythagoreans found in music.   Here again there are many technicalities that it is needless to discuss, but it is agreed that the mathematical discoveries of Pythagoras, and also his translation of mathematics into a wider philosophy, were closely connected with his investigation of musical intervals and concords, supported by experiments with the strings of the

lyre. To Pythagoras (ably supported by Plato) music owes its traditional place in education, and to Pythagoras the modern doctor of
music owes his degree. And just as musical degrees are awarded for
theoretical understanding rather than for executive skill or (as some
would unkindly add) for ability to compose anything worth hearing, so
Pythagoras would doubtless have understood by " music " something
that the general public would rather have described as a mathematical
exercise. On the other hand, music as sheer sound had always its
wider appeal, and in early days, long before anything we should
recognize as artistic had appeared, its " orgiastic " influence must
have been tremendous. In comparison with their eminence in other
arts, the Greeks never made much headway in music, but when surprise is expressed that Plato, in his *Republic*, should attribute such
powerful effects to an art so rudimentary, the point is entirely missed.
It was just because the music was so elementary that its power to excite
violent emotions, likely to affect moral conduct, was so great. Yet
music could be not only a stimulus of excitement but also a remedy.
Its use as a catharsis, or purgation, was apparently known to the
Pythagoreans, and thus in some degree they anticipated Aristotle's
famous pronouncement on the function of tragedy.

If, then, we would conjure up a vision of this early band of " philosophers ", we must begin by banishing from our minds all thought of the
modern environment appropriate to persons so described. Not in
lecture-rooms and dusty libraries shall we find the successors of the
Pythagoreans; but if we go out into the streets and chance to fall in
with a procession of men and women attired in a kind of military
uniform, beating drums and blowing lustily on instruments of brass, it
will be worth while to follow them. And presently, when it appears
that what they are offering to the public with so much vigorous
advertisement is nothing less than " salvation ", we may be certain
that we are on the right track. Every genuine sect of philosophers
has been a " salvation army ", but in one particular a meeting of the
body thus commonly entitled (a body of which I desire to speak with
all respect) will disappoint us. To complete the resemblance to the
first philosophers we should have to place at the head of the company
a handful of accomplished mathematicians, and, if one of peculiar
eminence were appointed to represent Pythagoras himself, he should
mark the pace and rhythm of the procession with regular strokes on
the simple instrument known as a " triangle ", invented, surely, as a
perfect symbol of the mystical union between music and mathematics.

But music was not the only link between the intelligentsia and the

humble disciples. Still more momentous was the Pythagorean discovery or formal recognition of the soul. The earliest traces of *psyche*
can be discerned, of course, in far more primitive days, but to the
Pythagoreans we may fairly attribute the first hint of a theory, the first
considerable attempt to disentangle soul from body, to contemplate its
moral destiny, and in some sense to proclaim its immunity from death.
But here again it would be wrong to suppose that beliefs which were
afterwards to take philosophical shape or to find their way into religious
doctrine, were born of purely intellectual meditation. They were not,
so to speak, by-products of the Pythagorean mathematics, but in some
way or other (for once more the evidence is deficient) they sprang from
mystical experience, and then, no doubt, had to be much refined and
clarified before they could acquire the form in which the poets and
philosophers of Greece have handed them down. How much tincture
of mysticism there was in Pythagoras himself, or whence he derived it,
we do not know. If, as Burnet observes, Apollo, rather than Dionysus,
was the peculiar god of the Pythagoreans, it would not be accurate to
describe them as Bacchants, but it is certain that with Orphicism (itself
of dim and doubtful origin) their sympathy was profound. From that
religion, presumably, came their belief in successive rebirths of the
soul (palingenesis), the vision of judgement after death, and all the
material so magnificently fashioned by Plato into "myths", foreshadowing the doctrines of Purgatory and Hell. Orphic, too, is the
injunction of secrecy about the mysteries reserved for the initiated, and
here it is especially important to note the tales of penalties suffered by
faithless Pythagoreans for revealing to profane persons the secrets of
mathematics. Even if the actual stories are legendary, their invention
is, none the less, good evidence that knowledge itself (the *gnosis* of
the adept) could be regarded as a mystery. The same notion, per-
sisting throughout the ages, is illustrated not only by the vigilant
guardians of religious formulas or by " the wonderful piff and paff "
of charlatans, but even by those " secrets of craftsmanship " which were
often the genuine secrets of a guild or a group of families and for that
reason have sometimes been lost. In more ways than one, then, we
find approximation and interaction of elements superficially incompatible. That the Orphic beliefs about the soul could even be made
to supply a kind of rational interpretation of the taboos is possible, but,
without pressing that argument, we are clearly warranted in concluding
that the religious side of Pythagoreanism reacted upon the scientific,
and that in mystical experience, which at first must have been wild,
ecstatic, and to all appearances completely irrational, were already

C

latent the germs of doctrines to be elaborated one day with all the resources of an advanced philosophy.

In the previous chapter I stated without hesitation that the trend of early Greek philosophy was not theological and that the ancient quarrel (as Plato calls it) with Homer and retailers of myths was not inspired by any religious motive. As applied to the Pythagoreans, that statement does not cease to be true, but it needs reconsideration. In them we have found an association of men differing widely in intellectual capacity, and in the religious practices of the society we have found the rudiments of doctrines afterwards raised to the level of formal theology; but what we do not find is any perceptible link between Pythagorean science and a theistic interpretation of the world. *De Rerum Natura* was the motto of all the philosophy loosely classified as pre-Socratic. To get behind and beyond the manifold of appearances, down to the very stuff and substance of the cosmos, and to maintain, in the teeth of common sense and common opinion, that all this wondrous variety of objects round about us was a perpetual manifestation of one and the same original " nature " was the ambition of all alike. What, then, was this " nature " ? Could it be single: just water, for instance, and nothing else ? Or must we postulate a conflict of two opposites, the mutations of four elements, or perchance the attractions and repulsions of an infinite multitude of atoms in the void ? Many hypotheses of this type were current in the time of Pythagoras, or not much later, but he would have none of them. Things, he declared, are numbers, and out of numbers alone he was ready to construct the world.

It was the boldest of all answers to the fundamental question, and also, if we allow for the vast difference between ancient and modern science, the most prophetic. How exactly the cardinal doctrine was to be interpreted became at a very early date a matter of dispute, but we may take it as pretty certain that Pythagoras meant what he said, and that he would not have welcomed the disposition of some of his more timorous successors to affirm only that things were like numbers—the kind of compromise that was really more difficult than the original unqualified pronouncement. The intricacies of the subject, however, I cannot offer to discuss. The only point I would emphasize is that no interpretation suitable to the age of Pythagoras would have suggested a possible transition from this identification of things with numbers to some kind of theism. We can, if we please, call the doctrine " physical ", in the sense that it obliterates the distinction between mathematics and physics. Possibly, though with less propriety, we might call it " metaphysical ", on the ground that numbers were said to be the ultimate reality; but I doubt if that later adjective can rightly be applied to any theory which does not allow that reality may be not only incorporeal but also entirely beyond the range of number and measurement; and, as long as " things " in their very essence were declared to be numbers, there could be no room for any such suggestion. And again, before the Supreme Being could be characterized as the One, and thereupon either identified with or (it might be) distinguished from, God, it would be necessary to form a conception of unity which in fact would have nothing to do with mathematics. Speculations of that type were one day to become familiar, and Pythagoras may unwittingly have contributed something to their origination, but to himself and his earlier disciples they were unknown.

At the same time Pythagoreanism was always more than a mathematical or physical theory. It was " philosophy ", not only because its " method " or way of life made room for mystical experience, and thus for certain beliefs about the soul, but also because knowledge itself was felt to be a mode of purification and because numbers were not thought of as creatures of abstraction, interesting only to a few specialists, but as the sum and substance of reality, the very nature of things. The upshot is that in Pythagoreanism we can discern something more than the two most obviously contrasted elements, science and ecstatic religion. Out of the harmonization of these arises a third competitor, and perhaps a fourth. A time was bound to come when philosophy, claiming to go beyond mathematics, would deny that numbers exhausted the nature of " being ", and a time when theology, critical of both science and popular religion, would assert its own sovereign rights. At that point must arise the further question whether theology and philosophy—given that both were of wider range than exact science—could be independent and autonomous disciplines, or whether the choice must lie between their perfect fusion and the destruction of one by the other. Religion as mystical experience is one thing; science, cold, dispassionate, impersonal, is another; but when Pythagoreanism or any other philosophy undertakes to blend and order both in a single rule of life, must it not, in its fundamental principles, be either theology or deliberate atheism ? How can there be two claimants to ultimate knowledge when the universe itself can be only one ? Yet, if we examine the legends on the banners under which men have ranged themselves for battle, we shall find science, philosophy, theology distinguished as three competitors, allies, or enemies, while religion wanders uneasily to and fro amid their rivalries, demanding bread from each in turn, and receiving all too often a stone.   All this was latent, though far from explicit, in the theory and practice of Pythagoras.   What he did bequeath to posterity was the firm conviction that truth and salvation were inseparable, and that man had a soul to be saved.

Nor must one further legacy, however unintentional, be overlooked; the solemn warning against any attempt to establish by force of law a " philosophy " which to the multitude is unintelligible and probably distasteful.   Sincerely convinced that his own " method " was the way of liberty, and finding that, under the political conditions of Samos it could not be pursued, Pythagoras was resolved to set up an autonomous community elsewhere.   But when he translated this legitimate ambition into a *coup d'état*, and assumed that it was right and proper to impose the Pythagorean rule of life on a mixed body of citizens who shared neither his knowledge nor his faith, he created a precedent for the most tragic of political blunders, anticipated religious persecution, and dimly foreshadowed the bitter conflict associated long afterwards with the names of Church and State.

3

The Invention of Theology

"THEOLOGY" is another good example of a name which cannot be adequately interpreted either by etymological analysis or by reference to its earliest usage. Wherever, indeed, the influence of the Greek word *logos* makes itself felt, there is need of the utmost caution. Often enough (as in Aristotle's writings) the right translation of it is hard to determine, and as we trace its gradual modification by a long succession of authors, we seem almost to have an index to the whole development of Greek philosophy. In compound words, such as "psychology" or "geology", it is usually (though not always) safe to assume that the termination implies the purpose of "giving an account of" the soul, the earth, or whatever it may be; but in the case of "theology" the account thus promised by the bare form of the word may still be ambiguous. Just as *logos*, in its early days, might signify no more than a story (the *Iliad*, perhaps), so the original "theologians" were simply men who told tales about the gods, and most of the tales were crude and fantastic products of barbarism, devoid of any quality that might seem to anticipate the conversion of *logos* into "reason". It is in this primitive sense that Aristotle sometimes uses the name, contrasting "theologians" with "physicists", with some slight recognition of an intermediate class, the writers who mixed a small dose of science with the tales commonly known as "myths". But when we also find in Aristotle that "theology" can serve as an alternative name for the "first philosophy", afterwards to be called "metaphysics", it is evident that a great transformation of meaning was coming to pass. In Aristotle himself this nomenclature is now thought to be characteristic only of his earlier philosophical attitude, and it is not unlikely that he became less and less of a "theologian" as he gradually emancipated himself from the influence of Plato. Be this as it may, his terminology is still good evidence that the possibility of giving an account of God (or gods), which had nothing to do with myths, had now been recognized in principle, and that something palpably

23

lacking in the philosophy of Pythagoras was thus in a fair way to be supplied.

That all religion is of popular origin is one of those loose and plausible statements that it might be far from easy to confirm.   Let us be content with the safer hypothesis that no religion can fulfil its proper mission unless it makes an immediate appeal to something in human nature far more common than intellectual curiosity; to which we may add that, if religion is to overstep the bounds of locality, kinship, and nationality, it must admit of great variety in its modes of expression. Nothing less than universal validity is claimed by the higher religions and, since mankind will always be occupied in the main with everyday affairs and simple ways of thinking, a religion intelligible only to the highly gifted and highly educated must fail to make good the claim.   From these rather obvious premises there has been a tendency to draw the entirely false conclusion that theology is either a corruption of pure religion or at least a superfluous burden imposed on the faithful.   To this there is more than one answer, but the most decisive is, once more, the claim of religion to universality; for the catholicity of any creed or system offered as a way of salvation must be vindicated not only by its indifference to geographical, racial, or political boundaries, but also by its power to convince all sorts and conditions of men; and, though the causes which split up the map of the world into variously coloured sections are a serious obstacle to community of ideas, they hardly indicate so profound a division of mind and spirit as may often be found in two natives of the same country living next door to each other. Religion, we agree, must appeal to all, and therefore must find a way to the heart of the multitude.   But were it thus debarred from access to the understanding—had it no message for Plato or Plotinus, for Augustine or Aquinas or Spinoza, to say nothing of thousands less known to fame but not less resolute in the search for truth—why, then, religion would be no more catholic in its genius than if its efficacy were confined to Aryans or Europeans, to Englishmen or Jews.   Theology exists for the same reason that natural science exists, because there are men who desire to understand and are content with nothing less than truth.   The religion which begins with the fear of " numinous " places and things, with mysterious taboos, and, it may be, with dark and horrible rites, may advance by slow degrees to sober piety and bloodless sacrifice to solemn ritual, to the sanctification of priests and temples, perhaps to the fire of prophecy and the heroic inspiration of crusades; but with all this impressive display of power, it may still be walking in darkness, and still may lack the only weapon that can protect it against sceptical assault. Not that we are bound to accept the plea, sometimes alleged by the half-hearted, that theology owes its very existence to the need for protective armour against the blows of rationalistic assailants. That is one of its functions, but not the source of its generation. It comes into being, I repeat, because if man must worship with the heart, he must worship with the understanding also; and the force of this contention becomes ever more apparent as we pass from the feeble gropings and dim presentiments of savages to the study of religions which from their earliest days can be viewed in the daylight of history.

There was a time when it was thought a mark of intelligence to maintain that religion was invented by priests; and though that particular form of nonsense has passed away, it may still be worth while to note that priests were equally innocent of giving birth to theology. About the origin of theology (in Europe at least) there happens to be no doubt at all. It was invented entirely by philosophers, and with only a slight touch of paradox one might even assert that it was invented as a protest against religion. To speak rather more accurately, the protest was neither against simple piety nor against belief in the existence of the traditional gods, but against the scandalous representation of their behaviour by Homer and other poets, and still more against the notion, diffused by quacks and " pardoners ", that bargains could be made with Divine Justice, and sins condoned or cancelled by suitable incantations or gifts. But, while it arose in truth from a far deeper sense of religion than was expressed in customary observance, this philosophical theology was not the fruit of meditation upon any pattern of divinity discoverable in the myths and legends which, in Greece, were the only available substitute for a creed. Without a reformation of popular religion no intelligent conception of God, no theoretical propositions about his nature, could be fashioned; thus from the very first the new theologians were faced with a dilemma from which there was never to be any escape. They neither believed in the religion of the vulgar nor were prepared to destroy it. Sincerely convinced that atheism or irreligion must be disastrous to the community, they were forced to admit (with the fate of Socrates as a constant warning) that criticism might always be mistaken for scepticism, and that simply to denounce the whole Olympian hierarchy as an imposture, or to deride the tales of supernatural beings far more primitive than Zeus or Apollo, would either provoke fanaticism or destroy religion itself. They were obliged, therefore, to fall back on compromise; to allow that truth could not be presented without disguise to the world at large, and that the disguise must be of a kind more or less agreeable to tradition. I am not, of course, pretending that all this was manifest from the outset, but there is evidence that the general character of the problem was understood almost as soon as " theology " began to imply something wholly different from the telling of idle tales.

So far as the authorship of this profound revolution can be ascribed to any one man, that man is Plato. Not only was he the first (in all probability) to use the term " theology " in the sense it was henceforward to bear but also, when all the relevant passages in the Republic, the Laws, the Timaeus, and other dialogues are collected and compared, many of the controversies fated to disturb the peace of later ages seem already to be taking shape. Nothing like an accurate study of this rich material can here be attempted, but some appreciation of the essential character of Platonism is an indispensable preface to the understanding of all subsequent philosophies, especially of the Christian position, which could not be defended without an open challenge to the wisdom of the Greeks.

The effect of Pythagoreanism, as we saw, was to establish a loose alliance between science and mystical religion, to suggest (if the anachronism may pass) that the science was also a kind of metaphysics, but not to indicate any way of transition from the philosophy of numbers to a theistic interpretation of the world. The extent of Plato's indebtedness to the first avowed " philosopher " is a controversial question, partly bound up with a further controversy about his representation of Socrates, but the existence of some affinity cannot reasonably be doubted, and it is clear that Plato resumed and amplified the same problems that the earlier master had stated or implied. Science, for Plato, meant little else but mathematics, and the Orphic beliefs about the soul, though he may not have taken them quite literally, he certainly accepted as a means of expounding his own doctrine. Just how near he came to reducing the essence of " things " to number is another highly disputable question, which, fortunately, it will not be necessary to discuss; but where he went far beyond Pythagoras was in his approach to philosophical monotheism and in his perception that no cosmology, nor any account of ultimate reality, could be sufficient unless it included the most earnest consideration of the being and nature of God.

The difficulties besetting Plato in the task with which he grappled so heroically were of more than one kind. Some were due to the elementary character of ordinary Greek religion, others to facts in human nature not peculiar to any age or country, while others—and these the most formidable—were inherent in his own intellectual convictions. As a religious reformer, he could not suddenly eradicate the popular notions of deity; as a philosopher he was well aware that the multitude would never be philosophical; but when, in the face of these obstacles, he set out to prepare a scheme for governing the state by means of philosophical wisdom he found in the very nature of the world, and in the radical structure of the human mind, a difficulty more insuperable than the spiritual deficiencies of any particular people or the mediocre ability of the ordinary man. The entire philosophy of Plato is permeated by the antithesis of " knowledge " and " opinion " or " belief ". I mention both the alternative renderings of the Greek word *doxa* because neither by itself is sufficient, and indeed both together fall short of equivalence with the original. Sometimes " opinion " is preferable, sometimes " belief ", but to insist on either, to the total exclusion of the other, is injudicious. In one famous passage of the *Republic* (Bk VI, 510–511) there are further refinements and subdivisions, but these, important as they are for a complete exposition of Plato's theory, do not oblige us to modify the general statement that his whole interpretation of reality and of human life is based on this sharp distinction between the knowledge which cannot err and an inferior mode of apprehension which, though far above sheer ignorance, can never yield more than sound judgement in practical affairs and wholesome beliefs which, like Butler's " probability ", can serve as the guide of life. And what more, we may ask, is needed? Even Socrates was sometimes tempted to put the same question, but the answer is not merely that opinion, though sometimes right, is often wrong, but that, even when right, it knows not why, but is like a traveller carrying a lantern through a twilight in which the forms of objects are vaguely apprehended, but never perfectly revealed as they would be by the radiance of the sun.

Even the simile may be questioned, for objects illuminated by sunlight must surely be apparent, and it is more than doubtful whether the objects of knowledge—in Plato's estimation the only realities—can properly be said to " appear ". And here, without pretending to cope with the famous doctrine of " ideas " or " forms ", I must emphasize one point essential to the right understanding of Plato. Our own use of the term " opinion " is vague enough, but as a rule, I fancy, we take it to mean a transient phase or makeshift, a state of mind which may at any time be replaced by knowledge. There is, of course, the " opinionated " man, tenacious and dogmatic, who will never admit that his views may be mistaken, but even he, if pressed, will hardly maintain that any " views " are certainties; indeed his very reluctance to listen to argument is no bad evidence that he would be glad to rise, if he could, from opinion to knowledge. Now in Plato's writings the original of " opinion " or " belief " occurs an immense number of times, and it would be rash to deny that his usage ever agrees with ours. But whenever he is carefully attending to his own theory of knowledge and reality, he does not mean by " opinion " a state of mental uncertainty (or, for that matter, a state of firm conviction) which might one day give place to knowledge. On the contrary, opinion can never be translated into knowledge, because it is essentially relative to a kind of object which cannot be known. In other words, opinion is not imperfect knowledge on its way to perfection, but apprehension of, or judgement about, that which is by nature unknowable.

The more we examine this position, the more difficult it appears. By " objects of opinion " Plato does not simply denote the innumerable facts which, for one reason or another, we cannot positively ascertain. He does not refer to paucity of historical evidence, to the scarcity of prophets, or (if we may anticipate) to the lack of microscopes and other instruments of precision. If we want common examples of these unknowable objects, we cannot do better than look out of the window. The garden is full of them, and so is the bustling street. In a word, the whole panorama of Nature, the multitudinous array of objects presented to us through the medium of our senses, and not otherwise discernible, belongs to this strange category; and thus the comfortable adage " seeing is believing " would be warmly endorsed by Plato, but with the additional comment that what we believe we cannot know.

What, then, are we to make of this puzzling doctrine, and what is its bearing on the philosophy which cares little, perhaps, for intellectual conundrums but seeks the wisdom which alone can point the way to the goal of human endeavour? Even among devout Platonists there has been much diversity of interpretation. In particular, it has proved almost impossible to extract from Plato a definite answer to the question whether this dualism of " phenomena " and intelligible realities can ultimately be resolved, or whether in the universe itself there is a recalcitrant element, a core of irrationality, which must simply be accepted as fact. This, however, is a problem which cannot be seen in its true proportions until we attempt to consider the relation of the Divine Intelligence to the world. On the human level at least, Plato shows no disposition to absorb the " object " of knowledge into the " subject ". The terms " realist " and " idealist " were not yet born, and since their birth they have suffered many fluctuations; but if we choose to classify Plato from this point of view, he belongs without a shadow of doubt to the realists. Neither the *esse est percipi* of the much libelled Berkeley nor the *esse est intelligi* of a wider idealism can pass as a Platonic formula. Realities exist in their own right, and our task is to get to know them. Thus far Plato agrees with a large company of philosophers, and also with the man in the street. But when he proceeds to declare that all the objects we see and smell and handle are neither pure entities nor pure nonentities, but something between the two, we naturally feel a little puzzled, and perhaps suspect him of merely forging a lively metaphor, as a means of describing our mental condition so long as we are content to take things as they come to us in haphazard coincidence or succession, without invoking the sciences to reduce them to order. But the problem goes much deeper than that, into waters that assuredly my own brief argument will not plumb. I can only repeat that we shall never understand Plato unless we take him to mean literally and most seriously that opinion or belief exists because there are objects of opinion or of belief which no science will ever enable us to know.

But what of knowledge itself? Is that simpler than opinion because its proper objects are at least indubitably real? The terminology of Plato is not very rigid and precise (for which we may be thankful), but for the most part the knowledge contrasted with opinion is the knowledge obtainable by the kind of science that admits of mathematical expression. Discursive reasoning and inference must therefore be expected, and nothing less than demonstration will satisfy the inquirer. But does it follow that without demonstration no genuine knowledge can be had? That is not in fact Plato's contention, but he does not rely on an evasion sometimes adopted by logicians who ought to know better. In modern books we often hear of both " mediate " and " immediate " knowledge, but the distinction is fallacious and the " mediate " variety is a figment of confused thinking. All knowledge, when you get it, is as immediate as toothache, but this does not mean that you will always get it without effort, without argument, or without delay. To enlarge on the point would be to digress too far into logical theory, and in relation to Plato, fortunately, the digression would be unprofitable. The clue to his recognition of a grade of knowledge above science is, once more, his assumption that each distinct kind of object requires a distinct mode of apprehension. The objects of opinion, as we have seen, are ranked below pure being (" that which really is "), but now we have to ask whether there can also be an object above being, knowable only by an act of mind more exalted than scientific thinking. Now this may sound even more difficult than the notion of objects hovering between being and not-being, and it must be allowed that Plato himself was hard put to it to find language adequate to his purpose. Actually there is only one passage (*Rep*. VI. 509) in which he boldly suggests that the Good is not in itself " being ", but above and beyond it; this passage, virtually ignored by Aristotle, may have been taken as only a " sublime hyperbole " (*Rep*. ibid.) until Plotinus and his successors gave it their serious attention. In order to understand it, or at least to make some approach to an interpretation, it will now be expedient to reconsider the part assigned by Plato to " theology ".

First of all, then, we must observe that his denunciation of the poets and his delineation of the " types " or elementary principles of theology occur in an early book of the *Republic* (Bk I), where his immediate concern is with the education of boys and girls not yet beyond their childhood. His statements, therefore, are simple in form, straightforward, and dogmatic. God is absolutely good, and therefore cannot be the author of anything evil; he is absolutely true, and therefore cannot, as the poets pretend, assume disguises and be accountable for human delusions; he is also morally unchangeable, and therefore cannot be deflected or cajoled by any kind of bribe. Something of this kind is what the young should be taught to believe, but to invite them to discuss the origin of pain and sorrow, the efficacy of prayer, or any other problem involved in the elements of theology, is far from Plato's intention, and would, indeed, have been extremely foolish. But when we pass on to the central section of the *Republic*, and to the education of men capable of aspiring to the highest grade of knowledge, we find that, instead of God, it is now the Good that holds the supreme place, and to this apparently impersonal abstraction is attributed the origin of all genuine knowledge and the being of all that really is. Hence arises the inevitable question whether God and the Good are identical, and, as every candid student of Plato is likely to confess, no perfectly conclusive answer has ever been given. Moreover, this profound uncertainty, though it first appears in Plato, and in connexion with a passage to which there is no exact parallel in his writings, is not peculiar to him, but reappears, in various shapes, so constantly in later ages that we are almost justified in setting aside as unimportant any philosophy which overlooks or deliberately ignores it. Fundamentally, the question is whether the God of religion, the object of faith and worship, can in any way be found out by the exercise of reason. There have been philosophers (and no mean ones) who have offered to " prove " the existence of God; others have been content

only to " postulate " it; others, avoiding the name of God, have preferred to speak of the One or the Absolute; others have declared
openly and sincerely for atheism. All of these, not excluding the
genuine atheists, have renewed the problem brought to light by Plato
when, in the same great dialogue, he first enunciates the principles of
theology, almost in the style of a creed, and then declares that science
is only a prelude to the " dialectic " by which we must strive to attain
to the vision of the Good which he frankly refuses to describe.

When the earlier and later stages in the education of Plato's imaginary
citizens are thus compared, and when we observe that the course
designed for a small intellectual aristocracy leads through a series of
mathematical steps, followed by a superior kind of " dialectic ", to
the search of a problematic Good, we naturally begin to wonder what
has become of religion, in so far as it was defined by the principles of a
theology which evidently has no place in the advanced curriculum.
Are we to infer that " theology " belongs only to an inferior state of
mental development, and that Plato has not, after all, transformed its
meaning, but merely improved its status by making it respectable,
without allowing it any part in the revelation of truth? Before
accepting or rejecting this disturbing conclusion we must examine the
whole situation more closely and, in particular, the remarkable
function of " myths " in Plato's philosophy. No sooner does Socrates
get to work on his educational scheme than he startles his audience by
observing that *Logoi* (here roughly equivalent to " stories ") are of
two kinds, the true and the false, and that children must begin with the
false. Since it is only by stories that their minds will be suitably im-
pressed, " myths " are indispensable, and though all myths are false,
in the sense that they are not true history, they can be composed in a
style that makes them vehicles of moral and religious truth. This is
where the poets have failed us, for their myths are not only fictions
but lies. Of gods and heroes they publish only a debased travesty,
thus corrupting the souls of their readers and poisoning their minds.
At this point Socrates introduces the " types of theology " which are
to serve as a model for all future poets licensed to tell tales of the gods.

It is a great misfortune that Plato never wrote a complete dialogue
on the subject of myths. As it is, we can piece together a few statements of theory and, with great advantage, can study the myths of his
own invention. But many questions to which we should like to have
the Socratic answers are nowhere precisely formulated; this, no doubt,
is largely because in education, in politics, in religion, and theology,
many unpredictable things have happened since the *Republic* was com-

posed.   The first point to notice is that the common associations of the term " myth " in our own literature are by no means an adequate clue to its meaning in Plato.   Even in the particular context to which I have referred (*Rep.* II. 377), where Socrates does, of course, attack the kind of stories that we should call mythical, he is really asserting a principle which is not confined to religious instruction, but applicable, in various ways and various degrees, to the whole communication and acquisition of knowledge.   The essential points are that all abstract, general, or universal ideas must first be presented in concrete shape, and that, in all such presentation, there must be some features which cannot without qualification be said to represent the truth.   And though it is in the initial steps of elementary education that we find the most obvious illustrations, it is wrong to suppose that the principle holds good nowhere else.   From the myths employed for imparting the rudiments of theology to children it would be both easy and legitimate to pass on to very different subjects.   The whole function of symbols, for instance, in the most secular atmosphere of mathe-matics, is profoundly instructive, and the triangles or circles drawn by the schoolmaster on his blackboard might well be cited as admirable examples of " myth ".   Or again, if we leave the classroom for the wider arenas of business and politics, we are immediately confronted with the vast commercial empire of " advertisement " and the still more sinister triumphs of " propaganda ".   Had the artists of ancient Greece been engaged by enterprising tradesmen to push the sale of their commodities, Plato would not have missed the opportunity for dis-crediting their perverted skill, but the use of " myth " for the propaga-tion of sound political opinions he does not disdain, but even commends and exemplifies in his own practice.

The theme, in fact, expands in too many directions, and we must confine our attention to the points most relevant to the problem of religious truth.   Myths, as Socrates roundly declares, are false stories, but there are two kinds of falsity, verbal and spiritual; a fiction may be positively beneficial so long as it does not generate " the lie in the soul ", and it is on this pattern that the official mythologists will be ordered to compose their poems.   Here, of course, there are tempting oppor-tunities for digression but, if we refrain from wandering into the philosophy of æsthetics, we shall at least escape the vociferous protests of young gentlemen who, as Henry James says, " know everything about art and nearly everything about life ".   That Homer is to be supplanted in the schoolroom by the writers of edifying hymns and ballads, is undeniable, and anyone who chooses to infer that Plato, supreme among artists, knew nothing about art, can only be advised to think again. But, though we avoid that interminable discussion, there are also unavoidable questions about truth and falsity, as represented by history and myth, and about the whole relation of Plato's argument to his estimate of religion. There are difficulties that he does not acknowledge, and indeed could not, by the dim light of Greek religion, be expected to perceive. First of all, we must note that the myths he proposes to make serviceable to morality and religion are not to be allegories. It is true that this formal rejection of allegory (*Rep.* II, 378) is applied only to the disreputable tales of the gods, which already, it seems, were being excused on the ground that they might have a hidden meaning and need not be taken at their face value; but the objection to this kind of apology—that the young will be unable to distinguish between the literal and the allegorical sense—clearly applies to all kinds of story. Plato, in fact, was wise enough to know that what boys and girls of a certain age demand is not only a story, but also assurance that the story is true. Once let them discover that " it never really happened " and a large part of its effect will be lost. Stories have no business to be sermons, and the detection of genuine medicine concealed in spurious jam will only discredit both alike. The myths, therefore, will have to pass as history, but the history, of course, will not be genuine, for in that case the argument would lose its point.

Now here, I think, Plato is making both true and false assumptions. He is right in supposing that stories about the gods will be taken literally by the innocent young, and will for that reason alone make a strong religious impression; for, if his schoolboys knew from the outset (like our own when they have a classical education) that the tales of Homer and Hesiod were only agreeable fictions, they would never take them as authoritative guides to conduct. But why, then, not tell them outright that we read the poets merely for entertainment, and so avoid the damage to religion? Because, as again Plato rightly assumes, you cannot dispense with the story, and because, as he is also aware, there are no true stories about the gods. That, as we shall understand more fully in due course, was the fatal dilemma for Plato and all Greek philosophers: they had to present the universal in the particular, the abstract in the concrete, the spiritual truth in the story; but all the stories were false. Either, then, belief in the gods must be abandoned, or myths, frankly described as " false *logoi* ", must be composed in such style as to pass for history and at the same time to justify the touch of deception by their moral and spiritual value.

Postponing any doubts we may feel about the honesty of this method, and remembering that it is primarily for the benefit of children, let us next inquire of Plato what is to happen when the children grow up. There would seem to be only two alternatives. Either they will never quite grow up in mind, and so may continue to believe in the old stories, or they will discover that they have been nutured on edifying fictions. In the former case Plato would probably be well content, but in the latter his hope would be that the kernel would survive the husk, that the adult would recognize the truth of the doctrine when its dependence on the narrative could no longer be alleged. But is it safe to count on this result? Sometimes, perhaps, but decidedly not always. It is at least equally probable that, when the myth is no longer mistaken for history, the moral or spiritual lesson will also cease to convince. The reaction may even be violent, for there is a familiar type of critical mind which rejoices in disillusionment, resents the taint of credulity, and is likely, therefore, to pour scorn on doctrines authenticated by a forged certificate, and insinuated, as will now be felt, into childish minds by means of a fraudulent dodge. In the end, however, the frequency of this disconcerting result is not the gravest objection to Plato's method. Given his two hypotheses (neither of which I should personally dispute), that all religion above the level of primitive superstition requires a theology, and that even the simplest theology must be presented to beginners in a form not perfectly representative of the truth, Plato might fairly argue that the risks were inevitable. But though we grant the need of " accommodation " to the capacity of the audience (and the teachers of almost any subject have to make this concession), we are obliged to press for an answer to a still more awkward question. Stories, he tells us, we must have, and the stories must be false, because no true ones are to be found. In other words, there is no historical evidence about the nature of God and his dealings with man. But how, then, do we know that God so much as exists, and on what grounds shall we affirm that he is good, true, immutable, or what you will? Incidentally, it is well to remember that in Greek education there was no such thing as the teaching of history. Before the date of the *Republic* the immortal books of Herodotus and Thucydides had, of course, been written, but there was no such thing as a text-book, and the bare notion of using history as an educational instrument was still unborn. Consequently, the only accepted pattern of truth was the mathematical; or, if Plato was now attempting to reach a higher level by the path of " dialectic ", this would carry him into a region yet more remote from the endless vicissitudes of human life. Hence to require of him evidence for the being of God, or justification for attributing to him any distinct character, is to demand either an exact demonstration or an arduous flight of speculative philosophy. Or if, again, we revert to his own antithesis of knowledge and opinion or belief, in which department is theology to be placed? Myths can only be believed, not known, and they may be defensible as adumbrations of truth. But what truth? Are they based on assured knowledge of God's existence, or are they only modes of embellishing a set of abstract propositions which otherwise would be too stark and dreary to touch the imagination and inspire the soul? In plain language, is God himself a myth?

After a short detour we thus come back to the point already noted, that whereas God appears in the early part of the Republic (and again in the tenth book, where the story of Er is confessedly a myth), in the central part, addressed to the intellectual few, we hear only of the Good. Now the intuition (or whatever we please to call it) of the Good is superior to scientific knowledge, but belief is definitely inferior, and its objects are below the level of pure being. And, since there is no question of demonstrating the existence of God by any mathematical method (for to Plato that would be an absurdity), he must be the object either of belief or of the supreme intuition, but surely not of both? In other words, the difficulty of identifying God with the Good—or one of the difficulties—is that it seems to involve a corresponding identification of two modes of apprehension which, in Plato's account of them, appear to be distinct and even incompatible. Much of the material for a fuller discussion of the question is contained in the Timaeus, a dialogue of unique historical importance because for many centuries an incomplete Latin version of it was the only work of Plato known to the European world, which had forgotten its Greek. For the moment, however, I shall barely touch that source of information, reserving for a later chapter certain problems which it has not yet been convenient to introduce. This much may be admitted at once, that in the Timaeus, no less than in the Republic, there are plausible grounds for maintaining that Plato's " theology ", when he speaks of God as personal, belongs to the region of " myth ".

What conclusion, then, is to be drawn from the evidence so far considered? Some flaw in the argument, some lack of coherence, we are obliged to suspect; but I doubt if any careful student of Plato will believe that all the language of religion, which he so frequently and so earnestly adopts, is nothing more than a concession to the vulgar, while in his own mind he only postulates the Good as an abstract ideal in which the union of knowledge and virtue is perfected and the meaning of the

D

universe explained.   To insist on the practical importance of religion without believing in its truth is, indeed, quite possible.   Machiavelli, for instance, sincerely regrets the decay of religion in Italy and denounces the corruption of the Church.   But while he urges princes to honour religion, he calmly adds that it matters nothing if they believe not a word of what they profess.   Religion is a safeguard of law and order, an instrument of policy, a title to respect, but its value does not depend on its truth.   Thus does Machiavelli expose the limitations of his own acute understanding, but Plato is no Machiavellian.   Of credulity and cynicism he is equally devoid.   He certainly believes in God, and is feeling his way towards monotheism, but the direction is not yet entirely clear.   Accepting from Pythagoras the broad conception of philosophy as a " method " or way of life, and approving in principle the incongruous association of mystics and mathematicians, he sets out to diminish the incongruity by attacking it from both sides. On the one hand, he substitutes a sober theology for Orphic legend and ecstasy; on the other, he shows that mathematical science, depending, as it does, on indemonstrable hypotheses, is not the final stage, but only a prelude to a higher mode of approaching the Good. Thus religion is made to appear more reasonable, while the supreme object of knowledge is shown to be also the supreme criterion of value and the sole infallible guide to the conduct of life.

At this point, however, comes the check to progress.   Knowledge and belief are unalterably distinct, nor does Plato imagine (and thus far he is right) that even in the most perfectly ordered republic the majority of the citizens will ever be qualified to reach the heights of " dialectic ".   He therefore proposes to govern the State by knowledge, but always through the medium of " orthodoxy "; for of that ominous term, still more clearly than of " theology ", Plato must be reckoned the author.   Now orthodoxy is really an expansion of the principle already exemplified in the function of myths.   What men cannot perfectly understand they can only believe, and in every formula of belief there will be an imperfect expression of truth, some trace of the misrepresentation which the famous antithesis of appearance and reality always seems to imply.   In this atmosphere, too, propaganda will flourish and the " medicinal lie " will always be legitimate, so long as a genuine physician compounds the dose.

Much that Plato says or implies in defence of orthodoxy is not peculiar to himself or his age.   On the contrary, it was the growth of a theology far more advanced than any he had dreamed of that made it imperative to provide authoritative statements of belief and plain rules of conduct which the majority of the faithful would be content to take on trust. Yet somehow he leaves us with the impression that he has never quite faced the crucial question whether the things he would have men believe about the nature of God are true. When orthodoxy means only that, for lack of ability or inclination to seek for proof, we are ready to accept all kinds of surprising statements on the authority of physicists, astronomers, and other men of science, we are not believing things essentially unknowable, but are merely recognizing a practical necessity, which, of course, is far more obvious to-day than in ancient Greece. But though it is natural to say that we then " believe " what is told us by persons wiser than ourselves, it is really in the persons that we believe, if their reputation inspires confidence, while the facts they impart to us are properly objects of knowledge. We all believe, for instance, that the earth goes round the sun, but comparatively few of us are familiar with the reasons that induced Copernicus to abandon the old astronomy. Yet the reasons are fully intelligible, and the facts, as an astronomer grasps them, are not in the least like Plato's " objects of belief ". This usage, therefore, of the term " orthodoxy " is decidedly ambiguous. When it means only that the higher education is beyond the reach of the multitude, and that philosophical kings will have to translate eternal truths into dogmatic laws before they can exercise mundane authority, we can allow that little more violence is thus done to truth than when we talk of " sunrise " and " sunset " or make an absolute contrast between " up " and " down ". So long, in fact, as orthodoxy is relative to the pursuit of knowledge which culminates ideally in vision of the Good, it is no worse than any other practical expedient. But when the name of God is introduced, when a theology supported by myths is propounded, and when no definite attempt is made to identify God with the Good, Plato surely provokes the suspicion that the orthodox are now being asked to believe something that can be only an " object of belief " for the sufficient reason that it can never be known.

In spite of this evident difficulty, I must again express my conviction that Plato does believe in the reality of God, and that he is not proposing to reduce the whole of religion to the level of myth. Much of the evidence I am obliged to omit, and certain points are intentionally reserved for later discussion, but without injustice we may now draw two important conclusions. First, then, Plato finds no manifestation of God in history, and therefore no historical evidence, no true narratives to take the place of the " false *logoi* ", otherwise known as myths. But since he also rejects allegory, and holds that myths, if they are to induce belief, must be made to sound like true stories, he is left in an uncomfortable situation. Secondly, when he moves on to higher regions of philosophy, where he feels, no doubt, that history is no longer relevant, he discovers the need of a mode of apprehension superior to the knowledge obtainable by exact science, but makes not the slightest suggestion of any affinity or connexion between this supreme intuition of the Good and the belief in God required by his theology and fostered by suitable myths. The upshot is that we cannot know God either through historical revelation or by faith.

4

The General Movement of Greek Philosophy

BETWEEN the death of Plato and the first visible signs of the inevitable conflict of Greek philosophy with the Christian " way " lies an interval of nearly five centuries; but from the very beginning of that long period the outline of the arena is discernible and some of the major events seem to cast their shadows before them. Theology and orthodoxy had arrived in close company, with authority at their heels, while reason, as represented by logical demonstration, had been subordinated to the idea of an intuition beyond hypotheses, the revelation of absolute truth. Anticipations, however, are apt to be equivocal, and it would be wrong to suppose that any of the terms thus used to describe Plato's position had yet acquired the whole of its predestined significance. When, for instance, we talk of " authority " in relation to the Christian religion, we take for granted the existence of two things, the Church and Canonical Scripture, to neither of which is there any real analogy in the ancient world. That Homer was " the Bible of the Greeks " is a favourite commonplace; but Plato, at least, had no use for this " Bible " and, when we remember that his educational myths will (in his own estimation) be neither history nor allegory, it is clear that he has no intention of basing religion on the authority of sacred books. Still more important is it to understand that Plato had not even the faintest conception of a Church which could be distinguished from the State. Yet to say that Church and State were identical in pagan times would be almost more misleading than to treat them as distinct; for it was not until the claim of a spiritual society to autonomous existence had been openly affirmed that doctrines like those of Erastus or Hobbes could have any meaning. What Plato does uphold is the difference between the authority of wisdom and the definitions of positive law. That any arbitrary decree of the State (no matter what its constitutional form) could fix the boundary between right and wrong he would flatly deny, but this in no way prevents him from invoking the aid of the law for the coercion of unruly citizens who decline to walk in the highway appointed by wisdom. Law cannot make or unmake justice, but when kings are philosophers, and when the laws represent, so far as possible, eternal truths, orthodoxy in religion becomes a civic duty, and to deny the existence of the gods, or to traduce their character, is to deserve the gravest penalties. Here, then, we have all the elements of the problem of " authority ", but without the peculiar complications involved in the visible embodiment of a Church. So, again, when we find in Plato a suggestion that reason (as the term has often been understood) may have its limitations, we must beware of forgetting that, from the Christian point of view, he has only a rudimentary notion of " faith ", and that, in so far as he connects theology with " belief ", this is no great compliment, and certainly no ground for exalting the theologian above the philosopher.

The main object of this chapter is to survey, in barest outline, the general movement of Greek philosophy towards the point at which its incompatibility with the new philosophy of the Christians was officially declared.   And here it may be useful to refer to an interpretation of history associated with the name of Auguste Comte, who believed there was a law of development in accordance with which there would be a normal transition from theology to philosophy, and from philosophy to positive science.   We must not, of course, demand a proof that each stage came to an end, at some precise date, before the next began— for that would be too obviously untrue—but the question is whether, as a broad interpretation of the past, Comte was justified in regarding theology as the infancy of speculation, philosophy as its youth, and science as its mature perfection.   Individual development on these lines is by no means uncommon; if we need an illustrious example, the life of Aristotle (as reconstructed in Jaeger's remarkable book) * will supply it.   In his earlier years, while still a convinced Platonist, Aristotle may have been even more theological than his master, for he was possibly untroubled by the suspicion that theology, as founded only on belief, must be inferior to knowledge.   Hence he could not only declare, in the *Eudemian Ethics*, that the supreme end of human action was the service and contemplation of God, but in the *Metaphysics* could present the eternal life of God, consisting in pure self-reflective activity of mind, as the explanation of the whole cosmic scheme, and therefore as the goal of all philosophical inquiry, beyond the reach of physics (the " second philosophy ") and attainable only by a " theology " which could rise above the endless sequence of cause and effect to contemplation of the Mover who is himself unmoved.   But, although this was the version of Aristotelianism destined to exercise most

* W. Jaeger, *Aristotle*, O.U.P.

influence on medieval theologians, there are grounds for believing that it was only a phase through which Aristotle passed to a philosophy of " being ", metaphysical but not in the least theological; while even this second moment in his intellectual history may have been only a preface to his final conversion to the organization of purely scientific research.

Many philosophers less famous than Aristotle, as well as a host of unpretentious amateurs, have doubtless experienced a similar transition; with a little ingenuity it may even be possible to select considerable periods of history in which the general tendency of intellectual progress would seem to agree pretty well with Comte's theory. As it happens, however, there is one and only one test case, and there his argument completely breaks down.   I refer, of course, to Greek philosophy, and I call it the only decisive test because it is the only chapter of a still unfinished chronicle which can be read from beginning to end.   Between medieval and modern philosophy there is no such clear-cut division as some of the historians have imagined, while we are too much in the thick of modern thought to prophesy with any confidence its future direction.   Greek philosophy, on the other hand, lies before us like a completed drama which can be studied from the first act until the fall of the curtain and the extinction of the lights.   It begins with the appearance of Thales, and, about eleven centuries later, it ends with an imperial decree.

Now when we survey this long stretch of time with the rise of one school after another, the affiliations and offshoots, and all the ebb and flow of competitive opinions, it may strike us that the acts of the drama are not, after all, very clearly distinguished.   Certainly there is no orderly procession of typical figures across the stage in what Comte would regard as the wrong direction.   Yet, when we patiently disentangle the plot and mark the general drift of the action, there can be little doubt that, in order to make the evolution of Greek philosophy square with his theory, Comte would be obliged to read the libretto backwards or upside down.   The plainest fact of all is that the first effort of Greek speculation was a hazardous and premature excursion into the field of natural science.   That the methods were confused, the implements rudimentary, the results, as tried by our own standards, inconsiderable, is not surprising, but no one of those deficiencies can obscure the fact that in aim and principle these masterful pioneers were men of science, forerunners of Newton and Galileo, determined to wrest from Nature her innermost secrets and to discover the hidden reality of which " phenomena " were at once the manifestation and the disguise.   Their outlook, too, was entirely secular and, though, as we have seen already, they expressed contempt for the fabulous theogonies which were the only existing " theology ", there could be no question of proposing science as a successor to an established philosophy, or to a still earlier dogmatic religion, for no such antecedents had ever existed.

The first stage, then, was in its essential character scientific, and by good fortune we have unimpeachable evidence of the revolution which initiated the second.   The *locus classicus* is the famous passage in the *Phaedo* (96–100) where Socrates, in the last hours of his life, dips into autobiography and tells the story of his disenchantment from the spell of natural science which had fallen upon him in his youth.   It happened that Plato was unable (as he tells us) to be present on this solemn occasion, and in no case could we suppose the dialogue to be a verbatim report.   Yet only a victim of the strange obsession that whatever Plato relates of Socrates must be fiction will doubt that in this passage we are brought face to face with a record of personal experience.   At the same time the reasons given by Socrates for dissatisfaction with naturalism do not depend on his idiosyncrasy; for in character and principle they are exactly the same reasons that might be offered to-day for refusing to admit that scientific explanations of the world can satisfy a philosophic mind.   What Socrates came to understand, as his power of criticism developed, was that the causes alleged by the naturalists were never reasons.   They told him how things happened, but not why: they described but did not explain.   The greatest of all disappointments was when he jumped at the offer of Anaxagoras to trace all natural processes to the agency of " mind ", only to find that, after all, the agents mostly discussed were not mind, but air, water, æther, and so forth; instruments required, no doubt, for effecting certain results, but instruments of a purpose wholly undisclosed.   Least of all could this type of explanation account for human behaviour.   When Socrates asks, for instance, why he sits down or gets up, an answer that merely describes the mechanism of his joints and sinews is sheer mockery.   Or if, again, he wants to know why he stays in prison instead of accepting a good offer to procure his escape, Anaxagoras and all the rest of them have nothing to say.

The language of Socrates is blunt and simple, and the whole episode is only a preface to another phase of the argument.   Naturally, therefore, it is easy to raise objections, and easier still to misrepresent his position.   The most likely criticism is that he is reproaching natural science for failing to do what it never ought to attempt.   Science, as

Bacon would say, has nothing to do with final causes. It does not look for reasons and purposes nor ask " what is the good of " natural laws and phenomena; its business is only to describe what normally happens, or, if it does go so far as to assert that the happening is necessary, the necessity will only be that of a sequence in which effects follow from causes either antecedent in time, or perhaps contemporary, but never located in the future like the ends of purposive human action. These admirable commonplaces (with variations due to scepticism about cause and effect) are not, however, a refutation of Socrates, but rather a confirmation of his point of view; for his contention is not that science has misconceived the character of its own kind of knowledge, but that knowledge thus conditioned is not what he wants. He is not demanding an impossibility, but, just because it is impossible for science, by its right and proper methods, to get beyond the investigation of sequences and mechanisms, he regretfully concludes that the things he would fain understand must remain inexplicable unless another kind of philosophy can come to the rescue. Then, as now, there doubtless were many who would reply that he was leaving solid ground to launch out into the void; but now, as then, the assertion that science alone possesses the key of knowledge and truth is not scientific, but belongs to a form of dogmatism that every true disciple of Socrates will repel.

A far more serious libel on Socrates has often been perpetrated by his friends. Again and again we read in books by authors otherwise reputable that what he did was simply to abandon science in favour of ethics. Had this been true, his accusers would have been able to charge him with a far graver offence than any contained in the actual indictment; but even their impudence fell short of that. Socrates was guilty of no such treason to the cause of philosophy, and the mere suggestion of it is enough to reduce the statements in the *Phaedo* to nonsense. What Socrates desired to understand was nothing less than the cosmic order, and, because he could not persuade himself that a description of the mechanism was a sufficient explanation, he turned away from physical science to look for something more helpful. But to suppose that the discovery of a neat little compartment in which men and women could walk up and down dusting the furniture in orderly fashion, with a bland indifference to the stars in their courses, would have satisfied his curiosity is to mistake the man who could inspire the composition of the *Phaedo* for a lecturer at some provincial university barely discoverable on the map. How far Socrates did advance towards the conception of the Good ascribed to him by Plato in the

Republic is, to be sure, a controversial question, too large for the present discussion, but who can doubt that the pupil was following towards the distant horizon the road already indicated by the master ?   At least it is agreed that Socrates was in the habit of maintaining that virtue was knowledge, and here again the critics have often been sadly wide of the mark.   They talk as though Socrates proposed to account for the frequency of theft and murder by suggesting that the culprits had (so to speak) never heard of the Decalogue, or had omitted to read the notice-boards warning trespassers of prosecution.   But Socrates was not quite such a simpleton as that.   The vicious are ignorant, not for lack of correct information, nor because their parents and nurses forgot to tell them to be good boys, but because nothing is truly known without a just appreciation of its worth.   Without knowledge there can be no valuation, and, conversely, without accurate valuation there is no genuine knowledge.   That is why, as Plato was in due course to observe, the supreme Good cannot properly be identified with knowledge, for, upon further inquiry, it must turn out that the requisite " knowledge " is nothing else but knowledge of the Good.   If, then, we would understand why Socrates protested that no man armed with perfect knowledge could deliberately prefer evil to good, we must first grasp his reasons for deserting a kind of knowledge that could tell him nothing about the meaning of the universe, and must accompany him in his search for the Good.   If, on the other hand, we imagine that he is merely exhorting us to give up the interpretation of the cosmos as a bad job and betake ourselves to ethics, we shall never even begin to understand what " philosophy " meant for Socrates and Plato, or what indeed it has meant for all men, even the humblest, who have striven to know where wisdom could be found.

Anaxagoras, as the patron of " mind ", had turned out to be something of an impostor, but the disappointment of Socrates is a valuable clue to one important aspect of the revolution effected at the time when philosophy—if we choose to preserve the style of Comte—was first differentiated from natural science.   Hitherto the common assumption had been (and the Pythagorean doctrine of " numbers " is no exception) that body alone was real; that, however great the difference between the original " nature " and the superficial flow of phenomena and however many alternative theories there might be about its constitution, at least it must have some kind of bulk or mass with three spatial dimensions.   Whether empty space was also necessary, possible, or (as some maintained) inconceivable, was a much-debated problem, equivalent, perhaps, to the paradoxical question whether " not-being " could " be "; but in all the lively controversies of the pre-Socratic age body retained its position as the unchallenged criterion by which all pretensions to reality must be judged. Let us beware, however, of selecting " materialism " as the appropriate label for that kind of thought. It is even doubtful (as Aristotle felt) whether any clear conception of " matter " had yet been formed, and it is certain that no one could be a materialist until the reality of mind or spirit had been asserted; and it is, of course, very far from true that the recognition of *psyche*, even when its importance was as great as the Pythagoreans allowed, must imply that bold assertion. Not until the dialogues of Plato do we find any genuine metaphysics, any clear affirmation, that is to say, of a reality which cannot be weighed, measured, or subjected to any test known to physical science. Once he had made his great discovery, it is not surprising that Plato should have swung over to the opposite extreme of maintaining that real objects, knowable only by pure intelligence, could not possibly be corporeal. It was not enough that all the phenomena immediately apprehended by the senses should be explicable in terms of invisible elements or atoms, for that was only what the physicists had taught. Upon himself and his successors Plato imposed the far heavier task of explaining the relation of phenomena to " ideas " or " forms ", which were the sole realities, and yet were eternally devoid of all corporeal attributes. Unless, then, the physical could either be derived from the metaphysical or dismissed as sheer illusion, there was an obvious danger of being left with a dualism of (let us say) matter and spirit, with no good reason for holding that one was more original or more real than the other. We must constantly bear in mind, too, that Plato was not, in the modern sense, an " idealist ". The real existence of the objects knowable by mind was in no way derived from, or dependent upon, the mind's activity; and, since Plato had no doubt whatever that mind itself was incorporeal, not even an unqualified declaration that the whole physical world was illusory would have saved him from the irreducible antithesis of subject and object (mind and " forms ") within the sphere of the indubitably real.

The only excuse for thus compressing into a few sentences the material of problems which required the whole history of Platonism for their full expansion is that the bare mention of them is enough to mark the immense distinction between philosophy as conceived by Plato and the precocious adventure of Ionian science. At the same time there was no question of hostility to science or of suppressing it (had that been possible) in the interests of a wholly different intellectual discipline. Not even succession of one defined epoch to another, but rather a gradual division of provinces, beneficial in the long run to all parties, is what we trace in the century most productive of original thought in Greece. To talk of philosophy as superseding science would, to Plato, have been as absurd as to pretend that the manœuvres of atoms in the void could account for the charm of the *Iliad* or the irony of Socrates. Similarly, when we turn to theology, the third of the competitors distinguished by Comte, we may reasonably hold that in merely chronological order it was the last to manifest its predominance; but at no time in the history of Greek speculation was it true that a secular philosophy had to come to an end before the theologians could disport themselves freely on the stage. We have learned already that the theology of the future, as contrasted with the fabulous theogonies of the past, was invented by Plato; but we have also noted the signs of an awkward gap between "belief" or "orthodoxy" on the one hand and the supreme intuition of mind on the other—corresponding to the imperfectly explained relation between the living God and the apparently impersonal Good. The later development of philosophy did not, however, take the form of a mortal conflict between those two ideals, but resulted in the gradual absorption of both into the Neoplatonist doctrine of the ineffable One. To describe that result either as the deification of the Good, or as the rejection of the mythical attributes sometimes assigned by Plato to God, would be possible; but at present I shall not go beyond the statement that philosophy thus became—at its highest level and without any concessions to the vulgar—more distinctly theological than at any time in its earlier history. There was no conscious desertion of philosophy for theology, any more than in Plato's own day there had been any formal repudiation of science on behalf of philosophy. It was simply that the scope of philosophy, as time went on, was constantly enlarged and its demands for an adequate explanation of the world less easily satisfied. All claimants to wisdom had to be cross-examined, and should it appear that the mathematicians, for instance, or the physicists had claimed too much, then search for a deeper kind of knowledge must be made. Or if, again, there was any truth in the pretensions of the mystics to illumination, a place must be found for mysticism, not by reverting to Pythagorean taboos, or even to Platonic myths, but by the discipline of mind and spirit which at rare moments might culminate in the ecstatic vision of something beyond the reach of demonstration or dialectic. The philosophers, in fact, would not admit that any kind of truth was outside their province; for all truth must contribute to wisdom, though not always in the way that specialists with a limited outlook had supposed.

But if Comte's reading of history, as illustrated by the development of Greek philosophy, is untenable, it would also be difficult to trace, in the schools of thought most prominent in the four or five centuries after the death of Plato, any clear and continuous movement towards the recognition of theory as the supreme mode of speculation. What we notice first of all is a change of atmosphere, a curious drop in the temperature, as though the philosophical pilgrim had strayed from the upward path and lost himself for a time in the mists enveloping the Slough of Despond. Not the least remarkable fact is the total failure to maintain any hold on the notion of incorporeal reality, which in the period covered by the great names of Socrates, Plato, and Aristotle had seemed to transform the whole character of philosophy and to point in the direction of a theistic interpretation of the world. However marked their differences in other respects, the Stoics and the Epicureans were alike in being " materialists ", at least in the sense that they failed to recognize in soul, mind, or spirit any substance devoid of corporeal attributes; and so widely did this hypothesis prevail in the Græco-Roman world that S. Augustine, as we learn from a well-known passage in the *Confessions*, was astonished to hear from the Platonists that any other view was possible. But, although in this respect the movement of thought was retrograde, there was no reversion to the stage commonly known as pre-Socratic. The genuine sciences, whether mathematical or experimental, seem to have been deflected into secondary channels, where their progress was not impeded either by exaggerated claims to universal wisdom or by conflicts with popular religion. Meanwhile the main stream of philosophy had to make its way through a troubled world, in which the ancient liberties of autonomous cities were being submerged by the weight of empires, and the ancient gods were passing through twilight into an ever-deepening gloom.

By " history ", of course, we are apt to mean just so much of the past as is recorded in books, and it is well to remember that the books surviving from classical antiquity reflect, for the most part, the thoughts of men sophisticated or disillusionized by education rather than the lives of peasants or artisans inhabiting a world unvexed by newspapers and other cheap modes of diffusing ideas. Hence to assert of the third century B.C., or, for that matter, of the third century A.D., that pagan religion was already exhausted would be extremely rash. Only in so far as we confine our attention to a rather limited circle is it safe to accept the evidence of philosophical books that the gods were moribund, or that a rationalized theology was supplanting the old, incoherent

medley of beliefs.   Even so, the evidence is rather ambiguous, and the
result, from a distinctly religious point of view, might often seem to be
negative.   The avowed sceptics, it is true, were more anxious to prove
the impotence of reason than to quarrel with any form of religious
orthodoxy; but the Epicureans, if unfairly branded as "atheists",
were certainly not more than deists who held that, since the gods did
not trouble themselves about human affairs, men might fairly return
the compliment by declining to trouble themselves about the gods.
The possibility of this cool indifference had already been noted and
condemned by Plato, but we cannot doubt that to minds of a type
common in every age of critical inquiry it brought a great sense of
relief.   Whenever religion is felt as a burden, whenever it is summarized in the uneasy thought that "there may be Heaven, there must
be Hell", no school of philosophy that offers to silence the *strepitus
Acherontis avari* will lack an audience.   Considered atheism is, in fact,
a form of theology, and we may go so far as to admit that it has sometimes been preferable to the theology against which it expressed a lively
protest.   It was not so much because the Epicureans were whole-
hearted atheists that they failed to make a deeper impression as because
they were not.   What chiefly discredited them, however, was their
recommendation of Pleasure as the Good; and, though here again both
their theory and their practice were often grossly misrepresented, it is
doubtful whether a more accurate interpretation would have improved
their status.   The genuine Epicurean was, indeed, no professional
debauchee.   On the contrary, he might be found dining contentedly
on porridge and water, and in his general regulation of appetite and
desire might rival the Stoic austerity.   But why?   Not because he
hated sin; not because he was training for an incorruptible crown, or
even a corruptible; but simply because luxury and self-indulgence did
not pay.   The pains might so easily outweigh the pleasures; the consequent headache was too great a price for the gusto of the wine.   In
the hedonism which means a reckless determination to make every
moment of life delicious there is profound delusion, but nothing quite
so ignoble as a frigid calculation that virtue is likely on the whole to be
less troublesome than vice.   Something loftier than this there must have
been in Epicureanism at its best, but even its warmest apologist will
hardly pretend that, as a rival to the Christian gospel, it had to be
seriously considered.

A far weightier matter was Stoicism, the one form of Greek philosophy which deeply influenced Roman society before the proper
genius of Rome—itself not philosophical—was dissolved into a cos-

mopolitan mixture of elements derived from every quarter of the civilized world. To the Roman age (though written, of course, in Greek) belong the two most famous documents of Stoicism, the *Discourses* of the slave Epictetus and the *Meditations* of the emperor Marcus Aurelius, while in the letters of Seneca (many of them nominally addressed to an Epicurean friend) we have ample materials for estimating the propriety of the legend which includes S. Paul among the writer's correspondents. That all those works were composed long after the founding of the school by Zeno is doubtless an important fact for historians, but from another point of view the quality of the later writings may be more significant than the exact form of the original doctrines. Nor is it merely that direct rivalry between Greek philosophy and the Christian gospel belongs inevitably to the Christian era. Quite apart from their bearing on the new religion, it is a remarkable fact that each of the three most famous Greek philosophies had to wait for centuries before coming into its own. Not that there is anything in the history of Stoicism closely analogous to the advent of Plotinus, or to the astonishing reappearance of Aristotle in the thirteenth century, but for its full expansion it does seem to have required the breadth of the Roman Empire, and it is no real injustice to Zeno and Cleanthes to judge their capacity for " saving " mankind by the presentation of their doctrines in authors comparatively late.

The question, in fact, is whether philosophy, in some such form as Epictetus or Marcus Aurelius had given it, could hold its own against the Christian alternative. Manifestly it did not, and, without pretending to touch more than the fringe of so large a subject, it may be possible to indicate briefly the main reasons for concluding that Stoicism, despite its great influence on the Græco-Roman world, was not only incapable of providing a universal religion, but was also in its intellectual quality so mediocre that it was likely to flourish only in an age when philosophical reflection of the highest order was more or less in abeyance. The importance of its contribution to the theory of will and conscience, and its unswerving faith in man's power to hold intact the citadel of his own soul, are unquestionable. Hence it is not surprising to find in Christian writings many admirable maxims of Stoic origin, and the story of a link between Seneca (Gallio's brother) and S. Paul does not cease to be interesting because no real evidence for it can be produced. One source of confusion, indeed, is the facility with which Stoic authors lend themselves to effective quotation. They are full of weighty aphorisms and moral epigrams which, removed from their proper atmosphere, have a Christian ring in the bare sound of them, and may seem to challenge comparison with precepts drawn from the New Testament. Yet to infer from such evidence that the Christians, after all, had nothing very new to say is almost as futile as to argue that Christ himself, in his discourses, was only repeating truths already enunciated by Jewish rabbis. The simplest cure for the belief that Stoic teaching is in essence identical with Christian is to open Epictetus or Marcus Aurelius at random and read any four or five consecutive pages. If anyone can imagine, after this brief experiment, that he has been reading a Christian book, the only possible conclusion will be that he is not yet acquainted with the rudiments of the Christian faith.

But again, we shall get a little deeper into the matter if we remember that " The Village called Morality " is by no means the spiritual home of Christians. " It is a mistake ", says Edwyn Bevan, " to suppose that the distinctive thing about Christianity was that it set before man a new code of conduct." What Bevan primarily means by this bold declaration is that the Old Law, as delivered to the Jews, was to be fulfilled rather than destroyed by the New Gospel; for it was to devout Jews, of course, not to adepts in Greek philosophy, that the gospel was first proclaimed. So rapid, however, was the missionary expansion that only a few years after the crucifixion S. Paul could find occasion to adapt his argument to the comprehension of Stoics and Epicureans. Had his theme been only morality, the adaptation (at least in the case of the Stoics) would have offered no great difficulty; and when, in later ages, the time arrived for a more deliberate comparison of the Christian philosophy with others, it was not because the pagan masters had failed to apprehend the nature of virtue and vice that they were judged to be inadequate guides. On the contrary, it was allowed not only that their precepts were often excellent, but that the principles of moral conduct, within the range, as one might say, of the cardinal virtues, required no special revelation. No better expression of the Christian tradition, at least in its more critical exponents, can be given than the text from the Epistle to the Romans (2. 14) which, nearly seventeen centuries afterwards, Bishop Butler prefixed to one of his Sermons on Human Nature: " For when the Gentiles, which have not the law, do by nature the things contained in the law, those, having not the law, are a law unto themselves ". What Stoic would not applaud ? Of the antithesis of Jew and Gentile he might, indeed, know nothing, but to be " a law unto himself ", to live " according to nature ", and therefore to obey conscience or " the ruling faculty ", was as much the purpose of every faithful disciple of Zeno as it was the ground of

Butler's weighty answer to those who pretended that, apart from the prohibitions of revealed religion, it was " natural " to indulge every appetite and desire.

All religion is either above the level of morality or below it, but never are the two identical.   Hence to search the pages of Stoic authors for points of correspondence with the New Testament, and perhaps to argue that a world converted to Stoicism would have been quite as well behaved as the Christian Church, is a rather pathetic waste of time.   Whether as a religion of universal efficacy or as a philosophy addressed to the intellectually gifted, Stoicism has obvious and fatal defects.   Faith, Hope, Charity are the three that " abide ", but of these " theological virtues " there is scarcely a gleam or glimmer in the wisdom of the Stoics.   Perhaps the most conspicuous absentee is Hope; for Stoicism, at bottom, is always the religion of desperate men resolved never to despair.   All things behave according to their nature, and all events come to pass in obedience to inexorable law.   Nothing independent of choice can be desirable or harmful.   Why, then, weep if our children die ?   Why encourage the grief of others by pity, or strive to assuage it with sympathy ?   Why be astonished or angry if our neighbours attempt to injure us, or if tyrants threaten us with death ?   As well might we abuse the gods because it rains or snows.   Such are the reiterated sentiments of this stern philosophy, and the result was always likely to be acquiescence, apathy, moral indifference, redeemed only by a touch of heroism in adversity, and supported by the final reflection that life, when it becomes too inconvenient, need never be prolonged; for merely to lie in a warm bath and open a vein will always (unless fuel be scarce) be one of the things dependent on choice.

Despite, too, its vaunted cosmopolitanism, its professed sympathy with all that is human, its cold approval of beneficence, Stoicism is utterly remote from the spirit of Christian charity.   It brings no message of love or consolation to the masses, and provides no more material for their salvation than any other Greek philosophy.   But since it never really pretended to undertake that kind of mission, let us next inquire whether its claim to have formulated a sufficient theology or " first philosophy " is more considerable.   Here again there can be only disappointment.   To students of logic and the theory of know-ledge there are points of interest in the Stoic technicalities, and behind the ethical teaching there is an official background of cosmology.   Yet the decline of speculation during the temporary eclipse of Platonism is as patent here as elsewhere.   Whichever of the two lines of develop-ment suggested by Plato we prefer to follow—whether we demand no

E

more than the systematic unity of a cosmos governed and penetrated by impersonal Reason, or whether, adopting the language of religion, we seek rather for a God who might be the object of adoration—the result will be only the discovery of a rather nebulous totality, a single substance which, in attempting, as it were, to be both body and spirit, fails to be either in any distinctive sense.   Pantheism, Materialism, Fatalism—with justice, perhaps, the Stoic will repudiate each of these labels, but for reasons far more cogent we may reply that the God of Stoicism is no more adequate to the needs of any genuine theism than was the " mind " of Anaxagoras to satisfy the curiosity of Socrates about the meaning of the world.

Could language alone suffice, it would, no doubt, be possible to gather from Epictetus (more easily than from Marcus Aurelius) many beautiful passages which might be mistaken for Christian expressions of devout resignation to the will of God.   But at any moment we might be suddenly and violently undeceived.   When, for instance, Epictetus exhorts us (Disc. IV. 7) to meet the approach of death with the reflection that " it is time for a compound piece of matter to be resolved back into its original ", we can scarcely fail to understand the immensity of the gulf that lies between the sentiment of that utterance and the feelings of the Christian mourner as he stands beside the open grave and hears the words " dust to dust, ashes to ashes " solemnly pronounced. Stoicism appears, in fact, to fall between two stools, if not three.   On the one hand, its cosmopolitanism and philanthropy are too intellectual to bring comfort to the simple; on the other, its speculative outlook and systematic thought are too hazy to satisfy the metaphysician; while to the theologian whose theology is grounded in religious experience it will seem that all he is offered, in the last resort, is a substance far more easily compared to the wind that bloweth where it listeth than to the spirit who must be worshipped in spirit and in truth.

Marcus Aurelius—most humane of men—persecuted Christianity, but only because he was ignorant of its nature, and certainly not because he imagined it would ever presume to meet his own philosophy on equal terms.   In a certain unexpected sense, too, he was right; for at no time was it probable that in the decisive struggle between Christian and pagan wisdom the pagan forces would be commanded by a Stoic. The reason, however, was not that Christianity was too humble an adversary, but that Stoicism itself did not carry enough guns.   Only Platonism, as revived and developed in the school of Plotinus, could be a serious competitor, because only Platonism was spiritual enough to touch the deepest religious instincts, and intellectual enough to reveal the essential points of sympathy and antipathy between its own doc-trines and those of the Church. On the religious side, however, so far as it was a question of providing for the needs of the common folk, no form of Platonism ever had the slightest chance of victory. In the centuries dividing Plotinus from his master the whole political structure of the world had been transformed. Instead of the petty dominions of Athens or Sparta, an empire acknowledging no rivals and, save for its own convenience, no boundaries, had arisen; while citizenship, once confined to a handful of residents who could meet at an hour's notice to debate a policy or pass a law, had been diffused among the freemen of three continents as the sign and warrant of imperial authority. Two results of this stupendous revolution were almost equally apparent, the utter impotence of traditional religion to provide a soul for so vast a body and the insufficiency of any philosophical Utopia like Plato's *Republic*, so long as its realization presupposed the limitations of a minute city. Gods, indeed, could always be multiplied, and to that extent the resources of polytheism were adequate to the demands of an indefinite number of localities. But when the need was felt for a deity fit to command the homage of an empire, the only plausible candidate turned out to be the emperor himself. How much political value there was in the cult of the imperial genius, or how far it did acquire any religious significance, it may not be easy to discover; but no one, surely, will be surprised if that kind of apotheosis was a little unconvincing to Jews and Christians, or even to pagan philosophers, if ever they desired to think of the empire as a single community sustained and sanctified by divine power.

Or again, if we turn to the religions imported by soldiers, travellers, or quacks from the eastern provinces, there is evidence that Isis and Mithras could satisfy the appetite for mystery which found no sustenance in the sober ritual of indigenous cults; but, though the prevalence of these and other oriental modes of worship helps to prove the insuffici-ency of classical paganism, it is no less evident that, when the conflict between Christian and Roman religion became acute, they counted for little or nothing. Whether we examine the last vain effort of Julian to stem the advancing tide or S. Augustine's refutation of the charge that Christian " atheism " was responsible for military disasters, it is clear that the exotic deities of Egypt and Asia were equally negligible as enemies or as allies. The only practical question was whether " the religion of Numa " could somehow be inspired with a new vitality and furnished with weapons less obsolete than those which moved Augustine to justifiable derision.   And thus it was that the Neoplatonists were drawn, perhaps reluctantly, into the arena of politics.   Left to themselves, they would have no serious inclination to translate the ideal of Plato's Republic into a scheme of imperial government;   for though Plotinus went so far as to meditate a Platonic reconstruction of a ruined city in the Campagna, his experiment, if accomplished, would have been only a kind of monastic retreat from the world.   A Platonic city was conceivable, but not a Platonic empire;   while as to popular religion, the tradition of the school, derived from Plato himself, would be to approve and encourage conventional piety, so long as it could be kept clear of discreditable myths.   The myths, however, had not been eradicated by philosophical criticism, and when the time came for a forlorn attempt to check the Christian invasion, there was nothing for it but to revert to allegory, the very expedient which Plato himself had wisely refused to adopt.   With much better reason than Plato, the Christians could pour scorn on Homeric tales and still darker legends, but if the philosophers could invent a sufficient number of allegorical interpretations, there might at least be a chance of raising Jupiter to the level of Jehovah, as depicted in the cruder parts of the Old Testament.   To produce anything fit for even the remotest comparison with the story of the Gospels was out of the question, and in any case there would remain the fatal objection (half-understood by Plato) that stories about the gods are always likely to miss the desired effect unless they are believed to be literally true.   As a political instrument, therefore, when the spread of Christianity became a menace to the structure of society, and perhaps to the authority of the State, Neoplatonism was useless.   As a philosophy, however, contesting the ground with another philosophy in the sphere of intellecutal speculation, its power was formidable, and our next step must be to examine the nature of that protracted struggle, which not only left its mark on the Church of the earlier centuries, but also, down to our own times at not infrequent intervals, has continued to colour the texture, and sometimes to cloud the purity, of Christian thought.

5

The Christian Rejection of Platonism
I. History and Faith

WHATEVER its variation in form, whatever its defects and back-slidings, Greek philosophy, at least in its essential character, was always what it professed to be. It was never a " subject ", but always a considered way of life, a search for wisdom, a quest of the final beatitude attainable only by knowledge of the Good. In principle, therefore, it was akin to the higher religions, and for this very reason the collision of Platonism with Christianity was not only as inevitable as the antithesis of Stoic and Epicurean but also infinitely more tragic and profound. From the outset, however, the issue was confused by partial resemblances, by the eagerness of many Christian writers to invoke the aid of Plato against materialism, to borrow his visions of judgement, and to express, in something like his terminology, doctrines which in truth were the negation of his own. As early as the second century A.D. there was a distinguished body of " Christian Platonists " at Alexandria, and in many subsequent centuries—the twelfth, the seventeenth, the twentieth—there have been successors to that equivocal title. But while these tributes to the genius of Plato are easily intelligible, " Christian Platonism ", if we propose to take the expression seriously, is nothing less than a contradiction in terms. As we range over the wide spaces of the immortal dialogues, or perhaps struggle across the thornier ground of the *Enneads*, we find, of course, a great variety of topics, and meet with a vast number of arguments which may be approved or questioned for reasons neither peculiar to any one philosophy, nor relevant, as it seems, to any particular creed. Nor can we fail to be conscious, in reading either Plato or Plotinus, of a certain nobility of tone, an exaltation of mind and spirit, which does in fact make Platonism more congenial than any other Greek philosophy to Christian thought and life. Nevertheless, the discrepancies between Christianity and Platonism, when we get down to first principles, are so radical that only by complete misunderstanding or wilful blindness is it possible to profess allegiance to both.

If we recall for a moment Plato's conception of theology, his proposed use of myth, and his general account of the relation between knowledge and belief, we shall remember that anxiety to provide for the needs of both the few and the many, the intellectual aristocracy and the unphilosophical multitude, obliges him to acquiesce in a division of provinces which looks rather like an evasion.   There are things that it is imperative to believe, and there are things that, ideally at least, it is possible to know; but the objects of belief and knowledge are by nature distinct, and there is no better warrant for expecting the myths required for the support of orthodoxy to be authenticated by science than for pretending that they are literally and historically true.   One result of this dualism is to leave it uncertain whether the God, who is the subject of theology, can be identified with the Good, which is alone the goal of aspiration, the source of knowledge, and the origin of whatever reality there is to be known.   Are the altars at which we " ignorantly worship " rightly dedicated to the one eternal Spirit, or do they merely consecrate a myth?   If Plato never answers, or indeed never asks, precisely this question, it may be because he does not count it vital.   Two things, however, are certain, that he seeks no manifestation of God in history, and that for a revelation of God beyond the scope of science he does not look to faith.   Here, then, are two cardinal points in the comparison of Platonism and Christianity at which their fundamental incompatibility begins to appear.   Let us briefly consider each in turn.

By expurgation of old myths and the invention of new ones Plato hoped to make religion respectable; but the replacement of fiction by historical truth was no part of his programme.   The most obvious reason, of course, for his frank acceptance of " false stories " was that no true ones could anywhere be found; but the most obvious facts are not always the most important, and if we assume that Plato would have welcomed historical evidence about the nature of God, and only had recourse to fiction because nothing better was available, we shall fail to grasp the meaning of his philosophy.   The manifestation of God in actual history Plato would neither expect nor even understand; for history belongs to the world of " becoming ", to the perpetual flux of appearances, which a Heraclitean might accept as the sum total of reality, an Eleatic might dismiss with a bold denial of the possibility of change, while a Platonist would take it as, at most, a disguise to be penetrated and a distortion of truth.   About the relation of the eternal to the temporal, Plato got into great difficulties, but at least we may be sure that in his search for an eternal and unchangeable God he would not direct his gaze towards the historical process of events. It was not merely that Greek theogonies were patently fabulous; it was no mere question of substituting good history for bad. The real point is that the very notion of an " historical religion " was utterly foreign to his mind. In this respect Christianity owes nothing at all to any form of Greek philosophy, nor was it possible in the pre-Christian era to anticipate or imagine the philosophical revolution that would one day be implied in the bare acceptance of a narrative—the story of Jesus of Nazareth—as historical fact. It is very doubtful, indeed, whether the doctrine of the Incarnation of the Logos would have meant anything at all to Plato; for all the diligent attempts to discover analogies in Greek mythology are sad examples of *docta ignorantia*, displaying in about equal proportions philosophical incompetence and ignorance of the Christian faith. But when the time did arrive for the statement that, " The Word was made flesh and dwelt among us ", it was inevitable that Platonists should reject it with scornful amazement. Myths they could tolerate by converting them (despite Plato's warning) into allegories, but history baffled them completely. Whether all or any of the events in the life of Jesus were actually verifiable by human testimony would be an almost negligible question: what they were bound to repudiate with indignation was the very thought of God descending into the sphere of corporeal existence and subjecting himself to the conditions of human life. If they were also shrewd enough to perceive that the gospel narrative could not be explained away as myth or allegory, they were at least superior in this respect to the bewildered " modernists " who maintain that Christianity in its essence has no dependence on historical truth. That is a contention appropriate to sundry Gnostics, and in principle (though not, of course, in its particular application) to Platonists, but of the Christian faith it is entirely destructive.

To discard all the historical affirmations to which the Church is committed, and then to offer the world a spiritualism beyond the reach of sceptical historians, is in effect to revert to the Platonic expedient of edifying myths. For myths, however, the Christian religion can find no place at all. The story of the life, death, and resurrection of Jesus is either good history or bad history, and bad history is an utterly different thing from myth. It would, for instance, be bad history to say that Tiberius reigned before Augustus, or that the battle of Waterloo was fought in 1816, but neither statement would properly be described as mythical. A myth, like a play or a novel, has its own internal order, but it has no dates in the calendar, and none of its recorded incidents occurs either before or after any historical event. Even when accepted quite uncritically by simple folk, it is only a story of what happened " ever so long ago ", and just how long it is pointless to inquire. Hence no such statement as " suffered under Pontius Pilate " can possibly be mythical: it can be only an assertion of historical fact, either true or false.   Now, Plato, of course, was not one of the simple folk.   He knew very well that myths were not history, but he also knew that their function was indispensable.   His attempted way of escape from the consequent dilemma we have already examined, but it is, I submit, a way that for Christians is absolutely barred; not only because the presentation of indoctrinated fiction as history is dishonest, but for the much deeper reason that, if the story be fiction, then the doctrine is false.   The very quintessence of Christianity is the substi-tution of history for myth.   It is not the discourses of Jesus that finally divide the Christian from all other religions, but the fact that he who lived the life of a man and died the death of a man, is yet worshipped as God.   Hence, if Platonism is to be put on the same level, its advocates must be prepared to deify Socrates, not as an extravagant metaphor, nor yet as a Roman Senate might decree divine honours to a defunct emperor, but as a solemn declaration that the eternal God had " come down from Heaven " into the sphere of the temporal and the perishable, to live there as " very man " without ceasing to be a " very God ". To an early Platonist such a doctrine would probably have been mean-ingless: to a disciple of Plotinus it could be only outrageous and profane.

Myth and allegory are by no means identical; but, since the Christian objection to the Platonic use of myth would also involve the repudiation of any attempt to convert the gospel narrative into allegory, some notice must be taken of the undoubted fact that allegorical interpretation of Scripture was not only practised from early times by Christian writers, but also came to be so firmly established that denial of the *sensus mysticus* would at one time have been positively unorthodox.   Moreover, the purpose of this allegorizing was often apologetic, and thus far indis-tinguishable in character from the attempts to mitigate the grossness of the old theogonies denounced by Greek philosophers.   There were many passages in the Old Testament about which thoughtful Christians felt decidedly uncomfortable, but when they betook themselves, rather incautiously, to allegorical interpretation, they at once provoked the retort that they were ashamed of their own sacred books.   Even the retort, however, was significant; for since the allegorizing of " sacred stories ", patently mythical, had long been familiar to pagans, the only ground for objecting to its novel application was that Christians were seriously committed to the assertion that their Scriptures were to be read as history.

A full discourse on allegory would take us much too far afield, but certain points deserve attention, particularly the broad distinction between allegory as a form of literary composition and allegorical interpretation—as a mode of apologetic—of books traditionally understood in a purely literal sense. Even in works admittedly composed as allegories there may, of course, be great variation in the degree of didactic intention. At one extreme the object may be only to make an experiment in a certain literary form; at the other, the story may be only the thinnest of disguises for a sermon. So again, it may be objected that when Homer (or perhaps the Book of Genesis) is defended on the ground that this or that passage is not to be taken literally, the implication may be that the author was an intentional composer of allegory. Despite these symptoms of overlapping, there does remain a serviceable distinction between conscious artists and apologists for " canonical " books, and in both classes Christian writers are numerous. Of one type the *Pilgrim's Progress* is a perfect example, and no reader of that immortal book is likely to have supposed that Mr and Mrs Christian were citizens and rate-payers, domiciled, perhaps, in the town where John Bunyan lived. On the other hand, when a mystical sense was discovered in words or acts ascribed to the Hebrew patriarchs, or perhaps to Jehovah, no Christian would infer that Moses and Aaron, and even the God of the Jews, were fabulous beings.

At this point, however, an entirely new distinction begins to appear. The Christian employment of allegory as a defensive weapon began in the early period when the Jewish Scriptures were allowed to be authoritative, but the narratives and epistles known to us as the New Testament had not yet been collected, much less canonized. But, though it was the early history of the Jews that gave rise to the apologetic use of allegory, the distinctive features of the Christian method were not fully revealed until the relation of the New Testament to the Old began to be considered, and only then did a problem, never discerned by pagan writers, largely supersede the older disputes about the function of allegory. When Greek myths were allegorized because of their impropriety, the avowed object was to argue that their " literal " sense was never meant to be historical. And again, when Plato proposed the composition of edifying myths, the actual stories would, of course, no longer be scandalous, but Plato himself knew perfectly well that they would be fictitious. In a word, neither the apologists nor Plato attached the slightest importance to history as such.

Now, when " the Bible " had been compiled, and when the miscellany contained in it had been scrutinized, not indeed with the eyes of a modern critic, but with considerable care, it became obvious that many passages, and possibly some entire books, were not intended to be read as history.   The Psalms, though full of historical allusions, were poetry, and the Song of Solomon (so at least it was believed) was a deliberate allegory.   More than this, the parables in the Gospels were evidently not fragments of history: no one imagined, for instance, that the Prodigal Son was a dissolute young man who lived in Galilee or thereabouts.   Thus the biblical use of poetry or fable, in which the " literal " sense was not in the least historical, came to be freely recognized; and in this respect an allegorical work of fiction like the *Pilgrim's Progress* would be only an exemplification of a method already familiar to intelligent readers of the Bible.   Nevertheless, the Old Testament does relate the history of the Jews, and no one could seriously believe that the whole account of their adventures and sufferings was meant to be an allegorical romance.   Whether some portions of the narrative were open to critical doubts, or whether other portions (such as the accounts of Creation) could properly be called historical, were secondary questions.   The fact of vital importance was that Christians, when they began to survey the Old Testament from their own point of view, discerned a mystical sense in the actual history of the Chosen People.   To interpret the story of the garden of Eden and the Fall allegorically would, in principle, be no novelty; but when a chronicle which could not possibly be myth, but must be either good or bad history, was found to have a mystical as well as a literal sense, the whole theory of allegory was revolutionized, and the true significance of the revolution was that Christians, in a manner unknown to Greek religion and unintelligible to Greek philosophers, believed in the historical manifestation of God.   Nor was it only the Greeks who were thus left behind, but also the Jews.   To believe that the cause of human history is subject to divine providence is compatible with most religions and with many philosophies; to believe that the destiny of one par- ticular race is the special concern of God is characteristic of the Jews; but to believe that Jewish history is a mystical foreshadowing of the life of the Church—that the Old Testament is to be interpreted by the New —is an expression of Christian faith, possible only to those who believe that in the human life of Jesus was revealed the incarnate Son of God.

Strange as it may seem that faith in the Incarnation should generate a new conception of allegory, it is certainly a fact.   Hitherto the dis- tinction of literal and allegorical senses had by no means implied that the

" literal " was historically true. The " literal " sense of " Orpheus with his lute ", for instance, was just the story as related in poetry or legend; and, however freely it might come to be admitted that Orpheus was only a mythical figure, the " literal " sense of the story would in no way be impaired. But when the Church began to read the Old Testament allegorically, the case was entirely different. Take as illustrations two famous episodes in Jewish history, the coming out of Egypt and the Babylonish captivity, of which mystical interpretations were common. If the Israelites never did shake off the yoke of Pharaoh, if they never did hang up their harps by the waters of Babylon, Handel and Palestrina could still have composed great music appropriate to those themes, but the Christian allegories, as based on historical facts, would entirely lose their point. Dante, as it happens, has twice selected the psalm *In exitu Israel* as an illustration of the allegorical and other hidden senses underlying the " literal ". Now Dante knew very well (and explicitly noted) that the psalms should be read as poetry, and equally well did he understand that myths could with strict propriety be said to have a " literal " sense. Yet that particular psalm does commemorate an historical event, and if the history were proved to be spurious, the mystical superstructure erected by Dante would simply collapse. This does not mean, of course, that exposition of that type was never applied to incidents wrongly supposed to be historical, but it does mean that the distinctive addition to the theory of allegory made by Christian writers was the mystical interpretation of historical facts recorded in the Old Testament, as prophetically foreshadowing the life of the Church; the true foundation of this new reading of history was the doctrine of the Incarnation, which no Platonist would accept, or even try to understand.

In the Platonic philosophy, as we have noted already, " belief " is properly relative to facts that cannot be known, and what surprises us most, when we begin to read Plato, is that these unknowable objects of belief are not invisible entities, beyond the reach of ordinary experience, but just the things and events directly and perpetually apprehended by our senses. In other words, belief is operative in precisely that field of experience which constitutes either history or the raw material of history, according as we understand the term in a primary or a derivative sense. In its most fundamental sense, history is the entire process of phenomenal events, and in the expression " natural history " we are still keeping close to this meaning. In another sense, perhaps more common, " history " is the record of human events for which there is human testimony, the " history " dealt with by " historians " in their books. But, though every historian must make inferences and interpretations which go beyond brute fact, it remains true in principle that the " historical " is that which can be actually experienced by means of our ordinary senses, and only in this vast realm of phenomena, according to Plato, does belief exercise its natural function and find its proper sphere.

Contrast with this, the famous definition in the Epistle to the Hebrews: " Faith is the substance of things hoped for, the evidence of things unseen ". Nobody will pretend that the statement—especially the first half—is easy, but for the purpose of comparison with Platonism it is enough to attend to the words " things unseen ". There is a sense, of course, in which Greek philosophers (Aristotle in particular) could argue that all knowledge must begin with apprehension of the sensible, and thus pass, with the aid of hypothesis and inference, to knowledge of the intelligible; but no theory of that kind brought them any nearer to the doctrine that belief or faith had for its proper object things not only invisible but also actually of a higher order than the facts demonstrable by science; and, though Plato did affirm the existence of a mode of intuition superior to science, he was by no means prepared to identify this synoptic grasp of " all time and existence " with the mental activity known to him as *doxa*. The Christian term is not *doxa* but *pistis*, and this makes it all the more interesting to observe that where Plato does assign a special status to *pistis* (as in *Rep*. VI, 510–511) he relates it to objects which, far from being unseen, are simply the most obvious " things ", which in our least philosophical moments we are content to accept as ultimately real. The man who walks by faith,. in the Platonic sense, is the kind of man who prides himself on his common sense. Shadows and images, he allows, are deceptive, so that a dog, or perchance even a man, may be fool enough to drop the bone for the sake of its empty reflection; but once you hold the bone in your teeth, your grasp of reality is indubitable, and what more can any sensible man want? *Pistis*, in fact, is only a subdivision of *doxa*, and its usage by Plato, when he does happen to employ the term, positively accentuates the contrast with the Christian notion of faith. To suggest that faith was the prerequisite, and means, of insight into truths beyond the range of science, and was the guarantee of a certitude more profound than any obtainable by demonstration, would, for Plato, have been impossible and even absurd.

In this respect, however, the original teaching of Plato was modified in almost startling fashion by some of his later disciples. Thus Proclus declares in more than one place that *pistis* is above *gnosis* because only by means of faith is it possible to reach the Good. Evidently, then, there must be a distinction between a lower form of belief and a higher (between *doxa* and *pistis*) which Plato himself never recognized, but which made it possible for Pico della Mirandola, a Platonist of the Renaissance, to summarize the position of Proclus in the remarkable statement, quoted by Whittaker in his book on the Neoplatonists: *sicut fides, quae est credulitas, est infra intellectum ; ita fides, quae est vere fides, est supersubstantialiter supra scientiam et intellectum, nos Deo immediate coniungeus.** Much has been written about the debt of Christianity to Platonism, but it does not always seem to have occurred to " Christian Platonists " that Greek Philosophy, when it was beginning to struggle for bare existence, was inevitably driven to present itself in the form most likely to be effective against its all too formidable rival. The Christian virtue of faith has no genuine Greek ancestry; if Proclus thought fit to discover a new variety of *pistis*, superior to science, it is highly probable, if not certain, that Christian influence was responsbile for this remarkable divergence from the original doctrine of Plato. Even so, the assimilation to the Christian doctrine is only superficial; for when the Platonist contrasts a superior faith with an inferior credulity, he is still assuming that only those who have repudiated " phenomena " and passed through the hierarchy of the sciences will be qualified to enjoy the higher mode of insight. This " faith ", in fact, will be operative quite outside the realm of history and ordinary experience, and will be reserved for the intellectual *élite*. On the other hand, the Christian Church maintains that the faith which, in Pico's phrase, " conjoins us immediately with God " is no privilege of the philosophical few, but an experience granted to the humblest believer; and further, that theology, however difficult it may sound, is only the articulate expression, or attempted expression, of the revelation granted to all who share in this common faith. And again, if the Platonist couples " belief " with history, it is because he despises both, but if the Christian couples them, it is because he believes that God has manifested himself in the visible and historical life, death, and resurrection of Jesus of Nazareth.

And here it may be well to take note of a certain variation in the Christian use of the term " faith " which may be slightly confusing. According to one common application of the term, " the faith " is roughly equivalent to the statements contained in the creeds or other authoritative pronouncements. Thus in the document known as the Athanasian Creed we actually find the phrase, " And the Catholic

* T. W. Whittaker, *Neo-Platonists*, C.U.P.

Faith is this ", followed by a series of propositions, many of them intelligible only to advanced students of theology. In the creeds more commonly recited the formula is only, " I believe ", but what follows is again a series of propositions which, at one time or another, it was found expedient to formulate as a declaration of what the Church believed. In this sense of the word, then, " the faith " signifies, not personal experience, but theology. On the other hand, when faith, hope, and charity are named as the distinctively Christian virtues; when faith is contrasted with works; when faith is said to move mountains; the reference is clearly to a personal assurance entirely distinct from any formula into which we may attempt to translate it. Of those two senses the latter is evidently the more fundamental. Without faith as personal assurance there could be no creeds or dogmas, and no creed or dogma can generate personal faith. Yet if we find that, not merely in common usage, but even in the works of professed theologians, there appears sometimes to be a rather casual transition from one sense to the other, no real ambiguity is implied: the variation is simply evidence of the fact, never fully understood by Platonists, that theology in its intellectual aspect is grounded in, and derived from, a kind of personal experience which does not demand exceptional gifts of intellect, but may be given to " unlearned and ignorant men ", to " babes and sucklings ", in fact to all.

The most radical distinction, however, between the Platonic and the Christian conception of faith has not yet clearly come to light. Though Plato himself was no frigid intellectualist; though he comes near sometimes to intimating that a kind of mystical love may carry us into regions inaccessible by any logical way of approach; it never ceases to be true that he thinks of *doxa* (be it " opinion ", " belief ", or " faith ") as a mental condition determined by and relative to a class of objects which, because they are not perfectly real, can never be perfectly known. Now the definition of faith as " the evidence of things unseen " may also sound Platonic, in the sense that its author appears to be describing a relation between a certain inward disposition and a certain class of things. Nor would it be right simply to repudiate this interpretation of his words, which is true, indeed, so far as it goes, yet is not the whole of the truth. What lies behind the Epistle to the Hebrews, and all similar documents, is the experience of a faith which is not in essence an attitude or mental condition relative to any kind of impersonal facts, but rather a vivid consciousness of absolute trust in a Person. When we talk, in quite untechnical fashion, of believing in a statesman, a doctor, or a friend, we are much nearer to the Christian notion of faith than we shall ever get by perusing a number of learned dissertations on the relation of opinion or belief to knowledge. And that is why Jewish prophets and poets, rather than Greek philosophers, are the true forerunners of Christian evangelists. Even when Proclus and other Neoplatonists are moved to recognize a " faith " superior to knowledge, they are still much more likely to relate it to the impersonal Good than to the God who tends to remain for them, in the Platonic sense, a myth.

To assert that the Jews from their most primitive days were always genuine monotheists would be both extravagant and superfluous. At what point in their history they passed from the militant proclamation that Jehovah was a God above all other gods to the firm conviction that there was and could be no other God but he, we must leave to the expert to decide. It cannot, however, be disputed, on a broad comparison between the Jewish Scriptures and the literature of the Greeks, that the Jews had a far stronger sense of the unity of God and of a relation to him which could not suitably be described as anything other than personal. And here, of course, we are promptly involved in the ancient dispute (which never ceases to be modern) about the meaning of " person " and the propriety of applying the term to God. To state with any precision what we mean by human " personality " is difficult enough, and when we dare to believe that the same mode of being may, without mere equivocation, be ascribed to God, we manifestly pass beyond the range of definitions. More than this, the Christian Church has boldly magnified the difficulty by declaring that within the unity of God are three persons, not on any account to be explained away as simply qualities, attributes, or variable aspects, such as we may discover within the complicated personality of any human being with whom we are intimately acquainted.

To reproduce even in outline the history of the term " person " in Christian theology would be an undertaking entirely beyond the scope of this book. Only one or two general observations will be possible, of which the first must be a warning against allowing ourselves to be disturbed by the familiar but empty charge of anthropomorphism. Not only all human religion but all human thinking is anthropomorphic. What else can it possibly be ? When Xenophanes sagaciously observed long ago that horses, oxen, and lions, if they took to religion, would make gods in their own likeness, he was entitled to some credit for what was then an original and forcible protest against modes of religious imagination which it was high time to discard. What he discovered, however, was little more than a truism; if he imagined that, by repudiating the childish imagery of savages, civilized man could fashion a conception of deity in no sense anthropomorphic, he was greatly mistaken. Or if, again, his suggestion was that, since religion must inevitably be anthropomorphic, it must always be spurious, he might just as well have argued that, since the ideals of science invariably reflect the character of the human mind, they, too, must always be delusive. Simple arithmetic, for instance, is almost blatantly anthropomorphic, but the difference between abstract thinking and religion is that the former reflects only a slice or a section of man's mental nature, while the latter (even in its crudest forms) represents an attempt to use the whole of his personality as a means of discovering something about the mysterious world in which he finds himself.

At the root of this traditional objection to anthropomorphic religion lies a confusion between an important truth and a fallacy. The important truth is that, if we want to discover the nature of a world not made by man, we must beware of prejudice, of emotional bias, of mere yearning to " remould it nearer to the heart's desire ": the fallacy springs from the assumption that in abstract thinking, from which all elements but the intellectual are, so far as possible, excluded, we cease to impose any of our own limitations on the universe, and simply accept the stamp of reality as it is in itself. So far is this assumption from being justifiable that it may even be nearer the truth to maintain that abstract thinking is the most " subjective " of all mental activities, because it is the most artificial, because it deliberately sets aside and ignores every aspect of concrete facts but the one that suits some special inquiry; above all, because it implies that, while human feelings and senses can be aware only of facts adapted to their nature, the human intellect suffers from no such restriction. For this complacent hypothesis, unfortunately, there is no genuine warrant. When we smile at the philosophy of Bradley's dog—" what smells is real; what does not smell does not exist "—we should do well to save a fragment of the smile for our own condition, and perhaps to re-write the canine metaphysic in some such form as, " whatever falls within my intellectual capacity is real; whatever lies outside it is not ".

Does it follow, then, that in all sciences we do but chase our own shadow? That we know nothing of objective reality, but must be content, if not with pure scepticism, at least with " subjective idealism " or something in that style? For my own part, I fail to see why any of these alarming consequences should be entailed. Suppose a dog really had no other clue to the nature of things but his sense of smell, why should it follow that the only facts he could then discover (his master's identity, for instance) must be illusory? Or suppose a man just " feels " the difference between iron and wool, why should the fact that his sensations are entirely his own prove that he has learnt nothing about the nature of those two different substances ? We must not, however, digress into that interminable controversy. The only point of importance is that when fear of anthropomorphism induces men to reject the idea of a personal God, and to substitute for it some product of abstract thinking, they simply delude themselves. What they propose is just as anthropomorphic as what they reject, and the only evident result will be that they have provided an inferior substitute for God. Whether it be the " unmoved Mover " of Aristotle, the *id quo maius nihil* of Anselm, or any similar abstraction, no hypothesis of that kind will ever prove anything but the failure of logical ingenuity to establish the existence of any Being who can be worshipped as God. The reason is that personality, however indefinable, is the highest " category " that we possess. Whenever we are promised something supra-personal, we may be certain that something infra-personal is what we shall get. Between divine and human personality the distance is doubtless immeasurable, but to attempt to improve the situation by taking refuge in the impersonal is a counsel of despair. " They have ears, and hear not: noses have they and smell not. They that make them are like unto them: and so are all such as put their trust in them." Exactly. The savage makes a debased idol because his notion of human personality is debased: and if, as Tennyson once humorously declared, there are still some of us who think of God as no more than " an immeasurable clergyman ", it must be confessed that the warnings of Xenophanes and the psalmist are not yet superfluous. Christians are not, however, confined to models reflecting only the weakness of their own imaginations. They believe that in the human life of Christ is to be found the clearest revelation of the nature of God that ever has been or, so long as the conditions of human life endure, ever can be made. If this be anthropomorphism, then to anthropomorphism the Church is irrevocably committed, for this is part at least of what the doctrine of the Incarnation means. When we speak of God as personal, it is not because we can imagine nothing more exalted than average men and women, but because, when God thought fit to make the supreme revelation of himself, he did it by taking our nature upon him; and again because, when we consider that nature in all its fullness, the comprehensive term " personality " appears to be the most effective way of indicating that not by reasoning alone, nor by any other isolated activity, but only by concentration of all the elements in their undivided unity, is it possible to discern, and in fullest measure to accept, the revelation of God.

F

By its recognition of history, by the bare thought of God descending into the sphere of phenomena to manifest his nature, the Christian Church assumed a position utterly incompatible with Platonism. And again, in the transformation of belief or faith from a confused apprehension of objects properly unknowable into a personal relation with a personal God, and in the contention that faith in this sense was not a consummation reserved for the elect who had exhausted the possibilities of *gnosis*, but an experience open to all, another wide divergence from Greek philosophical tradition was expressed. It remains to notice one curious and almost paradoxical result of these two developments, when their inter-relation is considered. That " no man hath seen God at any time " is a statement to which (in its most obvious sense) the Greek philosopher, the Jewish prophet, and the Christian believer would all be ready to subscribe. But when, in opposition to both Jew and Greek, the Christian boldly affirms that the *Logos* was incarnate in one who was no Gnostic phantom but, in all but his freedom from sin, like other men, does this mean that faith is thereby made easier, or that it ceases to be the evidence of things unseen? To both questions the answer, indubitably, is no. As we may fairly judge from a vast mass of historical evidence, some kind of belief in God or gods is comparatively easy so long as there is no actual epiphany to mortal eyes. True, there were plenty of myths in Greece and elsewhere about the way in which divine Beings used to show themselves and converse with mankind long ago; but long, very long ago, it was, and of a thousand who believed, perhaps, that groves and mountains were still haunted by unseen presences, not one would have received without open derision the assertion that to-day or yesterday a god was seen eating his dinner or working at his trade. It is often much harder to believe in the greatness of " great men " if you chance to meet them than while you know them only through newspapers or books. Particularly is this true when anything like sanctity is claimed for a human being, and if saints and scoundrels meet, as we are told, in the same prison, we never ought to be surprised. We may even go farther, and admit that this almost instinctive resentment of any human claim to divine attributes is itself an expression of religious feeling. Need we doubt, for instance, that when the High Priest cried out that Jesus had spoken blasphemy by claiming to be the Son of God, it was as a genuinely religious man that he was moved to indignation? It cannot, in fact, be doubted that to accept Jesus as the Christ was infinitely harder than to believe in God who, though he had spoken to Moses and the prophets, remained invisible, unapproachable, immeasurably remote from earth.

Moreover, the faith required of the disciples was still, and with added emphasis, " the evidence of things unseen ". How could anyone " see " that the young Nazarene, known to his neighbours from infancy, was the very image of the Father? Was it by superior eyesight, by a power of vision surpassing the eagle's? " Flesh and blood hath not revealed it to thee ", was the Master's own comment on Peter's stupendous confession. And, if it is only to the man of scientific genius that phenomena reveal the law of their occurrence, how much more astounding was it that in the words, the acts, the everyday life of a human companion, even the smallest handful of men should discover the revelation of God. Nor must we be misled by the mild rebuke addressed to Thomas: " because thou hast seen me thou hast believed; blessed are they that have not seen, and yet have believed ". What Thomas demanded was ocular evidence of a fact visible to all, but what he partly lacked was trust in a Person: in other words he had not perfectly discerned in the visible life of Jesus before his death " the evidence of things unseen ". To which it is fair to add that, had he totally lacked faith, not even the prints of the nails would have convinced him. An unbeliever would have seen in them only an ingenious fraud, and, as the disciples once had heard in the parable, there were many that would not believe " though one rose from the dead ". Thus to the Christian, as contrasted with the Platonist, history is not a mirage, an illusion, a distortion of reality, something to be dissolved into abstractions, with an obstinate residue of " brute fact " which resists dissolution. Rather is it the appointed vehicle of revelation, yet only to those who have faith.

6

The Christian Rejection of Platonism
II. Monotheism : Creation : The Body

" AND the Word was made flesh and dwelt among us." "Plotinus, the philosopher of our time, was like one ashamed of being in a body."

When the message of Christmas Day and Porphyry's brief summary of his master's creed are thus brought into direct comparison, it should be plain enough that they are totally incompatible; that no Christian can possibly be a Platonist, nor any Platonist a Christian; and of this elementary fact the Platonists, to do them justice, were perfectly aware. But while the doctrine of the Incarnation is at once the foundation of Christian theology and the rock of offence on which Platonism and all other philosophies are likely to be wrecked, it does not stand alone. Behind it are the two closely interwoven problems of Monotheism and Creation, and, in respect of both of these, the line of cleavage between pagan and Christian speculation has not always been clearly marked. That God is one, and that by him were all things created, may, indeed, be enunciated as dogmatic articles of faith, but since they will certainly be accepted by a Jew or a Moslem, and quite possibly by a Greek philosopher, much consideration of the sense in which they are to be interpreted is necessary before their true place in Christian thought can be understood. The bare antithesis of unity and plurality does not take us very far. If Jews and Moslems admit only one God, while pagans recognize many, will Christians, who declare that God is " three in one and one in three ", be welcomed as allies by either side ? In point of fact they were not. All Unitarians were bound to look askance at the doctrine of the Trinity; no pagan (with any understanding of the question) would offer to put Christ in the same category as Zeus and Apollo; while the Platonist, who for reasons of his own might dismiss traditional polytheism as mythology, would be as little disposed to base his monotheism on the testimony of a Jewish or Arabian prophet as to endorse the outrageous assertion that the Logos has become incarnate in Jesus of Nazareth. And again; when the

Jews denounced the gods of the heathen and avowed that the God of
Israel was the one God, their monotheism was undoubtedly coloured
by the racial theory, by the belief that Jehovah belonged in a peculiar
sense to the Chosen People. In course of time proselytes were
admitted, but their position was always rather anomalous. However
sincerely they might profess the Jewish religion, they could not, by
taking thought, revise their origin and transform themselves into the
seed of Abraham. Meanwhile the antagonism of Jew and Gentile
persisted, so that, even if Jesus had been accepted as the Messiah, the
Scribes and Pharisees would surely have protested that his advent was
promised to Jews alone, and we have only to read the early chapters
of the Acts of the Apostles to see how difficult it was at first for Christians
to break away from that tradition. Clearly, then, monotheism of this
restricted type falls far short of the Christian doctrine, and is also quite
distinct from any position towards which Greek philosophy might seem
to be moving.

No less susceptible of various interpretations is the doctrine of
Creation. In the Jewish Scriptures, of course, it is firmly asserted,
but not in opposition to any rival theory, not as a choice between
alternatives as plainly incompatible as worship of one God and pious
observance of twenty different cults. The speculative difficulties
involved in the very thought of Creation did not come to light until
philosophers had begun to meditate upon the concepts of matter, time,
and eternity; nor could the bearing of the question upon religion be
evident until something in the nature of Gnosticism or Manichæism
had been compared and contrasted with the Christian faith. It must
also be observed that no dogmatic propositions have ever been put
forward as a means of solving the philosophical problems—particularly
that of time and eternity—which continue to baffle the acutest intellects.
Hence, if we find no definite guidance in Plato or in later Greek philosophy, we must not be surprised to discover the same perplexities in
Christian writers of various dates. What we can, however, more
reasonably anticipate is a better understanding of the intimate connexion between monotheism and Creation, and of the relation of both
to the articles of Christian faith most repugnant to Platonism, namely,
the Incarnation and the Resurrection of the Body.

Beginning with Plato himself, we have now to give most of our
attention to the *Timæus*, and therefore to the difficult question whether
the theology of that astounding work is to be taken as anything more
than " myth ". And here we may rashly jump, though apparently
with Plato's sanction, to a most doubtful conclusion; for it is Plato

himself who expressly declares that the general atmosphere in which the discussion is to be conducted can be only that of myths or " likely tales ", without any pretence of demonstration.   Hence, if the subject of the dialogue were only, or even chiefly, the nature and action of God, we might be justified in concluding that he was only inventing an edifying story about matters beyond the reach of knowledge, but for practical purposes highly important.   This is not, however, a sufficient estimate of the facts.   The bulk of the discourse (for there is very little dialogue) is put into the mouth of Timæus, who is selected for the explicit reason that he is " the most astronomical " of the company and the one likely to know most " about the nature of the whole ". In other words, the subject is not so much theology as cosmology, and the argument ranges through various sciences, with a constant flavour, it is true, of mythical language, but with an intention none the less serious.   But why, then, we may be inclined to object, confuse science with mythology, and why not omit the theology altogether ?   The answer is twofold.   In the first place, Plato does not regard anything but mathematics as science in the strictest sense.   Consequently, the greater part of what we should now include under the head of natural science is only a " likely tale " ; or, as we might prefer to say, is pro-ductive of results not more than probable.   Astronomy, indeed, has a strongly mathematical side to it, and Plato himself suggests, in the course of the Timæus, that the whole physical cosmos may rest on a mathematical basis.   Nevertheless, it remains true that the natural sciences as a whole are grounded in observation of phenomena, that their methods are necessarily, and rightly, empirical, and that a higher or lower degree of probability, rather than mathematical certainty, is all that can properly be claimed for their conclusions.   Such is Plato's estimate of the situation, and how far this was due to the rudi-mentary condition of the natural sciences, or how far to a distant anticipation of the most recent position of modern thinkers, we must not stay to inquire.   The main fact at the moment is this, that if we propose to set aside the theology of the Timæus on the ground that it is intended to be only " myth ", we shall be obliged, for exactly the same reason, to conclude that Plato declined to take the natural sciences seriously.   But this will not do at all.   Those who would study the question thoroughly must consult Professor Taylor and other authorities,* but at least we are safe in assuming that when Plato presents a subject in the garment of myth he does not by any means imply that it is unworthy of sober consideration.

* A. E. Taylor, Commenting on Plato's Timæus, O.U.P.

Let us now turn to the second point, of no less importance.   If we are still disposed to wonder why the " myths " of theology and scientific cosmology should be mixed up together, we must bear in mind (not forgetting the statements of Socrates in the *Phædo*) that Plato does not believe that any kind of scientific thinking is ultimately sufficient.   Sometimes he observes that science always rests on hypotheses, and never arrives at an " unhypothetical principle "; sometimes he seeks for the origin of motion and change, and decides that it cannot be found in corporeal elements and mechanical causes, but only in self-moving soul.   Whenever, in fact, we aspire to discover the origin of all that is and all that happens, we are driven towards something beyond the reach of scientific hypothesis and method, something indemonstrable yet absolutely certain.   But what manner of thing can this be ? Plato does not profess to know.   He has no " revelation " to guide him, no authoritative creed or scripture, no " faith " as Christians understand the word, and certainly no hope of any historical manifestation of deity, such as the Incarnation of the Logos could provide.   His choice lay between two alternatives, the impersonal " form of the good ", which we find in the *Republic,* and a self-moving soul or spirit, fit to receive the name of God, which is what we discern in the " myth " of *Timæus.*   Whether there is any way of fusing the two alternatives into one is, as we have seen already, a problem suggested, but not examined, in the *Republic;* and in the *Timæus* it is bound to recur. Only this much can be affirmed with confidence, that if the Good and the self-moving soul have to be left unreconciled, then the God of Plato, whenever he speaks as a monotheist, must be identified with Soul. God is not an " idea " or " form ", but is either a living Being or a myth and nothing more.

The explanation, then, of the somewhat perplexing mixture of theology and science in the *Timæus* is partly the fact that in neither does Plato look for more than probability; but partly, too, his conviction that no cosmology can be adequate without inquiry into the origin of the cosmos and the reasons, beyond the scope of science, for its existence.   With this preliminary estimate of the work in our minds, we can now proceed to ask whether Plato is in truth a monotheist, whether " creation " is the right term to apply to his account of the genesis of the world, and whether he perceives any necessary connexion between the unity of God and his creative power.   Now, first of all, there is a difficulty, always likely to mislead a modern reader, inherent in the wide and rather ambiguous use of the word *Theos* in Greek literature. When, for instance, Socrates protests (in the *Apology*) against the confusion of his own views with those of Anaxagoras, and implies that, like everyone else, he regards the sun as divine, this does not mean that he (or any Greek) was a sun-worshipper, or that he accepted a kind of poetical identification of the sun with Apollo. Perhaps he is only evading a frivolous charge; but, if his statement is serious, it probably means that he regards the heavenly bodies as imperishable, or possibly that he believes them to be animated with immortal souls. Bad physics or astronomy, rather than bad theology, is what we might thus impute to him; but perhaps a fairer comment is simply that the term " god " may signify no more than immunity from the causes of change and decay which perpetually destroy terrestrial things, or at least transform them into a new condition. Now in the *Timæus*, as elsewhere, Plato often " talks with the vulgar ". Almost in the same breath he will speak of " gods " and of God, and actually his distinctive name for what some of our cautious forefathers liked to call the " Supreme Being " is not *Theos*, but *Demiourgos*, usually anglicized as Demiurge. Moreover, if we grant, as the most probable hypothesis, that the Demiurge is to be taken as the one and only God, this does not prevent him from introducing, at a certain point in the story, a number of second-class gods, created by himself, who in fact are simply the stars and planets, to which he assigns certain functions in the cosmic process. Plato (or Timæus) treats the gods of traditional mythology with solemn irony, recommending us to seek their credentials from the families reputedly descended from them, who surely ought to know the truth about their own ancestors. This last point may, indeed, be significant, for it might be interpreted as Plato's polite way of repudiating the ordinary polytheism of his time. Even so, it must be allowed that polished irony is a very different thing from the emphatic denial of plurality that we should expect from a Christian or a Jew. Plato, in fact, is conscious of no iconoclastic mission, of no religious duty to denounce polytheism as disastrous error or mortal sin. In the *Timæus*, as elsewhere, he is probably content to judge that, however clearly philosophers may perceive the absurdity of multiplying gods, the common religion will do very well for the common folk, provided they abjure the poetic travesties of divine behaviour which in the *Republic* are condemned as morally degrading, and in the *Laws* are ranked as punishable offences.

If, then, no incontestable proof of Plato's monotheism can be extracted from his use of the term *Theos*, if, on the other hand, it is also reasonable to argue that the Demiurge is God in a sense not applicable to any other being, the next step will be to inquire whether he is properly to be described as the Creator, and what " creation " means. Once more there is nothing decisive, nothing sacrosanct, in the terminology. *Demiourgos* is a common name for a craftsman, and though Plato speaks also of the " Father ", the " Maker ", or sometimes the " Composer ", in none of these alternative titles is there a necessary implication of unique creative power. The adjective " demiourgic " is applied to impersonal causes; and, when the inferior gods are instructed in their duties, they are advised to imitate in their " demiurgy," the power of their author, though with the qualification (of which there are curious echoes in the Middle Ages) that whatever they " create ", as contrasted with the work of the Demiurge, is bound to be mortal. To the Demiurge, however, is ascribed the origination of the cosmos or *Ouranos* which is certainly single and unique. There cannot, as we should say, be more than one " universe ", but it is not without hesitation that we can adopt that term as precisely equivalent to the cosmic totality depicted in the *Timæus*. Apart from God himself (for only a pantheist would deny that exception), the " universe " should include the whole of reality—everything that properly has " being "—but this is by no means evidently true of the world " created " by the Demiurge. The whole argument starts from Plato's familiar antithesis of that which eternally " is " and that which " becomes ", and it is at once decided that the cosmos they are about to examine has " become ". Now this means in effect that what " the most astronomical " Timæus is going to set forth is the genesis and nature of the physical and phenomenal world, not of the eternal being (" ideas " or " forms ", perhaps) which cannot rightly be said to " become ", but is rather to be presupposed as a pattern in accordance with which the phenomenal order is constructed. There is, however, one serious complication. The cosmic body, we learn, is to be endowed with a soul, and of the soul's existence the Demiurge is the author. And further, this soul is to be intelligent, or, as it is once expressed, *nous* is to be placed in soul. Is *nous*, then, also created? To this question we find no distinct answer; but in any case the difficulty of bringing all reality down to the level of the phenomenal world which " becomes " is insuperable. Whatever may have been Plato's attitude at this time (or at any other time) to the theory of " ideas ", it is indubitable, that in the *Timæus* he recognizes an order of timeless being altogether outside the realm of " becoming ", and therefore outside the cosmos, originated by the Demiurge, which Timæus undertakes to describe. In later times, when Christian philosophers had lost touch with the bulk of Plato's writings, some of them believed that he had definitely made the " ideas " independent, and this view they were obliged to reject.   On the other hand, they allowed the existence of " ideas " as patterns or exemplars within the mind of God, and it seemed possible to interpret the *Timæus* in that sense.   As genuine Platonism, however, it will hardly pass; for an incidental suggestion in the *Parmenides* that " ideas " might be thoughts or, in the language of a later age, " concepts " is promptly dismissed, and is indeed out of keeping with Plato's " realistic " position.   Whatever, then, was Plato's exact intention in the *Timæus*, it must be allowed that he leaves us in some uncertainty about the scope of the " creation " accomplished by the Demiurge.

There is also another passage that demands careful attention.   At a certain stage in the argument, when it might be thought that all the elements harmonized in the cosmic order had already been enumerated, Timæus suddenly revises his account of creation and introduces an entirely new factor, more radical than anything hitherto regarded by Greek science as elemental; something, in fact, which, in the light of later terminology, can only be called " matter ", though in Plato's vocabulary this familiar word has no special place.   The " matter " of the *Timæus* is not in the least like any of the " elements " which either ancient or modern science has thus classified.   It is entirely incorporeal, and, though described as the mother and nurse of all genesis, is in itself devoid of all specific form.   It is, in fact, indistinguishable from space and is doubtless meant to express Plato's belief that the physical world can somehow be fashioned out of the material pertaining in its most obvious aspect to geometry.   We are not, however, concerned with that possibility, but only with the indeterminate metaphysical status of this hybrid, and with the question whether it is created.   It is not, we are told, a possible object of sense-perception, nor is it properly knowable by pure intellect, but only by a kind of " bastard reasoning ", an expression not covered by Plato's habitual distinction between opinion and knowledge.   Does it, then, belong to the world of " becoming " ?   Or is it, like the objects of pure thought, timeless, original, and therefore independent, perhaps, of the Demiurge and his creative energy ?   In all probability we should be wrong in attributing to Plato any such invincible dualism, but it is easy to see that he might be thought to favour this suggestion of a limitation to the power of the Demiurge, especially when he speaks of it as having been in existence before the *Ouranos*, and also observes that necessity, as well as *nous*, plays its part in the moulding of the cosmos; as though, in modelling the world according to an eternal pattern, the Demiurge had to contend with something not entirely under his control, something which at least had to be " persuaded " (a word used by Plato) to adapt itself to the cosmic design.   Nor does the most positive and dogmatic rejection of this version of Platonism remove the suspicion that between the Demiurge of the *Timæus* and the Creator as represented in Christian thought there is a considerable gap.   More than this, we shall find that Plotinus, without openly dissenting from his master, does not regard the Demiurge as the author of the cosmos, but only as a figure symbolizing the second phase in the process.   Important as it is for an exponent of Plato to determine the original meaning of the text, there are often good reasons for attributing greater historical importance to interpretations and developments which afterwards prevailed;   nor is it always unfair to make an ancient author partly responsible for versions of his teaching which he did not anticipate, and might even heartily dislike.   And so it is with the author of the *Timæus*.   Protest as much as you please that he was a devout monotheist, that the Demiurge was the genuine Creator, that neither eternal " ideas " nor an elusive impalpable " matter " implied an original kind of being that needed no creation;   it will still be true that Plato did not think it worth while to make a direct assault on polytheism;   that he did not expound, with his own matchless literary art, the relation of the Good to God or of timeless reality to that which " becomes ";   and that he left his successors with at least a fair excuse for looking upon matter as something alien from, and possibly hostile to, the cosmos which bears the imprint of God's supreme handiwork and benevolent design.

Of the benevolence there is more to be said, but at this point it will be convenient to offer a few brief notes on the system of Plotinus. Accepting Plato as almost infallible, and seldom deviating consciously from his scriptural authority, he produced, nevertheless, a philosophy which not only absorbed many elements drawn from Aristotle and later sources, but also worked into a coherent whole all the tentative or imperfectly expounded doctrines which Plato never fully unified in a series of dialogues of which each was composed to suit its own peculiar atmosphere and from some special point of view.   Thus when Plotinus elaborates, for instance, the so-called Neoplatonist trinity of the One, *Nous*, and *Psyche* (a trinity in which the three " hypostases " are by no means Persons and by no means equal), it is easy for him to find support in the language of the *Timæus*, but the result is something that Plato might well have hesitated to recognize as his own.   So it is with the whole development of the later Platonism out of its original.   Time alone, with the perpetual modification of human life and thought through five or six centuries, accounts for much, yet for less than the inexplicable differences between two men of genius, which make it possible for the later to borrow almost any quantity of his predecessor's material, and then to fashion it into an edifice as distinct from the earlier structure as the fantasies of a Moorish Alhambra from the austerity of the Parthenon itself.   Plotinus, in all his individuality, can no more be deduced from Plato than Beethoven from Mozart or Haydn; but it may be worth while to add that, whatever his racial origin, his spiritual lineage is definitely Hellenic; and, though it is true, of course, that in his own day the world was far more infected with oriental " heresies " than in Plato's, the vague talk of orientalism in his philosophy has little more to commend it than the dubious assumption that all mysticism must come from the East.   There is no need, however, to digress into that complicated field of research.   It is enough that Plotinus took up all the problems about the unity of God and the origin of the world initiated by Plato and that he believed his own solutions to be genuinely Platonic.

If language alone were a sufficient index, we might judge that Plotinus was no more scrupulous than Plato in avoiding reference to a plurality of gods.   The truth is rather that traditional polytheism was no longer likely to be taken literally by any audience capable of listening to Plotinus.   As symbolism and allegory it might still have its uses, but no one was going to delate a lecturer to the magistrates for impiety because he failed to offer incense at a dozen altars; and for the same reason viewed from another angle, the lecturer could speak of gods in the plural without being suspected of disloyalty to his own mono-theistic teaching.   It is also true that, in name at least, God is not the centre round which the thought of Plotinus most evidently moves.   Everything in his philosophy, everything, let us rather say, in the uni-verse of which he strives to penetrate the mystery, is overshadowed by the invisible presence of the One.   Plotinus, if we may borrow and alter the famous description of Spinoza, is " the One-intoxicated man ".   To the exaltation of its ineffable majesty he devotes the whole resources of his commanding intellect, and in the hopes of ecstatic union with it— perhaps twice or thrice in a lifetime—he presses on with an ardour scarcely surpassed by any saintly mystic within the Catholic Church.   Hard, indeed, is it to find anything in the whole range of comparable literature more profoundly moving than the final pages of the sixth *Ennead*, which culminate in that bleak, impersonal, yet sublime descrip-tion of the soul's last journey as " the flight of the alone to the Alone ".

In order to establish the supremacy of this absolute One, Plotinus has, first of all, to lay hold on that single phrase of Plato's in which the Good is declared to be above and beyond " being ", but also the sole and sufficient origin of all that is.   Out of that solitary and unexplained utterance in the *Republic* was developed not only the central theme of Neoplatonism but also most of the " negative theology " that we encounter in the Middle Ages.   Of the identity of the Good and the One there could be no doubt; but, before we can safely add that Plotinus likewise identifies the indivisible Unity with God, we must observe that this could be effected only by a bold treatment of the *Timæus*, involving the relegation of the Demiurge to a lower place, to the rank of a derivative or medium through which the overflow of the original Goodness is transmitted to all the subordinate parts of the cosmos.   Thus when, disclaiming rash novelty, Plotinus appeals to earlier philosophers, and even to mythology, for precedents, he states explicitly (*Enn.* V. 1) that, for Plato, the Demiurge is *Nous*, while *Nous* itself springs from the King or Father of all: out of the Good comes forth *Nous*, and out of *Nous* comes *Psyche*.   But in that case the Demiurge is certainly not God, and (without returning to the *Timæus* to question this interpretation of the evidence) we can only conclude that for Plotinus—unless we prefer to call him an atheist—the only possible God is the One.

Does this mean, then, that his doctrine, in this respect at least, agrees entirely with the Christian?   Far from it.   Just as we have already noted, when examining Plato or when glancing at Judaism and Islam, that the mere antithesis of unity and plurality, of one God and many, is an insufficient characterization of any theology, so do we learn from the study of Plotinus that his unfaltering, almost fanatical mono-theism must involve the absolute rejection of every vital clause in the creed of the church.   The doctrines of the Trinity, of the Incarnation, of the Resurrection of the body, Plotinus could only repudiate with horror.   The bare protestation of the unity of God is, in fact, ex-tremely ambiguous until you have pondered long and deeply the meaning of " one ".   As an illustration, drawn from an age when polytheism was no longer a possible alternative, take the case of Spinoza, who more than once declares, in the course of his various writings, that " only with the greatest impropriety " can God be described as One.   Briefly stated, his objection is that between the nature of God and any usage of " one " in mathematics, or in ordinary parlance, there is no resemblance at all.   We have no room to pursue the subject; but, if we borrow a hint from Spinoza's criticism and demand from Plotinus some indication of the characteristics proper to the One, his startling answer will be that there are none. No qualities or attributes, no definable activities, can possibly be assigned to it without destroying the absolute unity. Unaffected by relations to time, space, or the phenomenal cosmos, it cannot so much as meditate upon itself without lapsing into the duality of subject and object; it cannot even, " without the greatest impropriety ", be said to exist. Moreover, the counsel of Plotinus to those who aspire to ecstatic union with the One is to imitate its nakedness. " Take away everything ", he says; strip yourself of sensibility, of imagination, of your innermost thought and reflection; only thus may you hope to be absorbed for an instant, which will also be an eternity, into the fount of illumination, the absolute identity, which dare not even be identical with itself. Only through some such language as this (for I am not quoting exact phrases) can we dimly form a notion of that which Plotinus worships as the unutterable Glory, but which, to those who find in themselves no kindred spark of mysticism, will be indistinguishable from the dark night of nothingness in which the human spirit can only faint and die.

Out of the One which is not proceeds, nevertheless, all that is. First, *Nous* emerges, then *Psyche*; below *Psyche* is Body, and last of all formless matter. Now if we ask why this genesis comes about, we must first return to the *Timæus*, where Plato accounts for the origin of the cosmos in a manner that brings him closer to Christian doctrine than anything else in his theology. It was, he says, because of the infinite goodness of God and the total absence of envy in him that he willed the existence of creatures and their likeness, so far as might be, to himself. Between this account of the matter and the statement in Genesis 1. 31, that when the Creator surveyed his creation he found it very good, the resemblance was close enough to secure Christian approval, while Plotinus, though he could only regard the story of the Demiurge as a myth portraying the activity of *Nous*, agreed entirely with the doctrine that all things spiritual and corporeal had their origin in the Good. The consequent difficulty of finding any place for evil in the cosmic order will in due course have to be faced, but if we inquire first not merely why but how this creation was effected, it must frankly be confessed that neither from Platonists nor from Christians is any clear answer forthcoming. The plain fact is that it never has been possible, nor ever will be, for human beings to visualize or imagine the creative act in any way that lends itself to expression in language adapted only to the description of " making " things, as an artist or craftsman may fashion them out of materials which can themselves be handled and described.   The very formula, *creatio ex nihilo*, which Christian writers adopt as the most suitable, tends to suggest that " nothing " is a kind of material; indeed " matter ", when it means *materia prima*, as conceived by Aristotle and many others, is so nearly equivalent to " nothing " that even Christians have to be on their guard against an ill-concealed dualism, as though the Creator had only introduced order into a pre-existing chaos.   Hence if we object, as creationists, to the statement in the *Timæus* (30.a) that God " took all the visible, which was not at rest but in a state of inharmonious and disorderly motion, and reduced it to order ", we shall with equal justice be called upon to explain the words of Genesis 1. 2, " and the earth was without form and void, and darkness was upon the face of the deep ".   The Biblical story, of course, is far more remote from science than the *Timæus*, but that fact is of little importance, for science cannot and does not pretend to deal with absolute origins, and in its proper vocabulary the phrase *ex nihilo* does not occur.

Another invincible difficulty appears in the total absence of any definable relation between eternity and time.   Even if eternity meant no more than endless time (itself a perplexing thought), no common measure of the eternal and the temporal would be discoverable; no multiplication of finite periods like days and hours would bring us an inch nearer to infinity.   But when, striving to banish time altogether, we accept something like the famous definition of Boethius, *æternitas est interminabilis vitæ tota simul et perfecta possessio*, it becomes still more evident that to insist on either of two alternatives, that the created world is eternal, or that there was a time before it began to be, is hazardous and unwise.   It is therefore not surprising to find that when a thinker as acute as S. Thomas Aquinas denies the eternity of the world, he makes no claim to prove his point.   *Nundum non semper fuisse*, he says, *sola fide tenetur, et demonstrative probari non potest* (*Summa Theol.* 1, qu. XLVI, art. 2).

In vain, too, shall we seek for a term adequate to describe the act or process of creating.   Some writers have alleged that the distinction between Christian and Neoplatonist doctrine is reflected in the difference between " creation " and " emanation ", but for this opinion there is no good warrant.   Aquinas, for instance, does not object to " emanation ": *emanatio totius entis a causa universali* is a phrase of his own (*Summa Theol.* 1, qu. XLV. art. 1), " and this emanation ", he adds, " we designate by the name of creation ".   Terminology of some sort there must be, but when once we start describing the emergence *ex nihilo*, we are likely to end with something as ludicrous as Milton's picture of the newly created animals struggling out of the ground, and perhaps sticking half-way. It is fortunate, one feels, that there did not happen to be a hard frost at the time!

Neither by an accurate selection of terms, nor even by a mere list of formal propositions, is it easy to indicate the full extent of the difference between Platonists and Christians in respect of their monotheism or their accounts of the created world. Take a few of the cardinal points emphasized by any representative theologian of the Catholic Church; that God alone is self-existent, or, in more technical language, that in him alone are essence and existence identical; that, since God is perfect, he needs no created world; that all things created by him are therefore " new ", and other than himself; that to no creature is given the power to create; that whatever is created is " good ". Between these statements and what may be gathered from Plato and Plotinus there is much verbal agreement and no obvious discrepancy. Yet it is not difficult to perceive that the Demiurge of the *Timæus* is imperfectly conceived and altogether too mythical in style; and again, that the One of Plotinus is so utterly negative that even the primary attribute of self-existence is but doubtfully assigned to it, while any definite assertion that creation was an act of will, or any such corollary as that God loves his creatures, is wholly impossible. From these two ancient sources, however, there was an abundant influx of confused ideas into medieval theology. In particular, the spurious authority of " Dionysius the Areopagite ", who must have drawn much of his material from Proclus and other Platonists of that epoch, gave a respectable status to the negative theology, and helped to produce that astonishing work, the *De Divisione Naturæ* of John the Scot (surnamed Erigena or Eriugena), which is all the more astonishing because, despite all the hard things said of it, the author's Christianity is evident and sincere. John, indeed, was always suspect, and eventually his works were officially condemned; but marked traces of the Platonism which he presented in its most extravagant form can be found in many writers of unquestioned orthodoxy and high repute.

In writing down, as one of the Christian affirmations, that whatever is created is " good ", I purposely used inverted commas, because when the epithet " good " is applied to the whole cosmic order it seems to require a sense more expansive, and perhaps less definite, than it commonly bears. Not that it would be easy to discover, even in colloquial usage, any plain and invariable meaning. On the contrary, we seem to throw the word about in the most casual way, and with small regard for anything distinctively moral; and perhaps the fairest interpretation of the theological doctrine would be that the "good-ness" imputed to all existent things embraces and clarifies all the various shades of meaning which we distinguish in practice, but seldom trouble to compare. The indissoluble union of goodness, unity, and being is almost a commonplace of medieval theology, and mingled with Christian elements there is usually a strain derived from Plotinus. Neither he nor Plato can be rightly accused of dualism in the sense of believing in the existence of an original and intrinsically evil substance, outside and opposed to the Good. There is, indeed, a statement in the *Laws* (256) which has been thought to mean that Plato felt obliged to postulate an evil world-soul as well as a good, but that interpretation is now dis-credited; and, though Plotinus, as we shall see, got into serious difficulties about the nature of matter, his attack on certain Gnostic opinions shows that he refused to admit the presence in the cosmos of any power which actually set bounds to the permeation of every grade of being by the Good. The recognition of grades was, of course, not confined to Platonists. Though all things, as created by God, were good, it was no part of the Christian contention that all must be equal in honour. The ordering of the heavens, of the souls of the redeemed, of the angels themselves, in Dante's *Paradiso* is a faithful reflection of the accepted view that there must always be higher and lower, and that no diminution of divine justice or benevolence was thus implied. Similarly, there was, in principle, no Christian objection to a gradation within the economy of human nature, to the predominance of mind or spirit over other psychic functions, or to the assumption, common to almost all philosophies, that body was properly subordinate to soul. In spite, however, of this broad agreement on the universality of goodness, the problem of evil remained, and here it was that Christianity and Platonism fell very wide apart. Had there been no other question but the most difficult of all—how the origin of evil in any shape could be reconciled with the omnipotence and goodness of God—the discrepancy might have been less patent; for the truth is that no solution of that enigma is offered by Christian dogmatic theology, while the philosophical attempts to deal with it, whether pagan or Christian, have not been conspicuously unlike. Only when the distinction between the evils that we suffer (pain, poverty, and other afflictions) and the evil that we do has been clearly established, and only when the reality of moral guilt is allowed, does the contrast between Platonism and Christianity become remarkable. One effect, or concomitant result, of Plato's great discovery that reality could be incorporeal was to emphasize and magnify the antitheses of body and soul, sensibility and reason,

G

animal impulse and moral decision.   It was thus almost inevitable that when he began to consider virtue and vice, right and wrong, and the essential character of moral evil, he should turn first to the body in which (as he had heard from the Pythagoreans) the soul was imprisoned; and secondly, that, within the complexity of the soul, he should look to the non-rational parts or elements for an explanation of conduct which belied the nature of man as a rational being.   He did not, as we have already observed, admit that body, or some more fundamental " matter ", was intrinsically evil; nor did he favour the antinomian doctrine that the soul itself could never be stained with guilt; but he did assume that reason in its own nature was impeccable, that moral evil, therefore, must originate in the psychic region common to man and other animals, and that this animality was involved in the association of soul with body.

In Plotinus there is a much fuller development of the same principle, largely due to a corresponding development in the conception of Matter. When he surveys the cosmic hierarchy, with the steady degradation from the absolute Good through *Nous*, *Psyche*, and Body to formless Matter, and asks himself whence evil can come, the mature and deliberate answer of Plotinus—in a book placed in the first *Ennead* (I. 8) by Porphyry, but chronologically, it seems, much later—is that Matter alone can be accused.   Since the One, itself above all beings, is identical with the Good, nothing evil can belong to it; and though Spirit, Soul, and Body are inferior, in different degrees, to the Good, yet all are forms of being, and Plotinus steadfastly declines to allow that anything which genuinely is can be by nature bad.   But how, then, can evil be said, in any sense, to be?   Only because Matter, the recipient of all forms of measure and limit, is itself acosmic, and because it cannot, by virtue of anything proper to itself, partake of being.   That we should speak of it as existent is, indeed, an unavoidable accident of language, but its being is only equivocal (" homonymous "), the being of an " idol ", a wraith, a phantom; and in essence—if essence can be ascribed to it—it is only negation or, more accurately, privation of the goodness inherent in all that has genuine participation in the being that flows from the One.

Now defect or privation in some degree must be imputed to all that falls short of the absolute Good, and therefore it is natural that attempts should have been made to find the source of evil in some weakness or corruption of spirit, soul, or body; in ignorance, perhaps, and error, in the weakness of incontinence, or in the gross composition of body. Moreover, Plotinus himself explains that at each grade in the hierarchy below the One there is a relation with both the higher and the lower, each, as it were, looking upwards to the Good, but also imparting itself to what is below. Only thus can soul be spiritualized and body en-souled. In a sense, therefore, a declination or stooping—something vaguely analogous to the " fall " in Christian theology—will be found at every grade. In the case of *Nous* the distance from the sheer dis-order of matter is too great for any risk of contamination, but when soul is incorporated it does at least become entangled with that which stands next door to matter, while body itself without a contribution from matter cannot realize its own manner of being. Nevertheless, Plotinus holds fast to his contention that neither weakness of soul nor the essential composition of body is properly responsible for the intrusion of evil. If body appears to be causative of evil, it is still matter, not form, that works the mischief; and as we rise to soul, and upwards again to spirit, even the shadow of evil grows fainter, until finally it disappears. There is a sense, however, in which Plotinus allows that evil can never entirely vanish from the cosmos. Here he is considerably influenced by pas-sages in the *Theœtetus* and the *Timœus*, but partly too by a still older tradition of Greek philosophy, suggesting that the antithesis and conflict of " opposites " is fundamental in the nature of things. Freedom and Necessity thus stand over against each other. Wherever there is a highest, there must also be a lowest; if pure form, pure matter; if good, then likewise evil. This may sound, perhaps, as though he were need-lessly entangling himself in the meshes of dialectic, or were even lapsing into the kind of dualism that he persistently rejects; but, without pressing these criticisms, we are entitled to conclude that Plotinus never sees his way to dispensing entirely with this Matter which, in its own right, does not exist, and that the influence of evil, at least within the region where body and soul are somehow united, must therefore abide.

So wide and deep was the stream of Platonism that, whenever the original nature of evil is viewed as a cosmic problem, we are likely to find in Christian theologians many statements reminiscent of Plotinus, and this in spite of the fact that direct acquaintance with the *Enneads* was for a long while as extinct as knowledge of any Platonic dialogue except the *Timœus*. On the other hand, whenever the full implica-tions of the doctrine of Creation were grasped, and when at the same time it was understood that the nature of sin could not be discovered by treating evil as a kind of substance which, like body and matter, might (or might not) have its place in the structure of the universe, the result was a doctrine not only distinguishable from Platonism but entirely opposed to it. Of the function of matter in scientific or philosophical thinking more will be said in another context. At present it is only necessary to insist that moral or spiritual evil has nothing whatever to do with the cosmic status of matter, the nature of body, or anything of the kind. So far as man is " material ", or so far as he is of the same corporeal constitution as the rest of the physical world, he has not moral character at all. So far, again, as he lives like a vegetable, or even like an animal endowed with keen senses and feelings, he is still below the level at which moral judgements can be passed on his behaviour. And when, finally, he is viewed in the full complexity of his nature, with all the powers implied in rationality, yet still with animal needs and appe-tites, to seek for the origin of wrongdoing in the lower section of his activities is utterly to misapprehend the facts. Since no animal devoid of " reason " (though the word is inadequate) can without absurdity be charged with cruelty, immorality, injustice, or any offence that we condemn in human beings, it must, on the face of it, be equally absurd to look in the direction of animality for an explanation of human vice or sin. If we try to evade the difficulty by replying that conduct which in animals is only "natural" can yet in man become reprehensible, this is simply to admit that man (except in certain morbid conditions) never is a mere animal; in other words, that passions and appetites, animal, no doubt, in origin, are taken up into the unity of his nature, so that he becomes responsible for their use and control. And this, in fact, is to abandon the whole " ape-and-tiger " theory of moral evil; for it clearly means that its origination and nature must be sought in the loftiest of man's activities, in company with whatever makes him noble and sublime, nay, in his very power of knowing and worshipping God. Man rises (dare we say ?) by successive stages, from gross indulgence of appetites found in all animals to petty selfishness, to fraud, injustice, and all manner of crimes; to envy, hatred, and malice beyond the reach of the law, to spiritual pride and hypocrisy, to sins of thought and in-tention known only to God, and so at last to " evil be thou my Good " and all the perverted majesty of the Miltonic Satan. All of these may be " mortal " sins, but those nearest to the behaviour of mere animals are not the most deadly but the least.

There were two main reasons which made it impossible for Plato to anticipate, or for his later disciples to understand and accept, the profound revolution in moral values thus effected by Christian thought. The first was that Platonists, despite their bold assurance that reality could be incorporeal, were still affected by a mode of thinking derived from the earliest phase of Greek philosophy. Unwittingly, they still tended to think of good and evil in terms of cosmology, to look for substances or essences, for different modes, grades, or strata of " being ".   If there was a " form " of the Good, and if this form was not visible and measurable like geometrical figures, at least it must be something existing in its own independent right, not an image, a concept, or any kind of mental construction.   And then, again, if there was a form of the good, was there also a form of the evil ?   Or if not, was evil sheer illusion, something that did not really exist ?   In Plato's own writings some of the curious possibilities latent in this way of approaching the problem are not yet disclosed.   Except in that one small section of the *Timæus*, the notion of a primary matter, underlying all visible shapes and bodies, does not appear; but if evil could in any sense be located, Plato would certainly put it somewhere in the vicinity of body, and certainly not anywhere near reason, which dwelt in a world sacred to contemplation of the pure reality of " forms " or " ideas ". In the next generation the theory of matter was immensely developed by Aristotle, and again, before Plotinus came on the scene, there was a relapse into corporealism, so that philosophers could think of the soul as merely composed of finer stuff, a more subtle material, enabling it to slip away unharmed through pores or crevices, if perchance the body were crushed beneath the ruins of a house, but with no suggestion that it was essentially incorporeal.   To this degradation of soul Plotinus, of course, was vigorously opposed, but the result was to emphasize more and more the thought of diverse grades of strata in the cosmic hierarchy, as though spirit, soul, body, and, more dubiously, matter, were like inner and outer spheres encircling the Good, even as planets in the visible heavens revolved round the central fire.   Since every sphere of genuine being was illuminated by the source of light from which all things emanated, and therefore must by participation be good, the only possible home for evil was in the bosom of matter, whose very essence— if essence could be attributed to it—was the darkness of absolute privation.   With some such mental picture of the universe constantly before his inward vision how could Plotinus conceivably tolerate the suggestion that, whereas matter and body were for ever untainted by evil, soul and spirit might come to be utterly corrupt ?

The second obstacle debarring all Platonists from the Christian interpretation of evil was their half-hearted theism, and particularly their imperfect realization of what was involved in the belief that creation was the act of a living God.   The vague relation in Plato's theology between God and the Good, and the serious doubt whether the Demiurge, represented as a Person, could be more than mythical, prepared the way for the One of Plotinus which is as devoid, not merely of personality, but of all attributes whatever as matter itself.   Not that Christian philosophers made much progress in dealing with the conception of pure matter: in most respects their theory of it was little more than a legacy from Greece.   On one point, however, they were clear, that if matter had any kind of " being ", it was just as much the creature of God as anything else, and therefore could neither be evil in itself nor productive of evil in other things by fulfilling its proper function.   Still more evident was it that, if the Son of God could deign to become incarnate and live the embodied life of man, there could be nothing degrading in corporeal substance; from which it must follow that Plotinus, or anyone else, who " blushed to find himself in a body ", was blasphemously setting himself up to be superior to God.   The broad result, however, was not so much that Christians engaged in perpetual controversy with Platonists about different grades of being, but rather that they dropped altogether the cosmic point of view, and fastened upon the fact that evil, as something culpable, could be found only in the acts of beings endowed with intelligence and will. Properly speaking, no sins or vicious acts were bodily; but, if in common language some of them were so described, this was quite intelligible; for language, after all, was not framed to suit the critical doctrines of the theologians or philosophers; and it was true enough, too, that the body was the soul's instrument of expression, and that in some kinds of action this collaboration was more obvious than in others.

Before closing this chapter something must be said of one more Christian article of faith, the Resurrection of the body, which to Platonists was entirely preposterous.   Here again a firm grasp of the monotheism which carried with it the belief that creation was an act of the divine will, and that no created substance could be dishonourable, was an indispensable preliminary to understanding.   In the Platonic tradition, so far as it was still coloured by Pythagoreanism, the body was regarded as the tomb or prison of the soul, from which death was an emancipation, not necessarily final; for, if " palingenesis " was indeed a fact, another term of incarceration, and yet another, might have to be served.   That Plato himself took all this literally it would be rash to infer from the use he sometimes (as in the *Meno*) thought fit to make of it.   Yet there can be no doubt that he looked upon the body as a hindrance; and, when Socrates, in the *Republic*, astonished his audience by speaking of the soul as immortal, or when in the *Phaedo*, with his own death imminent, he bade them waste no tears on the corpse he would leave behind, " the resurrection of the body " was about the last thing he would have alleged or desired.   Before even the bare possibility of a meaning in that startling phrase could be allowed, it was necessary, first, to banish all suspicion that body was something unworthy of the Creator, and secondly, to understand that, if the incarnate Logos was to triumph over death and frustrate the victory of the grave, it could be done only by absolute rejection of what had hitherto been implied in " the immortality of the soul ".   No one with the smallest power of judging evidence can doubt that the Church was founded on the unshakeable conviction that Jesus had risen from the dead, and that what his resurrection meant for the disciples was not simply the appearance of a disembodied spirit, a " ghost story ", in fact, which anyone but a professional Sadducee might chance to believe.   To dismiss this fundamental article of the faith as incredible will always be possible, but to deny that it is what the apostles and other " witnesses " believed is remarkably like nonsense.

Again: it is no business of mine to offer here any interpretation of the body that is " raised incorruptible ", and if I go so far as to observe that neither in the Gospels nor in the language of S. Paul is it implied that the episode of death makes no difference, I shall only be mentioning a fact which can hardly be disputed.   The point more relevant to the present discussion is that immortality of the soul, *as Platonists would understand it*, is not a Christian doctrine.   The qualifying clause needs the emphasis of italics, for there has always been this difficulty, that no Christian could in so many words deny that version of immortality without involving himself in much ambiguity, or indeed without appearing to renounce his own faith.   That was one of the penalties of the enormous influence exercised by Platonism, supplemented, no doubt, by a popular way of regarding soul and body far older than philosophy or theology of any kind.   To believe in the finality of death has never been easy.   In such records of primitive man as can be pieced together we are never surprised to find traces of belief in some kind of shadowy survival.   And when the soul had been discovered, when the notion of it had been developed to the point at which the first contact between philosophy and mystical practices was established, what else could be expected, as soon as any form of doctrine became explicit, but the assumption that the soul's continued existence must depend on its power to escape from a body that visibly perished and crumbled into dust ?   " The soul doubtless is immortal, where a soul can be discerned ", says the poet, but the invisibility of the soul was the very reason why its immortality could be discerned by the eye of faith, and in due course asserted by philosophers who had discovered that body and reality were by no means equivalent terms. Thus if we write down successively the two phrases, " immortality of the soul " and " resurrection of the body ", that order is much more than an accident of chronology. To believe in the first is a comparatively primitive achievement; to believe in the second needs a far bolder venture of faith and a philosophy immeasurably more profound.

7

The Medieval Problem
I. Faith and Reason

AS an alternative to the Christian religion, Platonism, re-edited and re-fashioned by Plotinus, was dead: as an intellectual tradition it not only survived, but for more than six centuries after the suppression of the Academy was almost the only relic of that unfettered curiosity about the nature of things which Rome had never quite succeeded in carrying away with the other spoils of Greece. " Revivals " have been almost as common in philosophy as in religion, but it must be confessed that throughout the period of history stigmatized as the Dark Ages it would have needed a very industrious raking over of the ashes to discover so much as a single spark of intellectual light. With the advent of Charlemagne, an enthusiast for education, there was a visible flicker, and it is possible that the restoration of the old curriculum (ultimately derived from Plato) with its two stages of *trivium* and *quadrivium* helped to increase the prestige of " dialectic ", a study classed traditionally with grammar and rhetoric, rather than with the sciences. Unfortunately, the progress of education and the vigour of intellectual life are dependent upon many conditions. No Charlemagne could suddenly put an end to the disorders of Europe, and, despite the sensational episode of John the Scot, another two centuries of darkness or half-light had to be traversed before any persistent movement, any opening of a genuinely new chapter in the history of thought, could be remarked.

Just how and why any notable renascence of the human spirit does come to pass in any particular century, and whether our incurable habit of stamping each century with its own peculiar character is defensible, it would require a very strong committee of experts to decide. No brief generalization can be adequate, but when we survey the broad advance of Christian thought in the Middle Ages, it is possible to distinguish three or four factors to which something roughly analogous may be discovered in any period of marked development. Even in the most revolutionary movement there will be signs of " palingenesis ", for it is only the dull and the ignorant who find nothing admirable in the past.   Equally true is it, of course, that no revival is mere resuscitation of the dead.   Originality there must be, of the kind that cannot be produced by imitation, antiquarianism, erudition, or indeed by any kind of education.   Yet some provision of opportunity, some common effort in a not unfriendly atmosphere, seems also to be indispensable; and this implies a vague diffusion of nascent ideas, almost as hard to explain as the emergence of individual genius, but manifested sometimes in an attack on established beliefs, which rouses latent energy and converts even somnolent conservatives into lively partisans.   Those who have leisure to study the history of medieval thought will easily detect the presence of all these contributing causes.   Much retrospection was inevitable, for the only available instruments of culture were survivals of a past, dimly known to have been more glorious; and only in fragments of Plato and Aristotle, or in comparatively ancient authors like Boethius and S. Augustine, was there any material for philosophical discussion.   Dependence on the past did not, however, destroy all hope of novelty.   To name only two remarkable men belonging to the earlier half of the " scholastic " period, there were Anselm, whose " ontological proof " of God's existence initiated a new line of speculation, and Abelard, whose impetuous and scornful temperament brought sorrow upon himself, but imparted a new significance to dialectic and opened the eyes of many to the urgency of problems not to be settled by mere professions of loyalty to the Scriptures and the Church.   As to the formation of an environment favourable to intellectual progress, we note the gradual convergence of streams derived from sundry monasteries and cathedral-schools, with the consequent rise, at Paris and elsewhere, of universities which, for better or for worse, became so powerful that none could venture to ignore them, least of all the two great orders of Friars, whose saintly founders, when they set out to restore the purity of religion, were far from anticipating the intellectual supremacy which some of their most devout followers were destined before long to enjoy.   Nor, finally, shall we look in vain for special causes of disturbance, new provocations and challenges, which obliged the champions of Christian philosophy to take the field once more against opponents not to be crushed by anathemas or refuted by official decrees.

But here we must distinguish two phases, chronologically divisible (if any precise date could be satisfactory) at about the year 1200; but requiring more than the lapse of time to explain the true distinction of character.   When we compare the first few centuries of the Christian era with the Middle Ages as a whole, the most obvious point of contrast is that the original task of the Church was to vanquish an alien religion, backed by a mighty empire which was decidedly a " kingdom of this world ". To convert the heathen was a manifest duty, but to annex and wield the imperial sceptre was so remote from Christian ambition that, even a hundred years or so after the reign of Constantine, S. Augustine could assume (as it seems) that the intrinsic antagonism of the *civitas Dei* and the *secunda Babylon* must endure as long as the earthly pilgrimage of the Church. In the same spirit, and perhaps with less appearance of ignoring facts already conspicuous, he recognized in Greek philosophy an antagonist more spiritual, indeed, than Roman legions and more worthy of respect, but not less irreconcilable with the gospel of Christ. From that general situation (even if Augustine's interpretation of it was partly questionable) turn to the coronation of Charlemagne, the career of Hildebrand, the imperialism of Dante's *Monarchia*, or to any other conspicuous landmark of the Middle Ages, and the world itself will seem to have been turned upside down. Heathendom has vanished, the imperial crown is a Christian appurtenance. Greek philosophy, or what little remains of it, is a discipline for schoolboys, or perhaps a modest handmaid to the triumphant theology.

With many features of this surprising revolution we are not concerned, but what did affect the fortunes of medieval philosophy in its earlier phase was the lack of any stimulus from outside the circle of established beliefs and modes of thought. To the geographical area of Christendom, indeed, there still were limits, and therefore an excuse for the preaching of Crusades; but as yet there was nothing analogous to the struggle officially terminated by Justinian; there was no philosophy associated with a rival religion, or claiming, apart from any religion, to possess and teach the truth. The only probable encouragement to new speculations was the outbreak of heresy, and, as John the Scot sagely observes, " many men are roused from slumber by heretics that they may see the day of the Lord and rejoice ". In one respect, however, the value of heresy as a means of promoting the search for truth is limited; for the heretic, as contrasted with the avowed unbeliever, either claims to be orthodox or, if not precisely that, at least to be reviving some forgotten truth or interpreting Scripture in accordance with its original meaning, hitherto unaccountably overlooked. It follows that he can be suppressed by authority, and in a sense without injustice; for, where there is no dispute about first principles and fundamental premisses, the offender may resent the decision of the court, but can appeal to no other. The case of Abelard is a valuable illustration.   Few who study him will doubt the sincerity of his faith or his loyalty to the Church.   It was believed, however, by S. Bernard and others that some of his opinions were dangerous, and twice was sentence pronounced against him.   Whether such recantation as he afterwards made was more than a formality we cannot tell, but it is clear that he was never quite in the position of one prepared to uphold the cause of reason, no matter what ecclesiastical judgements might be pronounced.   Thus far his case is typical, and what it means is that no " heresy ", so long as the term is used in its traditional sense, can ever quite demand the reasoned exposition of the Christian faith which alone can furnish a relevant answer to Platonism or any pagan philosophy, to a rival religion which acknowledges no " authority " common to itself and the Church, or to a rationalism which may be positively atheistic.

We must not, however, go so far as to suppose that, without the aid of heretics, the earlier medieval doctors could produce nothing of interest.   The effect of Anselm's ontological proof, whatever we may think of its merits, was to raise the whole question of " pure reason "; whether it was possible, by sheer exercise of thought, to get back to the necessary principle of real existence, and whether it was even legitimate for Christians to seek rational confirmation of propositions usually accepted as articles of faith.   Moreover, if Anselm appeared, at first sight, to be exaggerating the function of reason, this impression was corrected by his frequent insistence upon another point, that understanding of the highest form of truth was dependent upon a preceding faith.   *Nisi credideritis, non intelligetis;* faith is not a substitute for understanding but a prior condition; you cannot argue yourself into believing, but only when you believe will your mind be illuminated and truth revealed.   Anselm, of course, was very far from being the first to make this discovery, but the interesting point was that he combined this emphasis on the priority of faith with the ontological argument which in itself had at once provoked the criticism that he was attempting to transform a purely logical postulate into the existence of the living God.

So again, if we return for a moment to Abelard, we shall not find that his influence was derived solely, or even chiefly, from his reputedly heretical opinions.   It was not for his famous *Sic et Non* that he was condemned; but in that treatise he gave a deeper meaning to the dialectic which hitherto had largely consisted in that " talking for victory " dear to students in all ages, but naturally exaggerated in schools where books were scarce and teaching often took the form of disputation.   By arranging on opposite sides utterances drawn from equally authoritative sources Abelard plainly hinted that the sanction of catholicity—*quod semper, quod ubique, quod ab omnibus*—could not easily be found for doctrinal truths. His own conclusions, however, were often left indeterminate, and he was careful to maintain that apparent contradictions in the text of Scripture could always be reconciled or removed by better interpretation. It is even possible that he did not himself perceive the full significance of a method which afterwards became almost standardized in the exposition both of Christian doctrine and of philosophical theses; but at least he brought it home to his contemporaries that they might at any time be confronted with difficulties not to be overcome without the critical exercise of reason. Thus both he and Anselm, in their very different ways, threw out a challenge to mental indolence; all that now was lacking was the external stimulus without which neither heresy nor mere love of disputation could enlarge domestic controversy into a fresh elucidation of truth, latent, no doubt, in the Christian philosophy from its earliest days, but not yet fully expressed.

In the whole history of European culture there is nothing so astonishing as the dramatic re-entry of Aristotle more than fifteen centuries after his death. As a logician, of course, he had always been preeminent, but even of his logic nothing was known for many centuries except one or two minor treatises, with such commentary as Boethius and Porphyry could supply. The recovery of the *Analytics* and *Topics* in the first half of the twelfth century fell in with the fashion of the time and encouraged the modern Peripatetics to exalt their " philosopher " above all others, but logic alone would have produced no great revolution, and it was only when translations of works like the *Physics*, *Metaphysics*, and *De Anima* began to reach Paris that the authorities were gravely disturbed. The history of prohibitions and repeated prohibitions, little more effective than Canute's ironical attempt to bar the advancing tide, we need not trouble to follow; it is only the reason for them that requires close attention. Why should the views of a pagan philosopher cause so much uproar? What could anyone have had to say in the fourth century B.C. that could affect the faith revealed by God and guarded by an infallible Church? The chief source of the trouble was not the bare text of Aristotle, nor yet corrupt translations; for the old story that the Latin translations never came direct from the Greek, but only from Arabic versions already tainted with earlier Syrian misconceptions, has long been discredited by modern research. What is true, however, is that the first general impression of the new system was coloured by its association with certain Arabic commentaries and by rumours of doctrines evidently hostile to the Christian faith. But here we must beware of an erroneous inference. The frequent antagonism of Christian to Mohammedan commentators on Aristotle was no part of the Crusade: it was never, I mean, an item in the conflict of two religions; and this for the excellent reason that the Aristotelians who wrote in Arabic (few of them Arabs by race) were neither missionaries by inclination nor well qualified to represent their own nominal faith. Their own position, relatively to orthodox Islam, was highly equivocal, and they were far too much occupied with vindicating their right to be philosophers to save any breath for attacks on Christianity. What they stood for was not any kind of faith, but reason; and thus it came about that the arrival in Paris of a particular brand of Aristotelianism, reputedly unfavourable in certain respects to Christianity, encouraged the dangerous opinion that faith and reason pointed to incompatible conclusions. That popes and chancellors should therefore object to the public exposition of Aristotle before a mixed crowd of juvenile students is not surprising, and perhaps we may add that their attempts to suppress it were, after all, less foolish than similar displays of intolerance by some of our own universities in comparatively recent times. Much more surprising is it that the new philosophy should have made such rapid headway, and that the true nature of the problem should have been so thoroughly comprehended.

For the origin of certain controversies, which figure largely in the literature of the thirteenth century, about the interpretation of Aristotle, we should have to go back to Greek commentators long anterior to any Mohammedan school of philosophy. Nor, of course, were the " Arabs " by any means unanimous, but as we cannot stay to investigate their differences, it must suffice to say that Averroes (as the Latins called him), whose influence, diffused from Spain, was much greater in Christendom than among his own people, interpreted some of Aristotle's doctrines in a sense that made them definitely anti-Christian, and that somehow or other (for the details are still rather obscure) there grew up a faction or sect of Christian Averroists who confessed that faith obliged them to turn a deaf ear to reason, or perhaps insinuated that a man might swallow two incompatible sets of propositions without moral indigestion. That arguments in this style must produce a crisis was obvious, but the question was how best to deal with them. To begin with, it was a great advantage—not always fully appreciated—that Averroism, so far as it meant the interpretation of a pagan by a modern, could not possibly be condemned as heresy.

Averroists, as you might find them at Paris or Bologna, were on a different footing, and some of them (like Siger of Brabant) did come to grief. Yet punitive action, whether good or bad policy, was no solution of a problem which, as Albert of Cologne and Thomas Aquinas were wise enough to see, could be dealt with only by meeting their opponents on common ground, not by appealing to principles which Christians, indeed, would accept as infallible, but neither Moslems nor rationalists could be expected to concede. " Hast thou appealed unto Cæsar ? Unto Cæsar shalt thou go." For " Cæsar " write " Reason ", and the words of Festus to the Apostle of the Gentiles will admirably serve to express the spirit in which S. Thomas set out to face the " Gentiles " of his own day and their professedly Christian satellites. Much more was at stake than the general right to study Aristotle or the interpretation of any particular passage in his writings. For the first time (I say it deliberately) in the history of the Church the whole relation of faith to reason had to be fully examined, and as the result of that examination the very meaning of the terms " theology " and " philosophy " was about to be revised. True as it is that the supremacy of reason had always in practice been challenged by faith in the Incarnation and Resurrection, it would be wrong to infer that, when Platonists and Christians joined battle many centuries before the birth of S. Thomas, the controversy in which he afterwards played the leading part must already have become explicit. Whether it was that Neo-platonism was itself too theological in tone, or too mystical in temper, to represent dispassionate reason ; or whether its factitious alliance with pagan religion obscured the issue ; the upshot was that the main engagement never quite took the form of a struggle between a religion avowedly based on faith and a philosophy trusting to reason alone. Much less had any occasion been found for allotting to reason an independent province, for estimating its value as a guide to the borders of faith, or for defining the limits beyond which it must be impotent either to affirm or deny. But now at last, when a philosophy imported from beyond the precincts of Catholicism, and advertised as the very embodiment of reason, appeared to conflict in some important respects with the Christian faith, the time had come for a fresh survey of the whole field of knowledge, without shirking the difficulties inherent in the Church's claim to possession of truth revealed by God. Bulls and anathemas, prohibitions and excommunications, were all very well, but they could not disturb Aristotle or Averroes, nor could they persuade an honest man to accept as infallible truth anything that his intellectual conscience obliged him to reject as false.

In breadth of outlook and lucidity of exposition S. Thomas easily surpasses all competitors, but the problem was many-sided, and even his position needs to be analysed with care. The foundation of his argument is a firm conviction of the unity and essential harmony of all truth. *Duplex veritatis modus* is an expression of his own, but the " duplicity " does not mean that what is true inside a church is false outside the door, that what science plainly demonstrates can be refuted by Scripture, or, in a word, that there is any genuine incompatibility between truths of reason and truths of faith. At the same time he is perfectly confident that both sorts exist. It is impossible to know " by the natural light of reason " that God is triune or that the Word was made flesh: it is equally impossible to know by divine inspiration that any two sides of a triangle are greater than the third. When we talk thus of impossibility, we no more question the divine omnipotence than when we perceive that it is impossible to hear a colour or to smell a sound. A certain ordered arrangement of facts is found in a world created by God. One of those facts, sufficiently obvious without any kind of religious convictions, is that much can be discovered and proved by science; and to suppose that this " natural light " is simply delusive is as blasphemous (had S. Thomas been in a position to use the analogy) as the tales quoted by Plato of gods disguising themselves in order to deceive mankind. Another fact less obvious but, as S. Thomas believes, equally certain, is that truths undiscoverable by reason may be revealed to the eye of faith. It is with these general presuppositions that he comes to inspect the new situation brought about by the reappearance of Aristotle as physicist and metaphysician.

That " reason " should be represented in the thirteenth century by a philosophy more than fifteen hundred years old was, of course, an unpredictable accident of history, but it had to be recognized as a fact, and on no other common hypothesis could S. Thomas meet the " Arabs " with arguments they were bound to respect. With Jews one can appeal to the Old Testament, with Christians to both Old and New, but pagans and Moslems *non conveniunt nobiscum in aliqua Scriptura*, and therefore nothing remains but the appeal to reason, which in matters relating to God is weak. Now an appeal to reason ought not to mean an appeal to any particular philosopher, and no one knew better than S. Thomas that " authority " of that kind was *locus infirmissimus*, not for a moment to be compared with the citation of any " scripture " which all parties recognized as inspired. But why, then, trouble about Aristotle? Why not dismiss him as an ignorant pagan who knew no better? For more than one reason, fortunately, this short way with philosophers was impracticable, not least because it would have been quite inconsistent with S. Thomas's own principle, that, when a writer acknowledged no dogmatic authority common to himself and Christians, it was useless to quote such "authority" against him. There were, in fact, only three possible courses: (1) to show that certain disputed questions were outside the province of reason, or at least beyond the range of demonstration; (2) to show that some of Aristotle's arguments, when critically tested, were unsound; (3) to show that he had been misinterpreted by the "Arabs". In different contexts and on different occasions S. Thomas employs all these methods: the one thing he never does is to assume that Aristotle must be right. The only Aristotelians in the thirteenth century (I say nothing of more degenerate times) who came near to taking the philosopher's words as gospel were the Averroists. If S. Thomas thought that Aristotle was wrong, or that he had been too confident about indemonstrable matters of opinion, he was quite prepared to say so. He had, however, a profound admiration for him, and it would be foolish to deny that, owing to the deplorable condition of natural science at the time, he accepted many theories now obsolete and even, as viewed through modern eyes, absurd. That misfortune was inevitable, but luckily it had little or no bearing on the central problems of the time; for it was not about physics and astronomy that the great controversies arose, but either about speculative questions not determinable by science or about the interpretation of Aristotle, a task for which S. Thomas was at least as well qualified as his rivals.

For the most part, of course, Aristotle could have nothing to say about matters proper to faith; or, if he did appear to assert the eternity of the world in a sense that would make creation superfluous, it was a fair reply that his argument could be only conjectural, since nothing demonstrative could be produced on either side. The most famous dispute, however, was not about the origin of the cosmos, but about the subject indicated by the title of S. Thomas's trenchant little work, *De Unitate Intellectus Contra Averroistas*. The technicalities of the argument are too minute for brief discussion, and only one or two very imperfect comments can be offered, of which the first will be that the statements in Aristotle's *De Anima* which gave rise to the controversy are so condensed and so obscure (perhaps because they were only a lecturer's notes) that their meaning is to this day not perfectly certain. The Averroists took him to mean that the intellect (*Nous*) not dependent on any bodily organ, and therefore immortal or eternal, is never an organic part of the soul which informs an individual human body, but a single

H

cosmic Intelligence, which somehow establishes a relation with the individual during his lifetime, but without in any way imparting its own eternity.   From the Christian point of view this doctrine was, of course, intolerable; for it meant that, for the individual, death was the end of all things, and that no judgement upon good or evil lives was to be expected.   Beyond doubt, too, this was " heresy ", wherever the term was applicable; but Moslems could not, strictly speaking, be heretics, and, what is far more important, it was not as heresy that S. Thomas thought fit to treat it when he attacked the Parisian Averroists, but primarily as a misinterpretation of Aristotle, and further, as a doctrine which could be refuted *sola ratione*, because, as he believed, there were sound arguments for the immortality of the soul.

But now a new complication begins to appear.   That faith and knowledge are not identical modes of experience is hardly a controversial statement; again, that certain articles of the Christian faith are indemonstrable by reason is a thesis that an atheist would be quite as ready as a Christian to admit.   Thus far, then, the position appears to be simple; for, if the provinces of faith and reason are entirely distinct, what fear can there be of any direct collision ?   A few men will be expert in theology, a few (possibly atheistic) in science; while the masses will jog along quietly, content with such faith as they have and such scraps of knowledge as they may chance to pick up.   Like many other simplifications, however, this epitome of the facts omits too much.   However true it may be that the doctrine of the Trinity can no more be proved or disproved by arithmetic than the motions of the planets can be deduced from the Athanasian Creed, S. Thomas, for one, was by no means prepared to admit that reason was, so to speak, atheistic, and that no intimation whatever of religious truth could be got by philosophical thinking.   This would have meant, from his point of view, that the Creator of the world had left no trace of himself in it, and that man, a rational being endowed with endless curiosity about the natural order and his own place in it, would have sought in vain for illumination, unless perchance he had the good fortune to be born a Jew.   Apart, too, from any *a priori* religious objections, there remained the fact that pagan philosophers had offered proofs of the existence of God which supplied at least a foundation for arguments which S. Thomas and many other Christians took to be valid.

Far from shirking the objections to this apparent overlapping of faith and reason, S. Thomas is at pains to formulate them.   Sometimes he argues that the *sacra doctrina* (the theology which presupposes the inspiration of Scripture) is not made superfluous by any philosophical discipline, sometimes that the revelation of God to the faithful does not annul or discredit the claim of reason to discover his existence.   Given that there is a kind of rational theology, few men have time, ability, or inclination to travel by that difficult road to the knowledge of God, and it cannot be the duty of every Christian to be a metaphysician.   On the other hand, if faith is necessary, and if no man is debarred from it by lack of intellectual gifts, we may be still inclined to ask what point there can be in elaborate demonstration of what we believe, and whether this trusting to reason may not even destroy the merit of faith.   It is in meeting this criticism that S. Thomas most clearly explains his own position.   The facts about God which reason can discover are not, he says, articles of faith, but only " preambles ".   We may prove that God exists and that he is one, but not that there are three Persons; we may find arguments for the immortality of the soul, but not (he might have added) for the resurrection of the body.   Faith, as he says again, " presupposes natural knowledge " and perfects it; and, though it is true that all Christians are required to believe, while only a few can be philosophers, those few will have the important task of refuting infidel rationalists with their own weapons.   If the articles of faith cannot be proved by reasoning, then neither can they be disproved; and it is for the Christian philosopher to show that arguments purporting to overthrow the creed of the Church, or perhaps even to disprove the existence of God, are intrinsically fallacious.   After all, then, it seems that the provinces of faith and reason do not overlap: the truth is rather that reason can establish conclusions preliminary to the fuller understanding that comes only through faith.

The general policy of S. Thomas was by no means universally approved.   Some of his critics, suspicious of the whole Aristotelian movement, would have been glad enough to involve him in the downfall of the Averroists, and doubtless he would have been himself astonished (if not horrified) to learn that six centuries later his own philosophy would almost be in danger of canonization.   Nevertheless, his grasp of his own system and his power of exposition are so remarkable that we are justified in taking him as representative, at least in this sense, that, if he failed to make out a good case for the *duplex veritatis modus*, no other medieval writer is likely to have succeeded.   Let us consider, then, whether he does in fact leave room for the autonomy of the sciences, and what position he assigns to " philosophy ", as compared with either ancient or modern usage of the term.   To begin with, we must observe that S. Thomas rarely, if ever, makes it his primary object to champion the cause of reason.   He addresses himself rather to the vindication of Christian theology, which admittedly depends on presuppositions peculiar to itself. He calls it a " science ", because, like all sciences, it has its own *principia*, but he calls it also *sapientia*, the supreme wisdom, and declares that in this capacity it is entitled to pass judgement on the principles of all other sciences and to condemn as false whatever in them is repugnant to theological truth (S. Th. I, qu. VI). Taken in isolation, a statement of this kind must sound fatal to the very existence of the sciences; for to grant them freedom of action, provided they were always careful to arrive at no conclusions incompatible with sound theology, would be sheer mockery. S. Thomas is not, however, proposing anything so absurd. As we have seen already, his basic assumption is that there cannot be any real contradiction between truths of reason and truths of faith. In the same spirit, he remarks on the very first page of the *Summa Theologica* that the *sacra doctrina* rests on the inspiration of Scripture, and that *scriptura divinitus inspirata non pertinet ad philosophicas disciplinas, quæ sunt secundum rationem humanum inventæ*. Thus the " irrelevance " of Scripture to all that reason can discover is at once the *raison d'être* of theology, and the charter of liberty to human science. But if there is no radical schism in the body of truth, and if science is unaffected by the assumptions of theology, what point can there be in claiming for the higher wisdom the right to supervise the inventions of reason and, if need be, to reject them as false ? Here we have to distinguish between the competence of reason in its own nature and the fallibility of human beings. In asserting the sufficiency of reason for its own business S. Thomas not only repudiates scepticism (in its proper sense), but is also more ready, perhaps, than a good many modern critics to assume the existence of certain self-evident principles, which are not the premisses of any distinctive science, but simply the groundwork of all coherent thinking. This doctrine he inherited from Aristotle and (apart from Scepticism) the main tradition of philosophy, and whatever difficulties there may be in the notion of " self-evidence ", he was thus enabled to fortify his conviction that the Creator would not furnish man with a " natural light " no better than an *ignis fatuus*.

The natural adequacy of reason, however, can no more guarantee the truth of a scientific theory, or the logical perfection of an argument, than sound eyesight can debar the possibility of inaccurate observation. *Humanum est errare*, and if nothing more than this ancient commonplace were needed to justify the superior attitude of theology, the case would be simple. But clearly there is more in it than this. No science, to be sure, is above criticism, but while the specialist is always

ready to consider objections framed by others as expert as himself, he
will pay no heed to amateurs, least of all, perhaps, to the theologian,
whose point of view is so utterly different from his own. In the end,
therefore, the only ground on which the theologian's right to dissent
from scientific conclusions can be upheld is that they are not scientific;
and this will not mean that the methods of the expert are unsound or
his reasoning sophistical, but merely that the province of genuine
science is not wide enough to embrace the questions belonging to
theology. In point of fact, too, no astronomer, or physicist, or
biologist, unless he has an unusual gift of impudence, is likely to pretend
that his own science can positively disprove any article of the Christian
faith. More probably he will argue, if so inclined, that God is a
superfluous hypothesis, that the mechanism of nature leaves no room
for personal agency, that the soul is only a function of the body, or more
generally, perhaps, that nothing beyond the reach of scientific verification is credible. Now these and other similar contentions are philosophical theses, not scientific truths; and whether or no we agree with
S. Thomas that theology is their appointed judge, it is certainly
sapientia of some kind that we need to save us from the dogmatism which
masquerades as science. Atheism may be the true philosophy;
materialism (a sadly ambiguous term) may be a sufficient explanation of
the cosmos; the Christian faith may rest on a collection of fables; but
none of these propositions can be scientifically demonstrated, nor does
any one of them even belong to the subject-matter proper to any natural
science.

Reflections of this kind are bound to carry us beyond the immediate
horizon of the thirteenth century. However broad his outlook, however liberal his intellectual principles, it is not to be supposed that the
problem of faith and reason could be presented to S. Thomas in its
full magnitude at a time when most of the sciences which have since
been thought most damaging to the Christian faith could scarcely yet
be said to exist. Tempting as it is to speculate on his probable reaction to various modern theories, we have no space for such digressions.
It is enough that in his actual contest with " Gentiles " from beyond the
pale, or with Latin Averroists who hinted that only in the teeth of
reason could they hold fast to their faith, he was prepared to waive the
appeal to authority, and to rely on philosophical arguments. If he
often did appeal to the " authority " of Aristotle, that was chiefly
because, in the estimation of his opponents, Aristotle was both the
nearest thing to " Scripture " and the embodiment of reason; and also
because he believed them to be misinterpreting, in some important

respects, their acknowledged master.   Undoubtedly, too, his own enthusiasm for the new philosophy must have helped to determine his general attitude towards the problem of reason and faith.   Had he agreed, for instance, with Averroes that Aristotle's theory of the intellect was fatal to the hope of personal immortality; or had he judged that the line of reasoning which led to the conception of the " Unmoved Mover " was no more convincing than Anselm's ontological proof; he might have felt less confidence in the positive value of reason as a preface to the higher revelation of truth.   It has always, in fact, been one of the probable criticisms of S. Thomas that he claimed for reason not too little, but too much.   Even in his own generation there were many who shook their heads over this covert rationalism, and we all know how roughly the traditional " proofs " of God's existence have since been handled.

Let us suppose, then, that in respect of " God, freedom, and immortality " S. Thomas did ask of reason more than it could give.   How far does this affect his general position?   As regards his faith and the theology derived from it, not at all;   for nowhere does he maintain or allow that articles of faith can fall within the province of reason, and, as we have noted already, he is careful to explain that the demonstrable facts about the Being and Unity of God are only " preambles " to deeper understanding.   To this extent he may seem almost to anticipate the opinion not uncommon in modern times that, while the so-called proofs of God's existence do indeed establish something, they provide no genuine way of transition from a metaphysical abstraction to a God whom man can love and adore.   It is most unlikely, however, that S. Thomas would have acquiesced in this compromise.   If persuaded that the particular arguments on which he had relied were dubious, he would have been more disposed to search for better ones than to abandon his conviction that the author of nature and the human mind would not have left himself without witness.   In its negative aspect at least, his position would still be unassailable;   for, if the failure of reason to justify any kind of theism must be ascribed, not to the weakness of any particular argument, but to its essential incapacity, then the case for a reasoned atheism must be equally inconclusive.   It would not even be fair to lay the *onus probandi* upon the theist, for where proof is, by the very nature of the case, impossible there is no such burden for either party to shoulder.   The most that could reasonably be demanded would be a comparison of hypotheses;   and, since S. Thomas himself rejects the *a priori* form of argument, only contending that the existence of God is required to account for the facts of experience, he may be said to adopt thus far the method of natural science.   It does not follow, however, that the agency of God is, from the scientific point of view, a legitimate mode of explanation, and so once more we are driven back to the same question, whether reason, if clearly excluded from the province of faith, can indeed contribute even a " preamble " to the apprehension of truths revealed only to believers and affirmed in the Creed of the Church.

No further progress can be made without a more critical scrutiny of one too facile assumption which underlies the whole antithesis of reason and faith. Not only in the Middle Ages, but also often enough in far more recent times, it seems to be taken for granted that the meaning of " reason " is too obvious to call for discussion. But is it ? The truth is rather that in the whole philosophical vocabulary there is scarcely a more ambiguous term. That our own word comes from *ratio*, and that *ratio* was chosen to represent the Greek *logos* is certain, but what complicates the interpretation of this simple pedigree is the elusive character of the original parent. In the history of *logos*, which has yet to be written, no chapter would be more difficult than the first; and in the slowly developing catalogue of meanings it is possible that " reason " would be the last to appear. But since it is impossible here to mention even the principal difficulties, I shall make only this one suggestion about the history of the subject, that when we look back to Greek philosophy for anticipations of " faith and reason ", we shall be well advised to disregard *logos* altogether. No real equivalent of the medieval antithesis will be discoverable, but the nearest thing to it will be the familiar distinction of knowledge and opinion. Now the difference between " knowledge " (as representing the Greek *episteme*) and " reason " is quite as great as the difference between " opinion " (the Greek *doxa*) and " faith " in the Christian sense. What you " opine " (or " believe ", if that translation be preferred) you do not " know ", and therefore it must remain doubtful, but what you " know " is absolutely certain. That was the position in the age of Plato and Aristotle; and, though many further refinements and distinctions were afterwards introduced, the old tradition persisted and, if I am not mistaken, confused both the medieval conception of " reason " and many later discussions. Philosophy has never quite recovered from its infant malady of mathematics. The pattern of certitude was first exhibited in geometrical reasoning, and when the still more abstract science of logic came into being, it was inevitable that " knowledge " should almost be identified with demonstration in the mathematical style. Almost, but not quite; for the need of indemonstrable presuppositions was also an early discovery, and thus the " axiom " was established, as a defence, first of all, against the risk of circular argument or the " infinite regress ", but also against the sceptic, who no sooner perceived the impossibility of proving everything than he proceeded to infer that nothing could be known.

To S. Thomas, as to any other good Aristotelian, the analysis of logical reasoning, leading on, perhaps, to questions that would now be called " epistemological ", could not fail to be interesting; but he may not have been aware that the scope of " reason ", or indeed of the whole controversy about the respective functions of reason and faith, was still in practice restricted by this Greek tradition which descended from an age when " faith ", in anything like its Christian sense, had not yet secured recognition. It was faith that exposed the insufficiency of knowledge and opinion as the sole alternatives; for faith is neither what Plato and Aristotle understood by " knowledge ", nor what they meant by " opinion "; neither the certitude of exact science nor the state of uncertainty which prevails when science is lacking; but (as Christians maintain) the key to " revelation ", to a spiritual illumination concerning matters beyond the range of demonstration; not because, like axioms, they are logically prior to discursive reasoning, but because faith is, first and foremost, a way of access to that knowledge of a Person, between which and the knowledge of abstract truth obtainable by science there is no real analogy. Whereas, in Plato's estimation, the objects of opinion are inferior to the objects of science because they are too concrete, in Christian estimation, on the contrary, the objects of science are inferior to the objects of faith because they are too abstract. And, since God alone is absolutely individual and unique, and therefore entirely outside all classes, kinds, and types, the revelation of him which comes by faith is, of all forms of experience, the most remote from that knowledge of the universal, manifesting itself in " particulars ", to which science perpetually aspires.

When " reason " is identified with knowledge, and " knowledge ", like the Greek *episteme*, with demonstrative science, the delimitation of the provinces of faith and reason may seem to be a comparatively simple matter, but neither to theologians nor to philosophers in general can it be satisfactory to accept a restriction of terminology which entails the omission of so many important facts. If Christian theology, as founded on faith, is outside the domain of " reason ", what this really implies is that to attempt to prove or disprove the articles of faith by scientific methods is just as irrational as to pretend that the weight of the moon can be determined by faith. But again, if Christians assent to a formula like Anselm's *nisi credideritis, non intelligetis*, they are not merely stating a fact of personal experience, but also endorsing a theory which they take to be reasonable, and must therefore be prepared to defend. Doubtless there is a sense in which nothing fairly to be described as " reason " can do the work of faith, but there is also a sense in which no doctrine concerning the nature of faith can evade criticism on the ground that rational argument is irrelevant. The concept of " reason " must therefore be enlarged; or if the critics of faith and theology are still disposed to insist that nothing can be accepted as truth until it is scientifically ascertained, they must at least be made to understand that this contention is not a truth established by any science, but a pre-supposition, a thesis, a dogma, or, in its own way, an act of faith. By the firm assurance of S. Thomas that there could be no internal discord within the unity of truth the situation was partly elucidated, but not, I think, entirely. A still more comprehensive survey of the field of knowledge was required, not merely to convince Averroists that any supposedly scientific conclusions inimical to the faith must be fallacious, but in order to escape from the traditional identification of " reason " with demonstrable science, and to formulate one great question of the future, whether " philosophy ", in a certain restricted sense of the word, must not disentangle itself from both science and theology, and assume the position of a *tertium quid*.

8

The Medieval Problem
II. The Invention of " Philosophy "

GREEK theology, as we saw, was invented by philosophers, and, except as a protest against degraded myths and superstitions, had originally nothing to do with established religion. It did not follow, of course, that all philosophers, or all schools of philosophy, were equally interested in speculations about the nature of deity, but even if recognition of the gods had been everywhere as perfunctory as in the garden of Epicurus, it would still have been true that, if you wished to find a theologian, you would have sought him vainly anywhere else but in the frequented haunts of philosophy. Christian theology, on the other hand, was primarily and essentially an attempt to give formal expression to the truths of the Christian religion, and could never be more than superficially intelligible to those untouched by the faith to which its very existence was due. In the early days of the Church, therefore, it was only natural that many Christians, not necessarily lacking in education or intelligence, should stand aside from all the disputes of the philosophers, or frankly condemn them as inane. They knew that faith could not be inspired by mere argument, and they knew that without faith it could never be revealed to any man that Jesus was the Son of God. What point, then, could there be in taking sides with Zeno or Epicurus about matters not pertaining to salvation, or in listening to the feeble theologies of men groping in the dark?

It was not long, however, before the insufficiency of this attitude was discovered. Just because of the separation of theology from religion in the pagan world, the Church was obliged to arm itself with two kinds of weapons. Men acquainted with the various tenets of philosophy began to be interested in the new religion, and some of them, whether attracted or repelled, were shrewd enough to detect the possibility of a new challenge to all who professed themselves votaries of wisdom. Hence arose the distinguished company of Christian Platonists or Platonizing Christians; hence, too, was accentuated the mistrust of philosophy in the minds of all who were indisposed to welcome any infusion of secular doctrines into the theology grounded in faith. The result was an ambiguous tradition, a wavering between the rejection of all philosophy as pretentious ignorance and the ambition to prove that only in the Church was to be found the wisdom sincerely, perhaps, but vainly pursued in the pagan schools. At no time, of course, was Christianity itself announced as a new philosophy; for that would have been, in the light of Greek tradition, to proclaim its divorce from the religion of common folk; but when Augustine, for instance, declares that *verus philosophus amator dei est*, he is not trifling with the meaning of a word, but expressing a sentiment which was to find many notable echoes in the course of the next thousand years.

From medieval theologians, were we to adopt the method of Abelard's *Sic et Non*, it would be easy to collect a number of these conflicting utterances about " philosophy ", and no less easy to be misled by the restricted sense in which the word was frequently used. It was not the whole pursuit of wisdom that most of the earlier writers had in mind, but chiefly " dialectic ", or the logic described as *sermotionalis*, to indicate that it dealt rather with words and their meanings than with the nature of things. Obviously, then, this art of disputation might be merely vexatious, a display of perverse ingenuity, which sober and responsible ecclesiastics would naturally distrust. So again, when philosophy in relation to theology is described by Peter Damian (*ob.* 1072) as *ancilla dominæ*, it sounds as though he were enslaving reason to authority, but in fact he does little more than assign to logic the instrumental function still implied in the title *Organon*, which editors bestowed on the collected logical works of Aristotle long ago. If, indeed, we choose to understand " theology " in its Aristotelian sense, as an alternative name for the " first philosophy " or metaphysics, the office of a handmaid is, approximately, what does belong to logic; which does not rank, in Aristotle's estimation, with the sciences, but is, at most, a study of their methods.

At the same time, there were other medieval authors who understood " philosophy " in a sense more in accordance with its etymology, and thus were ready to find the only perfect example of it in Christian life and thought. John of Salisbury, for example, derides the self-styled " pure philosophers " who can see no farther than the boundaries of logic, and does not hesitate, for his own part, to call philosophy " the guide to salvation ", not as a rival to faith, but rather as a discipline which without the help of faith cannot be perfectly exercised. John of Salisbury lived till 1180, by which time the new translations of Aristotle's *Analytics* had certainly increased the dignity of logic, but he was still too early for the great controversy provoked by Averroism, and, when faith and reason came to be directly contrasted, it would have been impossible to identify his " philosophy" with either. The whole situation, in fact, was so revolutionized by the new Aristotelianism that, when we begin to estimate the work of S. Thomas in its relation to the status of philosophy, little is gained by looking backwards, for the real question is whether his analysis of the contemporary problem makes adequate provision for the needs of the future. If we ask, for instance, whether this " reason ", about which there was so much disturbance, is synonymous with either " philosophy " or " science ", neither alternative can be decisively preferred. S. Thomas himself did not set up to be a prophet—not even in the style of Roger Bacon—and to pretend that he foresaw the consequences of discoveries made two or three centuries after his death would be merely ridiculous. Almost unwittingly, however, and by force of circumstances affecting his own generation, he did, I think, prepare the way for a new orientation of " reason ", and for the new grouping of intellectual disciplines already signified to some extent by the distinction of " faculties " within the new universities.

Without anachronism, it may be said that one effect of isolating the *sacra doctrina*, as the study occupied solely with the knowledge resulting from faith, was to set between theology and philosophy a dividing line unacknowledged in the ancient world, and even in the Christian era imperfectly marked hitherto. Thus at the very opening of the *Summa Theologica*, after formulating the " objection " that, since the ordinary philosophical disciplines cover the ground, no special doctrine about God is required, S. Thomas replies that the theology *quæ ad sacram doctrinam pertinet differt secundum genus ab illa quæ pars philosophiæ ponitur*. By the kind which is " part of philosophy " he means, of course, the " theology " which Aristotle had occasionally recognized by that name, and he rightly judges that the novelty originated by the Church is a theology definitely not of that genus. In a sense, therefore, he expels philosophy from theology; for if metaphysics, admitted by all Aristotelians to be the highest form of theoretical inquiry, has no sovereignty within the precincts of the *sacra doctrina*, much less will any inferior be qualified to intrude. One result of this demarcation is that S. Thomas appears to adopt the " handmaid " theory in a far more comprehensive style than Peter Damian. As superior to all other sciences, he says, the sacred doctrine makes use of them *tanquam inferioribus et ancillis*, not because of any defect in itself, but because of the infirmity of the human intellect, which needs the guidance of

" natural reason " to lead it on to the study of higher things. Yet, if
we hasten to infer that theology is thus authorized to dictate to the
sciences, to supply them with *principia*, or to regulate their conclusions,
we shall go completely astray.   Nothing is farther from the mind of
S. Thomas.   What he does mean is, first, that if the other sciences do
contribute anything to the theology which, by hypothesis, is derived
from faith, it can be only something of subordinate importance; and
this, after all, is obvious.   But secondly, he means also (as we saw in the
preceding chapter) that he allows the sufficiency of the " natural light "
for the first part of the journey, in which the establishment of God's
existence by rational argument is a prelude to such understanding of his
nature as can be obtained only through faith.   As to the terms " philosophy " and " science " it seems to be almost a matter of indifference to
S. Thomas which of the two he employs.   The *sacra doctrina* is a
" science " distinguished from the " philosophical disciplines "; but
these " disciplines " may just as correctly be called " sciences ", and
to metaphysics, no less than to arithmetic or geometry, that name may
be freely applied.

Now in our own day we must take it as certain that no one pro-
fessionally addicted to the study of " science " would feel called upon
to deal with arguments for or against the existence of God.   Sciences,
to be sure, are many, and no man will be master of more than one or
two.   Yet any specialist, however conscious of his own limitations,
would be confident that none of his scientific colleagues was housed in a
laboratory where his appointed task would be to expound or criticize
any theological hypothesis such as the origination of the cosmos by the
will of an omnipotent creator.   Or, if, again, we were to betake ourselves to the lecture-rooms of the " philosophers ", we might catch
one of them discoursing upon the *Ethics* of Spinoza; but, as likely as not,
he would begin by warning his audience that the author's exposition of
the argument *more geometrico* must not be mistaken for genuine demonstration.   Passing on to other metaphysicians, we might hear a great
variety of opinions about the scope and limitations of " reason ", but
on two points we should find general agreement, that philosophy and
science belonged to different faculties, and that natural or rational
theology, whatever the philosophers might choose to think of it, was
assuredly no science.

To quarrel with a medieval author because he uses the term
" science " in a manner no longer customary would be as unreasonable
as to cavil at expressions like " natural philosophy " and " experimental philosophy ", which linger on, in the titles of some of our

academic professorships, to remind us of an age when Science had not yet acquired a capital letter or begun to make authoritative pronouncements. The real difficulty, however, is more than verbal; for the thesis that faith and reason do not conflict, is actually far more easy to defend when " reason " is nearly equivalent to " science " than when it embraces the whole field of inquiry which would now be designated by the term " philosophy ". No one ever supposed there was a specifically Christian geometry, any more than a Buddhist arithmetic; nor do I personally doubt that S. Thomas would gladly have accepted the Copernican astronomy, as soon as he was convinced that it " saved the appearances " better than the older hypothesis. On the other hand, no Christian can admit that matter alone is a sufficient explanation of the origin of the world, that death is the absolute end of the individual soul, or that the determinism of cause and effect reduces all human action to a level at which moral judgements become absurd; and, in point of fact, it was largely questions of this kind that S. Thomas had in view when he allowed to reason a province to which the *sacra doctrina* did not pertain. But suppose we dissent from his estimate of certain arguments accepted in his day, and find ourselves convinced by later criticism that they are not philosophically valid—what then? Are we driven back to a kind of Averroism? Or is there an intermediate position, in which we neither agree with S. Thomas that the " theology " constructed by reason is a satisfactory preamble to the articles of faith, nor yet are forced to admit that only in defiance of reason can the truth of those articles be affirmed?

Strictly speaking, S. Thomas is not obliged by his principles to uphold at all costs any argument belonging to the sphere of reason, much less to adopt any complete system of philosophy (Aristotle's, for instance) as an indispensable safeguard of the faith. All he undertakes is to show that any argument ostensibly destructive of the Christian position is either fallacious or inconclusive. In practice, however, this purely critical attitude would greatly diminish the force of the contention that faith and reason are harmonious. *Duplex veritatis modus* is a promising formula, but if each mode, in relation to the other, is entirely negative; if there is no common body of truth to which each makes an organic contribution; it is almost certain that the result will be either open antagonism or a constant retreat by faith towards some citadel of irrationality which no one will trouble to assault.

The dilemma is not, however, by any means so formidable as, for controversial purposes, it can be made to appear. If we begin by assuming that " reason " is confined to the sphere of strictly demonstrable science, and then subjoin, as our minor premiss, that no religious faith is demonstrable, a conclusion highly agreeable to rationalists will follow. But let us scrutinize the premisses a little more closely. The minor, of course, is incontestable; for, a demonstrable creed is out of the question, and the religious value of so fantastic a hybrid would be nil. It is impossible to believe what you know. On the other hand, to confine " reason " to the strictly demonstrable would be as disastrous to the secular investigations of reality as to any religion. Some further observations on this point it will be convenient to reserve for another place, and for the moment I shall only attempt to gauge the consequences for the Christian religion of two admissions, already foreseen: the first, that none of the traditional " proofs " of God's existence is rightly so described; the second, that, even if their validity be allowed, they prove nothing distinctively Christian, but would serve as a preamble to any kind of monotheism, or, as one might rather say, to no kind of monotheism in which the attributes ascribed to God imply that he is more than a logical presupposition or postulate, such as The Supreme Being or The First Cause; while even in those colourless titles it is possible that the definite article surreptitiously introduces a conception of unity not warranted by the evidence.

Now what this means, first of all, is that so long as we assume that demonstrative science can be pushed to the very borders of faith, with no intermediate area, a partition of territory between faith and reason is of comparatively small importance. However true it may be that, on this assumption, there will be no collision between the two modes of truth, the only considerable result will be that science is thus left free to mind its own business, without ecclesiastical interference. Logically, no doubt, a like freedom is secured for theology, but even that will be a doubtful advantage if it implies that, in relation to what Christians believe, reason has no other office but the deduction of conclusions from premisses supplied by authority. Faith is indemonstrable, but it cannot afford to be irrational. The province of reason, in fact, must be more liberally measured. It must be wider, not merely than strict demonstration, but than the whole range of the natural sciences, many of which are necessarily empirical in method, and more concerned, therefore, with generalizations and probabilities than with mathematical certainty. Let us beware, too, of the spatial metaphors which, almost inevitably, we employ for the purpose of specific differentiation. Every science has its own subject-matter, its peculiar scope, or, as we say, its "field" or "province", or "domain". To make a point of avoiding such expressions would be needless pedantry; but, when we pass from the delineation of sciences by specialists to the wider questions involved in the problem of faith and reason, or in the assigning of theology, philosophy, and science to different academic faculties, there is a real danger of imposing arbitrary and misleading limitations. To bar the road against criticism, to erect a notice-board warning reason to advance thus far and no farther, may be merely to beg the question. Nor does this fatal policy operate in only one direction. When theology barricades itself in a sanctuary and denies admittance to all who lack the passport of orthodoxy, its own criticism of philosophies hatched in the profane wilderness is likely to fall to the level of arguments which, as S. Thomas says, are useful *ad solatium fidelium*, but leave the infidel unmoved.

I am not, of course, denying that Christian theology—the *sacra doctrina*—has its own problems, which can be discussed only on the basis of its own propositions, but the danger of confusing this fact with a very different question is real. There is a chapter in *Summa contra Gentiles* (II, 4) which has for its heading the statement *quod aliter considerat de creaturis philosophus et aliter theologus*. Now it will be observed that, while the philosopher and the theologian are explicitly distinguished, both of them are said to consider the same " creatures ", that is to say, the whole system of nature in its widest sense. Human philosophy, S. Thomas goes on to explain, considers things *in quantum huiusmodi*, the nature of fire, motion, or whatever it may be, as judged by their phenomenal properties and behaviour; but theology considers them only in their relation to the Creator. The theologian, he intimates, has no more to do with astronomical theory (as the critics of Copernicus might with advantage have noted) than the astronomer with the psalmist's declaration that the heavens declare the glory of God. So far, so good; but when S. Thomas, in the same context, compares the distinction of philosopher and theologian to the distinction between the physicist and the mathematician (in their respective accounts of a line) the illustration is unfortunate; for the distinction of aspects in the totality of " creatures " is, surely, an entirely different thing from the specialization of the sciences. Every natural science has its own work to do and its own branch of expert knowledge, but certain fundamental principles are common to all. When it does happen, therefore, that one science borrows the results of another, or when there is, in a sense, overlapping, there is no risk of wandering into something as irrelevant to the whole body of natural science as the poet's ecstatic vision of the heavens to the sober calculations of astronomy. And this, as it seems to me, is where the tendency, in the age of S.

Thomas, to make " reason " almost identical with " science " did somewhat confuse the situation and cause the antithesis of faith and reason to be imperfectly conceived.

Just as the ancient philosophers had invented the theology which belongs to the province of reason, so did the medieval theologians repay the debt by inventing the philosophy which is neither the theology derived from faith nor natural science; but they did it almost inadvertently and without perceiving the full import of their own achievement. That physics, astronomy, and all the other sciences, do not clash with the doctrines of the Trinity and the Incarnation is a fairly obvious fact, but in the long run not very important. On the other hand, the claim of the theologian to interpret all creatures—the entire phenomenal world —with relation to God is a challenge to "rationalists", which can neither be supported by appealing to the authority of faith nor met by invoking the authority of science. It must be freely allowed, too, that in this wide arena, where all philosophies meet as competitors on equal terms, there is no room for infallible proofs. The weapons employed are those of reason, but not of demonstration, nor yet of verification by experiments performed before the eyes of trained observers. All theories spring from experience, and all strive to interpret it, but the range of experience is so vast that the attempt to capture its authority for the benefit of one particular type of thought is only a controversial device. The mystic deals with experience just as truly as the chemist; and, though the chemist has a great advantage in the clarity of his experiments, this means only that his whole science deals with a simpler class of facts, and operates below the level of the larger philosophical problems. It is thus not two provinces that have to be recognized, but three; and it is in the third, which is neither science, as the term is now used, nor Christian theology, that the real problem of faith and reason has to be faced.

But here once more let us beware of spatial metaphors. When three counties or parishes are marked on the map, it means, of course, that they do not overlap; but when theology, philosophy, and science are handed over to different faculties, this does not imply that reason is active in one of them, or perhaps in two, but not in the third. Nor is it merely that reasoned argument is found in any and every type of inquiry, for that could hardly be disputed. The more important point is that the critical function of reason must operate everywhere, keeping constant watch lest the assumptions proper to each special branch of knowledge should be illegitimately construed as the basis of a philosophy far wider than the scientific terms of reference. Familiar examples

I

from one quarter are associated with terms like Materialism, Determinism, or Evolution, reminding us of sundry attempts to pass from valuable scientific hypotheses to philosophies of enormously wider range.   Similarly, there are questions not strictly theological, as that term might be applied to the doctrines of the Atonement or the Sacraments, yet so vital to religion that adherence to certain theories (Materialism, for instance) is evidently debarred.   And what this implies is that the Christian challenge to philosophy—its claim to be reasonable—must be upheld in an arena where neither the theologian nor the scientist can overthrow his adversaries by means of the expert knowledge proper to himself.

Herein, too, lurks another danger.   Given that there are speculative questions which can neither be ignored by Christians, nor settled by authority, there will then be a temptation to confer our official status upon whatever type of philosophy looks to be most favourable to the position of the Church.   A specious air of finality will thus be imparted to arguments relative to a bygone intellectual situation, and, instead of unfettered inquiry in which men are free to differ, we may get a new dogmatism from which it will be almost heresy to dissent. Whenever the Church has adopted or patronized a philosophy of secular origin, the result, sooner or later, has been disastrous.   The rhapsodical pseudo-Platonism of the pseudo-Dionysius was bad enough, but the most conspicuous example, of course, is the medieval Aristotelianism, which began as a stout fight for freedom, and ended with the brayings of the donkeys who attacked Galileo with the hoofs in which their brains would appear to have been located.   Incidentally, too, the figment of an orthodox Aristotelianism did a grievous injury to Aristotle himself.   The reaction, when it came, was almost as foolish as the previous servility, with the result that one of the world's greatest thinkers had to wait another three centuries before he could receive the critical appreciation that was his due.   Partly, no doubt, the harm done by confusing the letter of Aristotelianism with its spirit was due to imperfect discrimination between better and worse science, or between science in general and problems of another order.   Thus the scandalously bad astronomy (for even in Aristotle's own day it might have been much better) did not annul the pioneer work in biology which Darwin could heartily admire, nor did the erroneous physics prove that in the metaphysical speculations there could be nothing of value.   Yet a dogmatic system of metaphysics, just because it cannot be patently refuted by new discoveries, may in the long run be far more detrimental to Christianity than an obsolete astronomy.   To suggest, for instance, that the doctrine of the eucharist is bound up with a particular theory of " substance " is deplorable, especially if the theory is supposed to be derived from Aristotle, whose own account of that perplexing concept is decidedly confused. At the present time the principal danger (in certain quarters) is a kind of semi-dogmatic Thomism, which again is almost as unfair to a great thinker—even more handicapped than Aristotle by ignorance of things which he could not know—as it is damaging to the cause of religion. There is no more a Christian doctrine of substance than there is a Christian astronomy. There is no *philosophia perennis* upon which the security of the Christian faith depends. The only Christian philosophy is the Christian religion.

The eventual significance, then, of the great medieval controversy could hardly be measured by controversialists of the thirteenth century. When both faith and reason were regarded as modes of attaining to certainty, it was doubtless expedient to show that they did not clash. But the appetite for certainty, in whatever department of human thought or life it may chance to be displayed, is always likely to be a source of disturbing bias and mental confusion. No sooner are we convinced that in one realm of experience—be it religious, artistic, or scientific—the vision of absolute truth is ours than we press on to one or other of two further conclusions. Either we insist that the whole of reality can be interpreted in like manner or, if driven to confess that this is impossible, we then protest that only through one window does the light of heaven stream into us, while elsewhere all is dark.

> Beauty is truth, truth beauty, that is all
> Ye know on earth and all ye need to know.

When the poet makes this surprising assertion, not one reader, perhaps, in a thousand supposes him to be speaking literally, and not one in ten thousand stops to inquire what " literally " would mean. Yet in all probability Keats was expressing with perfect fidelity the innermost meaning of the world, as it was revealed to him. Analogous declarations in the language of religion would not be difficult to find, and these, too, are put aside by the general public either as metaphorical extravagances or as too " subjective " to pass as truth. When we turn to the affirmations of science, the case appears at first to be different, for now we are offered proofs or experimental verifications, not always intelligible to amateurs, but in principle always public, and often authenticated by impressive displays of mechanical power. Nevertheless, when the exponents of this kind of knowledge make sweeping claims to the sole possession of truth, they are likely to be at least as wide of the mark as the poet or the saint; and the very root of the error may be the fact that within their own province so much can be either verified or proved. It is no question of disputing any genuinely scientific hypothesis, or of rejecting conclusions based on good evidence. Any criticism of that type will be the business of scientific experts, and of no one else. A far deeper problem now comes into view, which may be briefly summarized in the question whether the possibility of proof is increased or diminished as we get nearer to the heart of reality and the meaning of the world. That the horizon always recedes as science advances is freely admitted by all the greater men of science; for it is only beginners who think they have reached the end. But that is not quite the point. The question at issue is whether the ideal (even if it never can be realized) is demonstration; the reduction of all knowledge to a form that is either mathematical or approximating thereto. Ever since the days of Pythagoras something like this ideal has, intermittently, been dangled before our eyes, but I for one believe it to be entirely fallacious, and make bold to assert, on the contrary, that, the nearer we get to the realization of it, the more certain will it be that we are omitting the most important facts.

Further consideration of the point does not, however, belong to this chapter. Here it is only necessary to maintain that neither the certitude belonging, as Christians believe, to the articles of faith, nor the more generally recognized certainty of science, nor yet both taken together, can abolish the wide field of speculation in which there are inescapable problems, undoubtedly affecting the position of Christianity, not to be solved either by the theology grounded in faith nor by " reason " in the limited sense of proof. In a word, Christians have to defend the approaches to faith neither by appeals to authority nor by trusting to " proofs " which are not proofs, but only by such means as Platonism, Hegelianism, Materialism, or any other philosophy may employ to substantiate its claims.

9

Faith, Science, and Materialism

DURING the first fifteen centuries of its history the Christian Church experienced many variable winds of doctrine within its own household, but may be said, with sufficient accuracy, to have encountered only two alien philosophies, the Platonic and the Aristotelian, with which it was necessary to come to terms. Each of these, however, when brought into contact with a faith unimaginable by its author, gave rise to problems defined in their immediate expression by transient conditions, but not in their nature peculiar to any epoch that we strive to include within particular dates. As against Platonism, Christianity laid a new emphasis on the thought of Creation, gave a new reality to the phenomenal world and history, conferred a new dignity on the body in which the eternal Logos had become incarnate, and revolutionized the whole conception of moral evil: as against Aristotelianism (in medieval garb) it vindicated the rights of a theology not derived from reason alone, and at the same time secured for reason perfect liberty of action in respect of truth discoverable by the " natural light ". So, at least from our distant post of observation, we may read the facts; but when we compare these hopeful premisses with the subsequent record of petty squabbles, dogmatic ignorance, obscurantism, heresy-hunting, and persecution, it becomes all too evident that other interpretations of them were possible. Inter-sectarian warfare, deeply tainted as it usually has been with political colours, is, fortunately, no part of our subject. What we have now to investigate is the relation of the Christian faith to " modern thought ", if we can succeed, without open violence to a huge miscellany of opinions, in giving any definite sense to that comprehensive term. About the common character pervading the differences of the ancient schools, or about certain qualities of medieval thought, it is excusable to risk one or two generalizations; but how shall we cope with the immense variety of modern philosophical literature, or how embrace in one synopsis, from the Christian point of view, a multitude of systems, hypotheses, and speculations, in which there is as yet no sign of finality, and little apparent community of aim?

The only clue provided by the recent course of the argument is the emergence of natural science as an intellectual discipline, not identical with philosophy yet loudly claiming to be the representative of reason, and indeed to be the predominant influence of the modern world. The discrimination of mental activities, already foreshadowed in the thirteenth century, was by no means a rapid process. Three centuries and more after the death of S. Thomas, when we come to Descartes, who in most histories of the subject is named as the fount of modern philosophy, we find, to all appearances, much the same confusion of elements that we associate with " scholastic " writers. The mind of Descartes is steeped in medievalism; so much so, indeed, that his detractors can plausibly maintain that, apart from his undoubted eminence in mathematics, there is nothing much in his philosophy but debts to his predecessors which he forgot to acknowledge. Men, however, like trees, are judged by their fruits. No matter what affinities to earlier utterances can be detected, it cannot be denied that out of the famous *cogito ergo sum* there sprang, for better or for worse, a growth of philosophical ideas never really anticipated in either ancient or medieval times. With what propriety Descartes has also been saluted as the father of " mechanistic " biology may be less certain; but, even apart from mathematics, there is clearly much in his work to link him up with the science of later generations. Only in his quasi-theology is he retrospective; for in his statement of the " ontological proof " there is little novelty, and whenever he begins to threaten God himself with prosecution for fraud if we cannot safely trust our natural intuition of the external world, his argument becomes almost grotesque. Why not complain of the shocking deception by which the human race was so firmly persuaded that the sun went round a motionless earth ?

It was not by the personal efforts of Descartes or any other individual thinker that the progressive divergence of philosophy and science was effected, but rather by the sheer weight of scientific discoveries and by the new conception of method thus introduced. Moreover, the increasing prevalence of the scientific temper, often exacerbated by vexatious opposition, did not, apparently, favour an amicable redistribution of provinces, but gave rise to new and militant philosophies; and, since the main object of this book is to define the attitude of the Christian religion towards rival claimants, I feel bound to express the opinion that, from this point of view, the systems either professedly based on natural science, or visibly affected by its influence, are more important than any other originated within the last three or four centuries. This does not mean that theories adorned with names like

Rationalism, Materialism, or possibly Naturalism are the most notable achievements of modern thought. On the contrary, it is doubtful whether any philosopher of the first order, from Descartes onwards, would accept that kind of label as a sufficient account of his work. It is often difficult, however, to say where the scientific influence begins and ends; for, if we inspect the facts from another angle, there has often been a curious failure to remark the bearing of philosophical theories upon the hypotheses of natural science. When, for instance, Descartes had decided that his own existence as a thinking being was the one inexpugnable certainty, the natural inference, surely, would be that upon that safe foundation the whole fabric of science would forthwith be erected. But does Descartes himself even pretend to do anything of the kind? What really happens is that he promptly finds himself cut off from direct access to Nature by a screen of " ideas ". Whereupon he exclaims, in good scriptural style, " with the help of my God I will leap over the wall ", and over he goes, leaving *cogito ergo sum* conveniently behind, and discovering science only when and where he can take the real existence of material things as indubitable fact. It was, in truth, from the hypothesis of independent material things, unrelated to any percipient mind, that natural science set out on its travels; but meanwhile the " ideas " embarked on a voyage of their own. To what a hopeless impasse Locke was brought by his efforts to prove that some at least of them resembled their originals; how Berkeley proposed to drop the originals altogether; and how Hume observed that the good bishop, in his anxiety to refute one kind of scepticism, had only prepared the way for another, may be read in any manual of philosophy. Nor was this the end of the story. A new chapter, far more profound, was opened by the *Critique of Pure Reason*, and with the aid of the Kantian criticism, followed by endless criticism of Kant, the conflict of realists and idealists has smouldered on to the present day, and can still flicker up now and again in the decent obscurity of learned periodicals and somnolent classrooms.

Not the least remarkable thing about this controversy, which for a long while was the central theme of modern philosophy, is that it never seems to have had the slightest effect on the actual work of science, nor to have disturbed the confidence of scientific men that they were dealing at first hand with reality, not with " ideas " or " appearances ", but with " things in themselves ". Still more surprising is it that when Hume proposed to annihilate the distinction between *post hoc* and *propter hoc*, the men of science were rather inclined to welcome him as an ally, and this, too, at a time when it was a fundamental article of scientific faith that every event in the course of nature was pre-determined by its causes.   No doubt it was the attack on miracles that pleased the advocates of immutable natural laws, but that Hume, as the philosophical champion of science, was at least as oddly placed as Saul among the prophets, does not seem to have occurred to them.   The object of these comments (which, of course, are far from novel) is not to disparage either philosophy or science, but merely to illustrate the fact that, in comparatively modern times, they could drift into spheres quite as vaguely related as faith and reason in an earlier age.   There has been, perhaps, no modernized Averroism.   No one, I think, has explicitly declared that the same hypotheses may be indispensable to science and philosophically untenable; or, conversely, that certain philosophical arguments would be unanswerable if they did not happen to be destructive to science.   Yet the actual situation has often suggested a *duplex veritatis modus* very much in that style.   Look, for instance, at Kant's perplexed and perplexing treatment of the problem of free will.   Accepting whole-heartedly the postulates (as he understood them) of Newtonian science, he insists that all our external acts must belong to the phenomenal world and find their place in the unbreakable sequence of causes and effects; but since he proceeds to exhort us, none the less, to adopt the one motive that can enable us to behave " as though " we were free, he is thus obliged—as he candidly allows—to deny knowledge in order to make room for faith; or, as an unfriendly critic might choose to put it, he encourages us to foster an illusion at the expense of the facts.   Kant, however, did at least perceive his own dilemma: he did not, like some of the more ingenious rationalists, simultaneously and cheerfully swallow the postulates of natural science and the scepticism which destroyed them.

While philosophy and science have thus often been content to amble along together in a spirit of mutual toleration or disregard, in what ways, let us next inquire, was the Christian faith most likely to be affected by either?   As regards the main stream of philosophy issuing from Descartes, theologians had at least as good an excuse as scientists for remaining indifferent.   It is not, of course, that, when a man becomes a Christian, he ceases to remark the distinction between better and worse arguments, or between falsity and truth: the point is simply that, on any religious hypothesis, many abstruse philosophical questions are purely secular, in the sense that none of the possible answers either strengthens or weakens the case for any particular creed, be it Christian, Jewish, Moslem, or what you will.   What, for instance, does it matter whether the distinction of " primary " and " secondary " qualities be genuine or spurious ?   Or who cares, from any religious point of view, if space and time, as Kant maintains, are no more than forms of perception ?   Berkeley, it might be replied, attempted to pass from *esse est percipi* to the existence of an omnipresent Spirit, and Kant's restriction of knowledge to the realm of " appearances " obliged him to reject the supposed proofs of God's existence.   That is true; and in respect of " preambles " to faith, as S. Thomas would say, most of the greater modern philosophers have made some kind of contribution.   Yet the tendency to separate the faculties of philosophy and theology has, on the whole, increased, and rarely has the consciousness of their interdependence been acute.   Did anyone (unless it was Berkeley himself) ever quite believe that the doctrine of *esse est percipi* and his faith in God were inseparable; in other words, that no Christian could be, in a philosophical sense, a "realist" ?   But since it is only when they write books—and not always then—that we can read the minds of individual philosophers or Christians, it is more profitable to generalize the problem, and this can hardly be done more effectively than by considering once more, and this time with special reference to the development of natural science, the old antithesis of reason and faith.

There is a logical fallacy still known in text-books by its ancient name of *ignoratic elenchi*; the fallacy of irrelevance, of refuting a proposition which your opponent does not uphold, or of proving something that he does not deny.   That name, it seems to me, ought to be written right across the long and dreary record of the controversies between science and religion.   And here, first of all, it is necessary to observe that science and the philosophy of science are very different things.   This, indeed, is fortunate; for, were it necessary, in defence of the Christian faith, to examine even the major scientific theories now established or provisionally adopted, few experts would be competent for such a task, and no layman could dream of undertaking it.   As it is, I shall make bold to assume and declare that nothing which science has ever yet discovered, nor anything that it will ever discover in future ages, can possibly clash with any article of the Christian faith or affect the question of its truth.   Nor would I base this assertion on an unreasonable demand that assent to scientific conclusions should be withheld until they are mathematically certain.   That would be very poor philosophy and, as a controversial weapon, most ineffective.   Even when a verifiable hypothesis is found to cover, so far as is known, all the revelant facts, its truth is not, indeed, strictly proved; for other facts, not thus explicable, may yet come to light, or perhaps some other hypothesis may provide an even better explanation.   But to stake the immunity of any religious belief from scientific criticism on the logical distinction between verification and proof would be the height of folly; nor, in truth, can there be any policy more unworthy of religion than the vain attempt to bolster up its own position by disparaging reason in general or the special manifestation of it in natural science.

Before explaining the grounds on which it may be so confidently assumed that the Christian faith has nothing to fear from science, some notice must be taken of the painfully evident fact that, again and again, ecclesiastics of high degree, as well as simpler folk, have been thrown into a panic by scientific discoveries or theories, and have thereupon proceeded, by any means in their power, to oppose the advance of knowledge. The explanation is partly moral or psychological, and partly intellectual. A few men, it seems, are born rebels or anarchists, but most of us instinctively dislike any violent upheaval threatening the stability of established customs and ideas. On the face of it, these two types of mind, the revolutionary and the conservative, are diametrically opposed, but in point of fact their consequences are not always dissimilar. Few revolutions, for instance, have been more sweeping than the Reformation, but what was the plea of its genuinely religious protagonists ? Simply that they desired to return to a purer tradition and to discard all these perilous innovations. Almost every great religious movement has been, in fact or in name, a " revival ", and often enough, too, in the field of political revolution the avowed motive has been the desire to recover certain original " rights ", perhaps scarcely less mythical than the golden age imagined by poets. Every society, in fact, clings to some sort of tradition, and it is not, after all, very surprising that the first reaction of Christians to theories apparently destructive of an established cosmology should have been blind opposition. There is also a genuine, if only partial, excuse for their attitude which is sometimes overlooked. Many of the obstinate prejudices which barred the way of progress were due quite as much to bad science as to bad theology. Thus in the stock example of astronomy, the geocentric hypothesis was by no means undisputed in ancient times and, if the Greek astronomers who more or less anticipated Copernicus had chanced to prevail, it is most improbable that the Church would ever have resented the thought of a planetary earth. So again, there seems to be no reason—or none but the inextricable complications of history —why the Darwinian theory should not have appeared within a hundred years of Aristotle's biological researches; in which case we might have been spared a more recent disturbance. Lack of a scientific geology was another source of trouble, and in all these cases devout Christians, neither more nor less than the rest of mankind, acquiesced in the existing state of knowledge or ignorance, and thus not unnaturally had fallen into the habit of supposing that the Church was committed to a dogmatic position in respect of purely scientific questions.

At this point, however, the excuse of custom reaches its limit; for, in order to show that the progress of science, no matter what startling forms it may take, can always be received with perfect equanimity by Christians, it is necessary to elucidate and compare two fundamentally different hypotheses. The only Christian philosophy, as I now repeat, is the Christian religion, and this implies two things, superficially incompatible : first, that the Christian Church does not require, for the support of its faith, any philosophical system or theory of secular origin; secondly, that its faith does undoubtedly determine its general attitude towards every manifestation of human reason, philosophical or scientific. Thus it is, on the one hand, a fatal error to bestow a kind of official sanction on the metaphysics of Plato, Aristotle, Aquinas, Kant, Hegel, or anyone else; but on the other hand, it is impossible to pretend that the Christian faith has no rational implications; as though every new brand of philosophy could be received with the same cool indifference as a new style of painting or music. Now, as regards the Christian relation to natural science, there is no question of disputing with experts about the truth of conclusions either proved or made highly probable by sufficient evidence, but only of examining presuppositions. That any philosophy, or the philosophy of science in particular, can wholly dispense with initial hypotheses is sheer delusion. Newton's *hypotheses non fingo* is an excellent principle in so far as it means that he indulged in no fanciful conjectures; but, if interpreted in the sense that he assumed nothing at all (about time and space, for instance), it is flatly untrue. Similarly, when we scrutinize the proposal of Descartes to begin by doubting everything, it is easy to see that he entirely failed to apply the process to some of his own most important concepts, especially substance and causation. Or, if we turn from individuals to schools of philosophy, none has boasted more loudly of starting with a blank sheet than Empiricism, and none is more obviously steeped in unwritten dogmas. Now the radical and *a priori* difference in outlook between Christian theology and natural science is not only far more profound than any that distinguishes the various schools of philosophy, but is, in truth, so complete that, paradoxically, it cancels their opposition. The transition from mythical theogonies to science was effected in principle by the early Greek philosophers as soon as they abandoned the hope of discovering the absolute origin of the world, and in its place assumed, openly or tacitly, the famous maxim (best known in its Latin form) *ex nihilo nihil*, which lies behind every known theory of " matter " and the entire search for natural causes.   Over against this motto is set the Christian formula, requiring the alteration of only one word.   *Ex nihilo nihil*, says Science: *ex nihilo omnia*, replies Theology.   All or Nothing: which is the truth?   The answer is—both.

In the work of fostering and magnifying the historic *ignoratio elenchi* which has vitiated reams of superfluous controversy, roughly equal shares may be attributed to the rationalists, who imagined themselves to be upholding the cause of reason, and to the apologists, who, with less excuse, believed themselves to be defending the Christian faith.   That the world is not eternal *sola fide tenetur*, as S. Thomas wisely allowed. In other words, it is an article of faith—and never can be anything else— that all things " visible and invisible " were created by God.   But does science deny or need to question this assertion?   Not if it knows its own business.   With creation, as the origin of something out of nothing, science has no possible concern.   Its work begins only when the existence of the world—of everything comprehended in " Nature " —is taken as fact, and as fact to be explained without invoking powers, agencies, or causes beyond the reach of human investigation.   At the same time there has always been a genuine sense in which its ambition has been to get back from what is to what was, to explain the present by the past, to analyse the complex into the simple, to reach, if possible, the single stuff of which all this infinite variety of things is made. Hence were fashioned the basic concepts of " matter " and " element ", of causation and natural law; and with all the marvellous transformations of older ideas brought about by modern discoveries, the broad and general type of explanation offered by science is the same to-day as when Thales declared that all things were made of water, or when Pythagoras was ready to construct the world out of numbers alone.

Of all the notions characteristic and constitutive of physical science it seems that " matter " is the most fundamental.   Even the " element ", as that which defies analysis, or the " atom ", as that which cannot be divided into parts, may either be absorbed into " matter ", or, if perchance identified with it, will thus acquire a new status and significance.   Hence it is not surprising that " Materialism " is the nearest thing to a general name for the kind of philosophy which either claims the authority of science or perhaps, more cautiously, maintains that the limits of profitable speculation are defined by the range and scope of scientific method.   Not that the name itself is free from ambiguity, or that it always denotes a comprehensive philosophy. Very often the implication is only moral. We call a man a " materialist " because he appears to care only for food and drink, for accumulating wealth, or for something that demands no imagination, no faith in things unseen. But a man of this type is very unlikely to be interested in metaphysics or any kind of intellectual theory; he is simply one who declines to think. And again, a man may be carelessly accused of materialism because he is a physicist by profession, and therefore declines, in his scientific investigations, any attempt to get behind and beyond the nature of matter. As well might you reproach an artist because, in his strictly professional capacity, he refuses to consider anything but the principles and practice of his art. The only materialism entitled to rank as a philosophy is quite definitely a metaphysical doctrine; and in this connexion it is worth while to observe that, from its very first appearance, the concept of " matter " wavered between physics and metaphysics, and indeed became, almost accidentally, metaphysical through the effort to provide an adequate basis for physics.

As we noted in earlier chapters, the pre-Socratic philosophers were corporealists, apparently unable to imagine that incorporeal " being " could mean anything but empty space; and it is their very incapacity for metaphysics that makes it inappropriate to describe them as " materialists ". Plato, of course, was in an entirely different position. Reality, for him, was essentially incorporeal, and this makes it all the more interesting to find that passage in the *Timæus* (mentioned in Chapter 6) where he postulates, as one factor in the generation of the cosmos, something more like the general concept of matter than had hitherto been suggested. It was left to Aristotle, however, to take out a patent for this great invention, and by the antithesis of matter and form, which permeates and saturates his philosophy, the future of an infinite deal of better and worse speculation was determined. Now in all its common exemplifications the Aristotelian " matter " is quite a simple notion. Everything is made of something—a statue of marble or bronze, a coat of wool or leather, a living body of blood, bones, tissues, and whatever else physiologists can discover—and in these, as in countless like examples, it is evident that the " matter " is always " informed ". Equally clear, too, is it that what serves as matter from one point of view is itself not formless. Marble, for instance, has its own specific nature, and this is rightly regarded as " informing " the matter of which it is composed. As distinguishable in thought, but inseparable in fact, matter and form are thus easily intelligible: only when we contemplate the possibility of either subsisting without the other do they become problematic.   The question of pure substantial forms we may pass over, but when we turn in the other direction, and begin to search for a *materia prima*, a matter underlying all forms, a raw material out of which the physical world and all its contents are to be fashioned, what manner of thing can it be?   For more than two thousand years physicists have been asking this question, but the only answer that satisfied Aristotle was useless to physics.   The defect, as he thought, of the pre-Socratics was that, however much their theories had differed, they had all attempted to extract a boundless variety of things out of a substance already " informed ".   In other words, their primitive stuff was not matter, but a concretion of matter and specific form, and therefore, as Aristotle held, its function of becoming all things indifferently could not be fulfilled.   The only remedy he could find was to reduce the primary matter to bare potentiality, with no pre-disposed bias towards one embodiment rather than another.   Manifestly, then, it could not be corporeal, for no kind of body is formless; and manifestly, too, it was quite useless to the physicist; for though one theory of matter has constantly been superseded by another, and though in the latest refinements of modern physics solidity and all the traditional attributes of body may seem to have melted away, it remains true that a " matter " entirely indescribable (for the sufficient reason that there is nothing to describe) can have no place in natural science. Moreover, a still more remarkable consequence of Aristotle's theory— as he was careful to point out—is that matter, in and by itself, is totally unknowable; there is simply nothing for the mind to grasp.

By this remarkable feat of abstract thinking two different lines of criticism are suggested.   Scientifically it may (or may not) be a sufficient objection that Aristotle was deceived by his belief in the rigidity of species, and that, if he had arrived at the modern concept of evolution, he would not have felt obliged to make his basic matter entirely form-less.   Even this, perhaps, is not a purely scientific problem, for in the end it may involve the wider question of what is an " explanation "; but let us ignore that difficulty, or at least postpone it until the representatives of science are unanimous in believing that everything in nature (including their own theories) can be evolved out of whatever is now supposed to be primitive " matter ".   Another type of criticism is provoked by the frequent confusion of physics and metaphysics, for which Aristotle's account of matter seems to be ultimately responsible.   Of this there is no better illustration than Berkeley's philosophy, together with the largely irrelevant criticism of it to which we are accustomed. Unquestionably, Berkeley was attacking the " materialists ", and against the very notion of " matter " his keenest shafts are directed. But what is this " matter "? Does the denial of its reality mean that the physicists are chasing a phantom, and that the most fundamental work of science is simply waste of time? Berkeley's own position, unfortunately, is somewhat equivocal, and it is certainly possible to collect from him statements that appear to have that crude implication. There are places, in fact, where he seems to confuse " matter " with " body ", and thus to stray from his true line of attack. But, whenever he takes pains to characterize the object of his animosity, it becomes clear that this nebulous " matter " is only a derivative of Aristotle's formless, featureless, unknowable entity, or nonentity, which to physicists is perfectly useless. Hence the real gist and point of his challenge to the type of thinker represented by Hylas in the *Dialogues* is that matter is entirely otiose, that it fails to explain anything whatever, and that its total abolition would leave the physicists no worse off than before, nay, much better off, because they would now be able to devote their attention to intelligible facts.

One rather strange consequence of reducing matter to mere potentiality, with no actual being, is that it seems thus almost to evade the formula *ex nihilo nihil* and to pose as an antecedent of creation. Technically, of course, it would not be correct to treat Aristotle's *materia prima* as equivalent to " nothing "; nor is Aristotle himself by any means a materialist; for he never dreams of admitting that matter alone is sufficient to account for the order of nature. Yet a perfectly formless and intrinsically unknowable x is, after all, remarkably like " nothing "; and when it is added that this same x is the germ of all things and a necessary constituent in whatever has concrete being, the problem of getting something out of nothing is not very far away. This, in fact, is just where avowed Materialism falls into ambiguity, and just where the great *ignoratio elenchi* begins to obscure both Christian and anti-Christian thoughts. The only kind of " matter " useful to science must have a definite character, an intelligible mode of behaviour, and a real existence. It must also, in a certain sense, be original; for were anything admitting of scientific description prior to it, that " thing " would itself be matter. If, however, we press the physicist to tell us how matter itself came into being, his proper answer will be that he neither knows nor cares. His work can be accomplished only on the supposition that the business of science is to start with observation of the actual, to analyse the complex, to investigate the history of whatever has come to be, and to derive, if possible, every kind of phenomena from the same " original " matter. But this ambition is not *Materialism*: there is not the faintest reason why the most orthodox of Christians should not study nature in this spirit, nor any risk of his ever discovering something that will drive him into a new Averroism and force him to admit that certain conclusions would be inevitable if they did not happen to contradict his faith. The Christian attitude in this respect is entirely determined by belief in Creation, a subject on which natural science, very properly, has nothing to say. Matter, if we are right in supposing it to have real existence, was created by God, and so was human reason. About the constitution of matter, however, nothing is " revealed " or laid down as an article of faith, but by the energy of reason much may be discovered. Let us set to work, then, and discover all we can. Materialism—the metaphysical thesis that matter is an eternal or self-created substance which makes God super-fluous—has no support in any scientific hypothesis, and its claim to be pre-eminently the scientific philosophy is totally fallacious.

It must be confessed, however, that the persistence of the fallacy is due quite as much to Christian apologists as to their adversaries. Never, it seems, will the ghost of Plato (or Plotinus) be exorcized; for there can be little doubt that most of the recurrent alarms excited among Christians by the progress of physics are revivals or survivals of the ancient belief that matter (or body) is the natural enemy of spirit, the very belief which the doctrines of Creation and Incarnation ought finally to have swept away. Matter, of course, is far from identical with body, but much of the traditional prejudice against it seems to arise from a feeling that its composition is corporeally gross. One rather ludicrous piece of evidence is the naïve delight sometimes exhibited by friends of religion when they hear that the solidity of matter is being whittled away by modern physics, as though Materialism would at any rate be less dangerous if only matter could be made decently thin. Possibly rations and war diet will be found to have helped! It makes, however, not the slightest difference whether matter is as hard as adamant, as stodgy as suet, as volatile as gas, as agile as electricity, or as naked as a mathematical formula. The only relevant question is whether it is self-existent or created by God; and this, as we cannot too often remind ourselves, is a question upon which natural science has nothing to say.

It remains to notice briefly one or two notorious controversies derived from the same general misapprehension. First of all there is the whole range of discussions and disputes loosely covered by the term " psycho-physical ". What is the relation of mind (soul or spirit) to body? Can there be direct interaction, or is it impossible for an incorporeal energy (" will ", perhaps) to set a body in motion? Is " parallelism ", then, the right solution, or shall we prefer Spinoza's alluring but difficult theory of a single substance manifesting itself both as *ordo rerum* and *ordo idearum*? Or must we take the more drastic step of reducing consciousness to an " epiphenomenon ", a by-product of matter, a sort of voiceless supernumerary, with no real part in the drama? Or would it not, after all, be simpler to dismiss it as an effete superstition—in which case, of course, our theories about it could only be nervous disturbances, or perhaps diseases of the liver? Although the literature of the subject is enormous, made up of contributions by physiologists, psychologists, materialists, and sundry philosophers, it is hard to point to any agreed conclusion. Much, indeed, in the problem remains obscure, but take the rival alternatives: (1) that mind (or spirit) requires no bodily instrument; (2) that, on the contrary, every mental act is either conditioned by, or at least registered in, the brain; and suppose that one or other of them is definitely proved. Why should the Christian faith then be affected for better or for worse? Once more, it seems, we have to beware of the non-Christian, and indeed anti-Christian, assumption, that in matter or body there is something essentially debased, something hostile to spirit, something alien from, and independent of, the creative power of God. Along with this gratuitous concession to pagan tradition goes a dubious conception of immortality, implying that the soul is a lodger or prisoner in the body, from which in due course it will take its leave. The difficulty of asserting that Christians do not believe in the immortality of the soul has already been allowed, but to make the validity of their faith depend upon a proof that mind, or any function of soul, can operate, during earthly life, without relation to any physical organ is, surely, the most egregious blunder.

Another famous controversy is associated with the concept of evolution, and more particularly with questions about the biological descent of man and the origin of life. Among biologists quite unhampered by religious prepossessions there is much room for differences of opinion. There are some who believe that the old maxim *omne vivum ex vivo* is no longer tenable; there are others who disagree. Or, again, it may or may not be strictly accurate to say that man is descended from apes, and there are many ways in which the original Darwinian account of the factors operative in evolution is constantly being modified by later researches. There is also the wider philosophical question—upon which biologists speak with no special authority—

K

kind of causation required by science than for being terrified at the
thought of matter and body.   What exactly science does demand is,
to be sure, a little uncertain.   For the last two hundred years or so the
theory of causation has been in such a state of chaos that we may well
be reminded of S. Augustine's remark about time, that he knew well
enough what it was until somebody asked him.   We talk of " necessary
sequence ", but, if the succession of events is identified with logical
sequence, it seems to evaporate, for in the timeless world of mathematics there is no such thing as an event.   Hence, as physics continues
to get more and more mathematical, the less reason does there seem to
be for troubling about causation.   Events in time, we may be inclined
to suggest, do not occur necessarily, but some of them occur more often
than others.   The main task of scientific logic, therefore, will be the
compilation of statistics, as the basis for the measurement of probability,
and substantially Hume's estimate of the situation was right.   What
does not " happen " at all belongs to mathematics, and is quite certain;
what has happened already belongs to history; what is going to happen
no man can tell with certainty, but there are often reasonably good
grounds for a modest bet.   In vain do we appeal to the calendar, with
its predictions of sunsets and eclipses; for in point of fact these are not
predictions at all; they are only deductions from given premises, and,
if one day an eclipse should arrive a little early or late, the logical
validity of the deductions would be in no way impaired.   So it is with
the whole calculation of probabilities.   The odds against a given event
occurring to-morrow are, let us suppose, a million to one; but if,
when to-morrow comes, the event does occur, the soundness of the
calculation will be quite unaffected, and the odds will still be a million
to one.   On the other hand, it is incompatible, surely, with the very
nature of science to admit that any occurrence is an irrational fluke.
As soon as any event has actually come to pass, we are bound to hold
that it followed inevitably from its cause or causes, of which, as it
happened, our knowledge was incomplete.   The total situation, then,
is decidedly strange; for: (1) the odds against the occurrence were
(and are) a million to one; (2) its occurrence was an absolute certainty.
Nor does it avail anything to reply that, given omniscience, the probability and the odds would vanish; for as soon as omniscience is
postulated, the distinction between past, present, and future will also
vanish; time becomes an illusion, and no longer are there any events.
Science, however, is no more disturbed by these philosophical conundrums than it was by the scepticism of Hume.   Its existence is justified
by results, and only when a bogus philosophy, disguised as science,

begins to dogmatize about metaphysical and theological questions are we obliged to point out that loose talk about mechanism and causation is no more alarming to Christians than the threats supposed to lurk in the nature of matter or body.

For like reasons, there is little that need be said about the insoluble problem of free will, so far as it comes within the range of the hypotheses required by natural science. It may be remembered that not long ago the discovery of what looked like indeterminacy in the atomic or sub-atomic world led to a gracious announcement that physicists, for their part, would no longer insist that our moral actions (or even, presumably, their own theories) must be mechanically predetermined. Intellectually, this solemn proclamation ranks with the suggestion that matter gets less dangerous when it becomes fluid or thin. Whether this reputed indeterminacy means anything more than the temporary lack of an explanation remains to be seen; but one thing is quite certain, that the existence (if genuine) in the physical world of a stratum where things happen, so to speak, without rhyme or reason is about the last thing that would strengthen one's belief in the reality of moral freedom. A human being who behaved like this giddy irresponsible x might be the perfect libertarian, but his proper home would be an asylum. The bare fact that an argument so futile could be propounded is, however, a fresh enforcement of the lesson, stamped in the largest letters on the philosophical record of the last two thousand years, that the permanent obstacle to the solution of the problem of freedom is the complete lack of agreement as to what the problem is. Would it even be extravagant to say that every argument advanced by either side in the long campaign has, sooner or later, been annexed by the other? To quote one minor example, the fact that men can be influenced by the prospect of reward or punishment is adduced by Aristotle as evidence that they are masters of their own actions; but the same fact is freely cited as evidence that they are not. Or if we pass to a wider question of principle, it is commonly assumed by determinists that freedom means motiveless action, so that the production of a motive is always sufficient to prove necessity; but it may also be held (and with much better reason) that the possibility of acting from motives is exactly what makes man free. Or again, a common interpretation of freedom (favoured almost equally by both sides) implies that when alternatives are presented, the free man must be just as likely, or at least equally competent, to choose one as the other; but, on the contrary, the truth may rather be that, when a man has attained to perfect freedom, his preference of the better course to the worse is absolutely certain.

10

Christianity and Modern "Ideologies"
I. The Scientific Way of Life

IN the course of the last three chapters the process by which philosophy was gradually reduced from a considered way of life to an academic "subject" has been roughly described; and indeed the very word "academic", if we compare the slightly contemptuous tone of its modern usage with the original prestige of the Academy, has become an expressive symbol of that melancholy decline. The two successive stages were: first, the stabilization of a theology grounded in faith; secondly, the rise of modern science and the vindication of its right to accept as true, without reference to any theological prepossessions, whatever conclusions could be ascertained by its own methods. Thus it was that, almost accidentally, room was made or left for an intermediate province, in which many speculative problems, pertaining neither to the *sacra doctrina* nor to any natural science, could be freely debated. Even if all the imposing "systems" constructed since the age of Descartes could be dismissed as empty show, there would still remain a function of criticism not to be suppressed by authority or annexed by any special department of knowledge. Wherever truth is said to reside, wherever knowledge of reality is claimed, there a door stands open for "reason", in one of its many guises, to enter and lodge objections. Yet this independent sphere of action, with all its genuine advantages, has been purchased at a heavy price. It is not only that, as critic, the philosopher has often failed to obtain a hearing; for that, perhaps, may have been because he was addressing adders proverbially deaf. The graver consequence is that when a modern pilgrim, travelling far and wide in search of wisdom, calls at the department of philosophy and asks for guidance towards the good "which every soul pursues", he will be politely informed that he has come to the wrong shop. Philosophy, it seems, does not deal in "goods", least of all in the good. Manuals of ethics, of course, are on sale at a moderate figure, but in the preface to each of them there is likely to be a plain declaration by the author that he is no evangelist, and that the question whether it is worth while to sell all you have for the sake of one priceless pearl, or whether any such jewel is more than a vain imagination, is no part of his business. Such, beyond doubt, is the general attitude of our modern philosophers and that is why " philosophy ", in its current sense, is an equivocal name, denoting, I will not say a flagrant imposture, but simply a group of highly technical studies, the totality of which has only a verbal identity with the philosophy invented and practised by the Greeks, or with the pursuit of wisdom under any other designation.

Let us beware, however, of doing injustice to individuals by generalization. No one acquainted with the facts will deny that many of those classed as " philosophers " during the last three or four centuries have believed in their profession as something more than an amusing hobby or a respectable means of earning a livelihood. The most illustrious example is Spinoza, whose life of patient abnegation when he was cast out of the synagogue (yet could not, by reason of his loyalty to truth, seek admission to the Church) is a pattern of excellence, worthy to be compared with the martyrdom of Socrates, who would neither conciliate his judges by soft words nor seek an unlawful way of escape from the death to which their blindness condemned him. But mark, too, the reflection of this life in Spinoza's most famous book. *Ethics*, he called it, but of all the works thus entitled or classified there is scarcely more than one—the *Ethics* of Aristotle—to which it has any real affinity; and the reason for the true kinship, despite immeasurable differences, of these two masterpieces is that neither is a treatise on " ethics ", as a sub-department of philosophy, but both alike (with occasional wavering on Aristotle's part) set forth what the author believes to be the way of salvation, the only way that leads to absolute good.

But, while Spinoza and doubtless many others, famous or obscure, have understood and practised philosophy in its most honourable sense, the general result of the modern differentiation of " faculties " is that when a man sets out on the hazardous voyage of life, in search of an eventual haven, the only chart he will get from our academic philosophers will strike him as remarkably blank. He will learn, perhaps, that, whatever his particular work may be, there will be things that it is " right " for him to do; that, in other words, he will always find " duties " to be performed because it is his duty, and for no further reason; and doubtless it is by inducing men to accept this dreary programme that we get the ordinary business of life carried on with tolerable success. But suppose a man happens to be inquisitive, imaginative, or adventurous; suppose he reads, incautiously, a little

Plato, or, worse still, the Gospels.   Is he likely then to be satisfied with the prospect?   And may he not even be disposed to think that " duty for duty's sake ", with no reference to any ultimate good, is so far from being the perfect motive that it is only the maxim of the spiritually barren or the last resort of morally desperate men?

Are there no philosophies, then, by which men who find no refuge in the Christian Church can strive to regulate their personal conduct, and perhaps to remodel the general structure of society?   Assuredly there are, but it is not in any analogue of the Academy, the Porch, or the Garden that we must expect to discover them.   No Stoics and Epicureans now compete for disciples, and in our own academic controversies there is nothing equivalent to the rival offers of those ancient schools to reveal the nature of the good.   Profane as it sounds, we may get a clearer hint from the newspapers; for most of the schemes of life now moulding the course of history are known as " ideologies ", and by journalists, above all others, that portentous neologism (scarcely yet acknowledged in the dictionaries) is greatly beloved.   In the language of an older convention, it is " political philosophy " that is now in the ascendant, but on a scale which virtually implies that all philosophy is political.   The modern " ideology " tends inevitably to be " totalitarian "; partly because it approves and demands an unlimited extension of public authority, but still more because it works up all manner of ideas into a single compound, and then seeks to devise a political machinery which, by force or by guile, will constrain all citizens alike to swallow the dose.   A " political philosophy " of this kind is therefore much more than a text-book subject which may engage the attention of students for a year or two, without prejudice to any moral or religious principles they may chance to possess.   An ideology, in fact, is nothing less than a creed; and so it is that, when we are looking round for rival alternatives to the Christian appreciation of life, we must turn our eyes chiefly in the direction from which the loudest noise (including the menacing note of guns and bombs) appears to proceed.

First of all, however, we must take account of a proposed way of life, not usually numbered with the " ideologies ", and not officially competing with Fascism, Bolshevism, or any similar ideal.   I refer once more to the possibility of a scientific philosophy; not, however, to the materialism which is mostly bad metaphysics, but to the belief entertained by a large and miscellaneous body of " experts ", that if once society could be ordered and managed in accordance with scientific principles, the only new Jerusalem worth having could forthwith be erected in England's green and pleasant land, or in any other con-

venient situation. In considering the merits (rather than the prac-
ticability) of this ideal there will be, as before, no attempt, and no desire,
to cast doubts on the truth of any strictly scientific theory. Criticism
of that kind will never be lacking, but, to be effective, it must come from
expert critics whose sole object is the advancement of science. It
must also be observed that there is at present no official version, no
" Atlantic Charter ", of the scientific gospel; and though some very
distinguished writers have expounded their views, it would not be
profitable to fix on any one of them as an authoritative spokesman.
The larger question at issue is quite untechnical, nor is it, in many of
its aspects, exclusively relative to the Christian point of view. For,
not only is it highly probable that adepts in other religions will be
dissatisfied with a purely scientific valuation of human life, but, apart
from any religious hypothesis, there will always be men of mark whose
notion of " the good " (little as they may be accustomed to use that
expression) will be as remote from the atmosphere of the Royal
Society as, let us say, the homilies of Ruskin from the verses of Omar
Khayyam. But since we cannot grapple with a multitude of individuals,
and have no commission to represent poets, painters, musicians,
historians, scholars, or any other profession likely to cherish its own
ideal, we must approach the question, which is essentially one of
valuation, in another way.

All expert knowledge, presumably, is delightful to those who possess
it, and in nearly all specialists there is a pardonable tendency to magnify
the importance of one particular class of facts. Yet some forms of
knowledge are manifestly more imposing than others, and in our own
day the popular appeal of natural science, by reason of its visible
achievements, is almost overwhelming. " ' Other things being
equal ', said Mr Saunders, ' I apprehend that the generation that
travels sixty miles an hour is at least five times as civilized as the
generation that travels only twelve.' ' But other things are not equal,'
said Mr Herbert.'' The quotation is from Mallock's *New Republic*, a
witty and caustic piece of satire written more than fifty years ago. " Mr
Herbert " is Ruskin, and " Mr Saunders " is probably meant for W. K.
Clifford. For the modest sixty miles per hour of those days we now
can substitute two or three hundred; doubtless the level of civilization,
as estimated by the Saunders type of mind, has been proportionately
raised. Meanwhile Ruskinism has gone sadly out of fashion, and no one
who suggested, for instance, that the invention of the aeroplane was one
of the major calamities in human history would be likely to get much
applause. But if wisdom does not exist in the championship of lost

causes, neither does the claim of natural science to prescribe the most excellent way of life get much support from a catalogue of inventions. Because we can pick up a receiver and converse with a friend a hundred or a thousand miles away, it does not follow that either of us has anything wise or witty to say; or if, like Puck, we shall soon be offering to put a girdle about the earth in forty minutes, it will at least be arguable that more could be learnt of life in the same forty minutes by reading the *Midsummer Night's Dream* or wandering (in search of Oberon and Titania) through leafy forest glades. In the plethora of mechanical inventions which have transformed the surface of life there are, of course, innumerable advantages of which we could not bear to be deprived, but to measure the progress of the human spirit in the style of " Mr Saunders " remains as devastatingly vulgar and inept as when Ruskin denounced it. When we compare the twentieth century with the Athens of Pericles, the Rome of the Antonines, or the Florence of the Medici, many good reasons will be found for preferring our own civilization, but the least convincing evidence, surely, will be the multiplication of mechanisms and speed.

Let us not seem to insinuate, however, that the prophets of the scientific millennium carry with them no better advertisement than a parcel of labour-saving devices and ingenious toys. Perhaps their most incontestable service to mankind has been in relation to the improvement and maintenance of bodily health; not merely by the wonderful progress of medicine and surgery, but by sanitation, drainage, purification of food, and all the various applications of hygienic principles. How our forefathers endured the insanitary horrors of a medieval city we can scarcely imagine, and in truth they did not, as a rule, endure them for very long. If longevity alone could be taken as a test, our modern superiority would be unquestionable; or, if mud could be regarded as a symbol of all that clogs the wheels of progress, those of us who remember the London of even fifty or sixty years ago will gladly confess that the elimination of the crossing-sweeper is no small advantage. But, while sound health and increased expectation of life are much greater contributions to human happiness than any mechanical invention, they must still rank as preliminary conditions rather than as ends in themselves. A perfectly healthy nation, with a guarantee that every member of it would come to fourscore years without labour and sorrow, might, after all, be nothing better than a formidable army of " blonde beasts ". A glimpse of that possibility has already been given us in the Nazi philosophy, and even in the most ordinary experience of life it is fairly obvious that (outside Samuel Butler's delightful *Erewhon*) the hygienic test of merit is insufficient. Moreover, there are not infrequent occasions when the importance of health, or of life itself, has to be weighed against values of another kind. To say nothing of war, or of the cases in which heroic sacrifices have been made for the advancement of science, we may lay it down as a general principle that the physician has no authority to pass moral verdicts on human behaviour. He may tell his patient frankly and truly that to persist in his present course will be fatal, but should the patient reply that ruined health and early death are preferable to abandoning his work, or even his pleasures, no medical knowledge can settle the question. The way of life condemned by the doctor may be idle debauchery, or, on the other hand, it may be unselfish service to mankind, but in neither case will a final estimate of its moral character be discoverable in the pharma-copœia. Again, if we peruse the biographies of men of genius, it is a nice question whether the world does not owe as much to the oppor-tunities created by physical infirmity as to robust constitutions. Even brevity of life, we may almost suspect, has sometimes an obscure association with brilliance of natural gifts. The evidence, of course, is faint and dubious, but is it quite certain that the kind of fire which glows in a Mozart or a Keats would have burned with the same intensity in a life that was destined to be long?

With health we often couple prosperity; here, too, no argument is needed to prove that the advance of science has increased and magnified our resources to an extent impossible in any earlier state of society. But with what results? The reflection common to all moralists on the deceitfulness of riches we may take leave to pass over, for that is a theme by no means peculiar to a scientific age. It will not, however, be disputed that one effect of the manifold inventions which have revolutionized the processes of industry and commerce has been to generate social and political problems of a kind, and on a scale, to which there is no complete parallel in the unscientific past. Though it would be the height of injustice to make science directly responsible for our present discontents, it is not unfair to observe that the application of expert knowledge to the production of wealth carries with it no moral guidance, no political wisdom, no principle of valuation, which enables either individuals or society at large to separate the gold from the dross. To prefer the " city of pigs " because civilization, in its outward aspect, entails new trials and dangers is the policy of despair, but to pretend that the science which increases beyond measure our " abundance of instruments " provides us also with a philosophy that will prevent the instruments from destroying us is vain. One good reason, in fact, for examining the scientific way of life in the same context as the avowedly political " ideologies " is that some at least of the creeds thus described are by-products of science, not devised, indeed, in any experimental laboratory, but offshoots, none the less, of a social development made possible only by all the novel implements of wealth.

Thus far, however, we have touched only the surface of the question. However imposing its outward and visible triumphs, no natural philosophy will be qualified to reform the world unless it can master the spirit of man by a new revelation of truth. Even the mechanical apparatus and all the marvellous devices are chiefly significant as refutations of the popular superstition that theory and practice are opposed. True as it is that the first hint of some memorable inventions has come from the rough-and-ready empiricism of daily life, it is only by the energy of abstract thinking, as remote from commercial interests as from military ambition, that the stupendous instruments of war and peace have been forged. Yet this is not enough. When business men have somehow been persuaded that science can improve the supply and quality of the goods in which they deal, they will be ready to subscribe for the erection of new laboratories, and may even indulge in a little complacent talk about higher education; but they will hardly think of themselves as missionaries, or rank their own substantial cheques with the widow's two humble mites. The true devotee of science, however, is no minister of commerce. Ready as he is to benefit mankind by improvements in many kinds of practice, his proper aim is the advancement of knowledge; and if he passes beyond the outlook of the specialist to the larger thought of a scientific philosophy, which may even amount to a new religion, it can be only because he believes himself to be pre-eminently an apostle of truth. With what justice, then, can this high pretension be alleged?

In one sense with absolute justice; for no one—not even a Grand Inquisitor in the golden age of persecution—would deny that science has had its inflexible martyrs; while, in less sensational style, many examples could be quoted in which it has required almost as much sincerity to abandon a favourite hypothesis as to part with life itself. It is not the intellectual honesty of scientific men, their renunciation of personal bias, or their unfaltering demand for objective facts that any reasonable critic will question. The deeper problem appears only when we proceed to investigate the character of the truth discoverable by this scrupulous devotion—when we fain would be assured that it is not only the truth, but also the way and the life. Truth is of many varieties and degrees. There is no saving grace in correct information;

whether the bare facts be gathered from *Bradshaw's Guide*, from *Whitaker's Almanack*, from a popular encyclopædia, or from a systematic course of astronomy, makes, thus far, no great difference. In scientific training, however, we pass from facts to method and principle, and from the mastering of principles may arise the conviction that only by one road is it possible to reach the goal. Knowledge then ripens into faith, and only when that sublimation is effected does the specialist assume the mantle of the prophet and call upon the ignorant to repent and be saved.

All knowledge is a mode of valuation, and that is why, in the old Greek way of expressing it, the last perfection of understanding is to be had only by knowledge of the good. In less formal language, we may estimate the different branches and types of knowledge partly by their range and extension—by the very multitude of facts they enable us to embrace in one synopsis—but partly also by the depth to which they penetrate and the degree in which they approximate to revelation, not of particular aspects and relations, but of a concrete whole. It is fairly obvious, too, when we compare some familiar examples, that breadth and depth often vary inversely; that our " universals ", and in a less degree our empirical generalizations, are obtained only by abstraction; in other words, by omission of most of the attributes (perhaps even of all) which belong to individual things. Thus, to take an extreme case, the proposition $2 + 2 = 4$, sometimes quoted as the pattern of certainty, may loosely be said to apply to anything and everything, but in point of fact is applicable to nothing, or to nothing but qualitatively indistinguishable units, which are merely serviceable creatures of human invention, more respectable and orderly than the traditional rats of delirium, but no whit more substantial. Abstract thinking, in fact, yields the maximum of certainty and the minimum of truth. A cosmos reduced to a mathematical expression could be inhabited only by unknown quantities and geometrical ghosts.

In their degree of abstractness the sciences differ widely, but all are departmental, and with the advance of knowledge the tendency to specialization becomes more marked. Nor, of course, is it suggested by those who would fain entrust the direction of human life to science that any one kind of specialist should be appointed dictator. It is rather by a systematic combination of experts that the public welfare would be secured, and just how the general design is to be contrived and realized is, perhaps, a little obscure. To demand exact information about a problematic ideal would, however, be unreasonable. What we can more reasonably propound, and test by experiment, is the

question whether here and now, in our imperfectly rationalized condition of life, it is possible, by invoking the joint assistance of all the
sciences, to illuminate the essence of some very ordinary things.
There is no need to go roaming about the abysses of space and time in
search of mysteries impervious to science; there is no need to step
outside the room in which at this very moment you chance to find
yourself. Take any common object, such as a book. Almost any
book will serve as well as any other, but let us select a very famous one,
Don Quixote; and let us now prepare to welcome a distinguished
company, appointed by the Royal Society to represent every branch of
natural science, and beg them to bring all their manifold resources to
bear upon this object which lies on the table. What is it? What is it
made of? What are its qualities and attributes? What is its meaning?
What is its worth? These sound like plain and straightforward questions, but it must be understood, of course, that what we require are
scientific answers. We are inviting the physicist, the chemist, the
astronomer, the physiologist, and each of the experts in turn, to apply
his proper methods and draw on his special knowledge in order to
explain to us what manner of being belongs to this object chosen for
inspection. We are full of expectancy, of appetite for knowledge,
of hope that words of oracular wisdom will be uttered. But life alas!
is full of disappointments; for the surprising fact is that the amount of
relevant information provided by this galaxy of experts turns out to be
—precisely nothing. True, the object is approximately oblong, and
about the properties of the oblong the geometrician will have something
to say. It also has weight, and therefore a discourse on gravitation, or
possibly a pair of scales, may be appropriate. It seems, too, to be
largely made of paper, encased in cloth or leather, while the interior
is spotted with ink; so that chemical analysis might be instructive, and
possibly the date at which the object was compounded might thus be
roughly determined. Meanwhile the physiologist and the botanist, by
their joint effort, will have decided that it never was alive, and human
artifice will be strongly suspected. Or again, the physicist, resolved
to go deeper into the matter, will brush aside trivialities like cloth and
paper, and, after reducing it to atoms or electrons, will add that,
strictly speaking, it is not a " thing " (for there is no such thing as a
" thing ") but only a complex system of events; while the astronomer
will implore us not to drop it, lest the equilibrium of the stars should be
disturbed. Now all this will be very interesting in its way, but what on
earth has it got to do with *Don Quixote*? How shall we know whether
the knight himself belongs to history or romance, whether Rozinante

could have been sold at Tattersall's for an old song, whether tilting at windmills is ridiculous or sublime, whether the author's intention was farcical or serious, whether the book is an immortal masterpiece or as worthless as the fantastic volumes that the curate pitched into the yard? The plain fact, as I say, is that to these and all similar questions no kind of scientific man, by virtue of his science, can supply any answer at all.

The implication of this little experiment is twofold. In its most obvious aspect it means that the entire interpretation of life through the medium of art is beyond the purview of natural science. To reply that art is only an agreeable by-path, or that, since truth and falsity are found only in propositions, it cannot reveal the nature of things, is easy enough; but assertions of that kind require much philosophical consideration, and it is certainly not within the power of any science to make them good. It is not, however, to that complicated problem that I desire chiefly to call attention. The deeper import of the failure of the experts to cope with *Don Quixote* has no special connexion with works of art: the real point of our random illustration is that individuality, no matter how or where presented, entirely baffles and defeats all attempts at scientific explanation. By the " individual " I mean the unique. Colloquially the word often means no more than single, and against colloquial usage it is idle to protest; with better reason, however, we may complain of logicians who sometimes fail to distinguish the " individual " from the " particular " which is commonly opposed to the " universal ". Outside logic that traditional terminology may now find little place in scientific literature, but in effect it remains the ambition of every science to discover the universal in the particular, to bring a plurality of facts under one and the same law, to combine and systematize, to grapple, as the Greeks would say in a still older terminology, with the problem of the one and the many; in a word, to prove that nothing, when fully understood, is unique. Failing the absolute universality which is confined, perhaps, to logic and pure mathematics, the next best thing is thought to be generalization; and though it may be a complete fallacy to suppose that generalization is a way of approach to the universal, it is evident that wherever a large number of separable facts or events are covered by a single formula it is not to the exceptional or the unique that we are attending, but only to some element or attribute common to all alike.

Both the propriety of this method and the immensity of its success are too evident to require illustration. Moreover, one great reason why knowledge of this type is so acceptable is that, every day and all day, it is corroborated by practical experience. It is in the atmo-

L

sphere, and by the agency, of generalities that we transact the business of life. Thus I have always suspected that the familiar title (if it has not been forgotten in these latter days) of the London *General Omnibus* Company was chosen by a philosopher, for it is in general or, at most, specific omnibuses that we ride. A man goes to and from his daily work by (let us suppose) a Number 6, and in that number the very essence of the omnibus is, for him, contained. The individual vehicle may be different every day of the week, and certain minor distinctions, such as an uncivil conductor or a new style of seat, he may chance to notice now and then, but nothing really counts but the route and destination for which the figure stands; and indeed it is surprising how seldom, when the facts are closely examined, we are concerned, either in thought or in action, with what is properly individual. When, for instance, you borrow an umbrella, the lender, of course, is individual, and only to him would it be sensible to return it. Yet the restitution is made not solely to Brown or Jones, but to the owner: it exemplifies, that is to say, a principle in which, as it happens, you and another man are involved, but which depends for its validity and motive power on neither of you, much less on the umbrella. On the other hand, there are many occasions when nothing less than individuality counts. For the society of your bosom friend, for the poem or the symphony you rate above all others, there is no substitute; and in truth all the finer appreciation of persons and things is of this character. Existence is supported by generalities, but for the zest of life we must strive our utmost for vision of the unique.

Science, however, is quite undisturbed by this duality of aim. Far from aspiring to knowledge of individuality as its supreme fulfilment, it habitually ignores and avoids it; nay, it even gets near to denying that there is any such thing. How much less wrangling and confusion there might have been about " miracles " if only the combatants had remembered that in the whole range of scientific comprehension there is no room for the unique. Considered in all its propriety, *Don Quixote* is an unpredictable portent: it falls under no rule, particularizes no universal, is explicable by no science (least of all by bogus psychology), and in fact has little or no right to exist! Once more, too, let us beware of being carried away by the magnificent success with which scientific theory is applied to all kinds of practice. Touch the switch of your radio, listen to the roar of the aeroplane, shoot up to the seventieth storey of the Empire State Building in the " elevator ", and with justice you will reflect that these are only three casual examples, to which a thousand might be added, of the powers conferred on man by the scientific mastery of natural law. Or, in another style, take a miscellaneous collection of trifles—a stick, a stone, a shell, a flower, a butterfly—and with no great difficulty you will find experts qualified to "tell you all about them". But how can this be, if never until this very moment was any one of them observed? Simply because they are specimens, because nothing, as estimated scientifically, is unique. That famous skyscraper is, to be sure, the tallest in the world, but even that proud claim to individuality is, from the scientific point of view, of no consequence. As an example of mechanical construction, the building may be of some interest, but its overtopping of all rival edifices is merely a private affectation, as insignificant as the tiniest idiosyncrasy in the colour of a daffodil or in the markings of a butterfly's wings. Or if variation itself is sometimes the special object of study, that is only in the hope of reducing it to rule. The species, the genus, the class, the order, the family, the law; and, in relation to these, the specimen, the example, the instance, the case, and perhaps, in a limited sense, the exception; such are the concepts and notions which make up the intellectual atmosphere of science; and the upshot, if we revert to the old logical terminology, is that science deals always with the universal and the particular, never with the individual and the unique.

More than once in the history of philosophy there has been a hint of a strange dilemma, involved in the two propositions: (1) that only the universal is knowable; (2) that only the individual is real. The conclusion, of course, would be most disconcerting; but, since both the premisses might be strongly contested, and since it is impossible here to embark on a metaphysical discussion of that magnitude, let us be content to observe that the scientific approach to reality is not the only one, and that the valuation of things obtainable by scientific methods is far from complete. There are, indeed, much larger omissions to be considered. In a society permeated and ordered by the principles of natural science room might be found, no doubt, for poetry and other imaginative arts, as harmless extras or amusing diversions, implying no distinct challenge to the orthodox conception of truth. But what of religion; not as the innocuous piety of the Græco-Roman world, nor as a form of respectability likely to diminish the work of the police, but as bound up with a theology which makes bold assertions about the character of the universe, and proposes an interpretation of human life for which no scientific evidence can possibly be adduced?

Let me quote here a sentence or two from William James, a most unorthodox philosopher in many ways, but surely not to be classed as unscientific. In an address delivered in 1895 (under the title *Is Life*

Worth Living ?) he intends, he says, to use the word " religion " in its " supernaturalist " sense, " as declaring that the so-called order of nature, which constitutes the world's experience, is only one portion of the universe, and that there stretches beyond the visible world an unseen world, of which we know nothing positive, but in its relation to which the true significance of our present mundane life consists ". A certain kind of " natural religion ", too, he regards as so bankrupt that he takes his stand, in the same address, with those for whom " the physical order of nature, taken simply as science knows it, cannot be held to reveal any one harmonious spiritual intent ". What theological dogmas (if any) James accepted I do not know, and there is, of course, nothing in the two statements quoted that would not agree with the philosophy of Plotinus or with various non-Christian religions. Nevertheless, they do, in a general way, represent the Christian point of view; for, though the word " supernaturalist " is rather questionable, because it so often begs the question, it is certain at least that the Christian account of the universe will never be verified by the methods and instruments of material science. And, if we are told in reply that fearless respect for scientifically verifiable truth is the beginning and end of wisdom, some of us will respectfully decline to agree. That position, in fact, is not in itself a demonstrated conclusion, but a mode of faith, very natural in men devoted to scientific work, yet very far from adequate to all the demands of the human spirit.

How one estimates the diverse inventions of man is partly a matter of temperament and taste. Should one chance, for instance, to feel that in *Hamlet* or *The Divine Comedy*, in the *B Minor Mass* or the picture of *Les Merinas*, there is a loftier manifestation of genius than in the speculative masterpieces of Newton or Darwin, there are no decisive arguments by which this judgement can be refuted or confirmed. On the other hand, when our primary interest is the acquisition of truth, nothing is easier than to point to the discoveries of science, and nothing harder (or perhaps less judicious) than to set up art as a rival mode of knowledge. Now religion is in neither of these positions. You cannot say that, like art, it neither asserts nor argues: you cannot say that, like science, it proves its assertions. Yet religion does claim to be an organ of truth, of truth about the unseen world, by relation to which, as William James declares, the true significance of our mundane existence here and now is determined. It does not, then, compete directly with science in a realm of experience common to both; nor is there any reason, as we have seen elsewhere, why any strictly scientific interpretation of phenomena should clash with any article of faith. Nor, I think, is it

true that the maxim *nisi credideritis, non intelligetis* completely differ-
entiates the religious attitude from the scientific; for, after all, if a man
had so little faith in the efficacy of science that he would not even attempt
to get any, one kind of illumination would certainly never fall to his
lot; and in the actual history of science there have been many occasions
when a new venture was hindered or delayed by dogmatic scepticism
or misplaced ridicule.

But, though we must put aside, as beyond the scope of this work,
many difficult questions about the nature of reality and the possible
modes of knowledge, it is clear that belief or unbelief in the reality of a
world beyond the range of scientific discovery is bound to have a
practical effect upon the conduct of personal life and upon any scheme
for the reconstruction and ordering of society. Thus, when we are
urged to commit our public and private welfare to the expert direction
of science, it is fair to assume that in the proposed millennium there
will be no "otherworldliness", but only a perfectly rationalized
kingdom of this world. And this, again, is a good reason for numbering
the scientific way of life with the "ideologies" now militant here on
earth; not because it is ostensibly political, but simply because it is
impossible, by the proper light of science, to pierce the veil of phenomena and look for a reality which no instruments of precision, let their
power be magnified to whatever degree you will, can ever reveal. In
what ways belief in the supreme importance of a world beyond "the
so-called order of nature" does, or should, affect the conduct of daily
life is a problem of infinite complexity, upon which the most diverse
judgements, leading to an astonishing variety of practical experiments,
have been recorded in the history of the Church. That it must, however, have some effect is certain, and therefore it is impossible to
expect perfect harmony between the Christian pursuit of wisdom and
any kind of ideology, scientific or political, which denies the reality,
or at least the relevance, of a "beyond", and measures progress in
terms of mechanical inventions, of economic reconstruction, of
"health and wealth", or of a mode of thinking dominated by the ideal
of demonstration, or at least of well-attested generalizations. It is
chiefly on this last point that I should desire, at the moment, to lay
emphasis. Just as, in the modern development of industry, the factory
leads to mass-production; just as, in modern politics, we are largely
governed by statistics which exhibit mass-behaviour; so does the
scientific valuation of truth and life favour mass-thinking; not, of
course, in the sense of encouraging popular notions (far from it), but
in the sense already noticed, that it strives perpetually to attain to the

universal, to reduce multiplicity to law, and thus to abolish or depreciate the individuality of persons and things. Now, this, I believe, is a very imperfect kind of philosophy, which may well be rejected on grounds not distinctively religious. Most clearly of all, however, is it incompatible with the Christian appreciation of truth and life.

11

Christianity and Modern "Ideologies"
II. The Political Problem

ANY discussion of the ideologies by which the world is now so grievously distracted must border, unfortunately, on "politics" in its most controversial sense. I must therefore begin by disclaiming all intention of comparing the merits or demerits of rival systems, whether established already in certain countries or still in search of a local habitation, and perhaps of an unequivocal name. What makes it easier, too, from a merely personal point of view, to keep clear of the more violent antagonisms is that my own distaste for all the competitors is approximately equal. The object of this chapter is not, however, to expound and defend any personal opinions about the ordinary newspaper topics, but to examine the very notion of an "ideology", in so far as it implies a "totalitarian" conception of the State; and further, to inquire whether that conception, no matter what constitutional form it may assume, is compatible with the Christian view of life. As to what totalitarianism does involve, it is advisable, first of all, to beware of one common misconception, greatly exaggerated by the circumstances of the present time. There is, I believe, no good reason for assuming that a totalitarian State must be aggressive, that it must profess the gospel of war, attack its neighbours, and perhaps aspire to domination of the world. Just as an Alexander or a Napoleon may dream of a boundless empire, without caring a rap for most of our sociological programmes, so is there no reason why a tiny nation, almost devoid of military power, should not attempt, in the ordering of its domestic life, the total subjugation of human activities to the authority and embodied purpose of the State. It is true, indeed, that the philosophy of militarism, as preached by Treitzschke and afterwards popularized by Bernhardi, could only be made effective by persuading the German people that the State was all in all, but if we proceed to infer that, once the militarist ideal is renounced, the danger of totalitarianism is at an end, we may find ourselves most disastrously mistaken.

The main question is whether the State can demand unlimited allegiance; not the mere habit of obedience to law, characteristic of all good citizens in any kind of State, but assent to an all-embracing system, which implies that all the mental, moral, and spiritual activities of man are functions of the State; a demand equivalent in the sphere of religion to the doctrine that the State itself is the highest object of worship, or, at least, that the interpretation of " the will of God " belongs only to the sovereign power.   Wherever, and with whatever varieties of form, this claim is advanced, it means that the business of the State is to embody in its laws a complete philosophy of life; and, though at the present time the term " ideology " is preferred to both " philosophy " and " religion ", the invention of a new label is not enough to disguise the fact that, in a State which thus dictates a complete and supposedly adequate rule of life, there is no room for any other appeal to " reason ", or for any recognition of a superhuman authority.   Looking at the facts from another angle, we must admit that the Christian religion might be treated as an " ideology ", and consequently, that a theocratic State, in which obedience was demanded on the ground that the laws of the realm were the official expression of Christian doctrine, would be identical in political type and principle with Fascism, Bolshevism, or any of the " ideologies " commonly so described.

The general character of the thesis opposed to totalitarianism may be summarized in these propositions: (1) that the cult of the State as an object of worship is a degraded form of idolatry; (2) that for the State to impose on its members any ideology whatever is an act of tyranny; (3) that the nearer the ideology actually preferred is to absolute truth, the less excuse is there for translating it into positive law; from which it follows that theocracy, that is to say, the virtual identification of Church and State, is, of all forms of government, the least defensible from the Christian point of view.

The number and variety of associations invented by man, the " political animal ", is almost infinite, but certain elementary facts are common to all.   Every society exists for the realization of an end; every society has rules which its members are expected to obey;   every society which can neither inspire nor enforce this obedience must be dissolved.   To mistake this skeleton anatomy for the essence of any actual society would be like reducing *Don Quixote* to a compound of paper and ink;   but, as soon as we begin to clothe the abstraction in circumstances, it does not take long to discover at least one vital fact peculiar to the State.   Of all other associations membership is voluntary; no one is obliged to join them, and any member, if so disposed, can leave them for good and all. In the case of the State neither option exists. You become a member automatically, either at birth or at an age determined by law, and you cannot cease to be a member except by becoming an exile, an outlaw, or a public enemy. True, there are some apparent exceptions. The laws regulating citizenship vary in different countries, and in most of them it has been possible to live as a resident alien. This does not, however, exempt a man from subjection to most of the laws; it only involves certain technical disabilities, which may, occasionally, be inconvenient, but may also facilitate avoidance of some civic obligations. A more important point, if we were considering the subject historically, is that the kind of State to which we are now accustomed has not always existed, and in the Middle Ages the whole situation was different. Or, again, it might be objected that infant baptism allows no option of joining the Church, and that, formally at least, no baptized person can leave it, unless by excommunication, which is not a voluntary act. But, though each of these cases might be important in other contexts, none of them, I think, is very relevant to a discussion of the State as we find it nowadays, in the age when ideologies flourish.

For practical purposes, then, we may take it as a genuine mark of distinction between the State and other societies that the citizen neither enters it voluntarily nor can leave it of his own accord. Herein, too, we discover the basis of a notable difference in respect of coercion. The rules of all societies are meant to be kept, and therefore penalties for breach of them may have to be exacted; but the coercive power of the State is far more serious than any other, not only because the punishment of transgression is heavier, or because it cannot be evaded by resignation of membership, but because the law has to be administered with a rigorous uniformity, to which exceptions can but rarely, and somewhat hazardously, be allowed. Some discretion, indeed, is usually within the power of a court, and some range of variation in the penalties imposed, but in the main it is true that, whenever the law has manifestly been broken, the offender must suffer; and the very fact that " law " (in its political sense) is a name properly reserved for the ordinances of the State connotes a grade of authority not belonging to the rules of any other association. Nothing, in fact, is " law " unless it is recognized as such in the courts. The State alone has " sovereignty ", and by its very nature sovereignty is absolute. Upon this point, however, there has been some regrettable confusion, and it is well to note that the difference between constitutional and autocratic government, which may deeply affect the happiness of the citizen, in no way alters the fact that against the final decision of the law there is no appeal. Legislation may be impossible except with the consent of a freely elected parliament, and against arbitrary interpretations of the law the citizen may be fully protected; but in the end his case must come before a tribunal above which there is no authority, and should he then resist the verdict, his act will be rebellion, and will be treated as such.

Totalitarianism, however, means much more than this. Were the State to reduce its own functions to the minimum, confining itself to the determination of foreign policy, the control of armed forces, and the suppression of crime, its sovereignty would still be absolute, but scarcely one of the problems now agitating the field of politics would arise. Under the conditions of life established in all civilized countries it is agreed that the use of physical force is a prerogative of the State, that no other society may declare war, and that no individual citizen may take the law into his own hands. Few States, however, if any, restrict their work to these modest dimensions, and the question now becoming more obtrusive and more urgent every day is whether there is any kind of human activity, economic, intellectual, moral, or spiritual, which cannot, or should not, be subjected to public direction and control. The totalitarian answer, of course, is that there is none: the State is all in all.

Let us glance first at one or two conspicuous illustrations. In commerce and business, for instance, the policy of *laissez faire* was at one time almost universally approved, but recently, as we all know, the pendulum has swung violently the other way, and the evils of unrestricted competition, or perhaps of all private enterprise, are loudly proclaimed. But, though nothing is more fashionable than a purely economic interpretation of human life, it would be possible to make the State entirely " socialistic " in that sense, and yet to stop far short of totalitarianism. A far graver matter is education, and here we can discern a number of possible variations in the attitude of the State. At one extreme the State may assume no function at all, but leave the whole task to other associations, or to private persons. At the next stage, it may be exacted by law that all children must go to school, and in order to make this possible some schools at least will have to be established and regulated by the State. At the same time, voluntary schools, in which there is no standardized method of curriculum, may still be allowed. In a further phase of development we may find that all schools are subjected to public authority, with fixed regulations about the course of studies; but even then it may be possible to devise a curriculum quite free from political bias, and it is only in the final stage of the advance towards totalitarianism that schools become instruments of policy, with the avowed object of fostering certain doctrines, and especially the cult of the State as an object of veneration.

Between education and religion there is a fairly close analogy, but also a considerable difference. Just as, at one extreme, the State may disregard education, so, of course, it may ignore religion entirely and confine its energies to strictly mundane affairs. Historically, however, the distinction between the two cases is this; that, whereas indifference to education was characteristic of the earlier stages in the development of the modern State, it was just in the earliest period that a similar indifference to religion was least possible. If we take the birth of autonomous national States as roughly coeval with the Reformation, politics and religion were then so closely intertwined that no nation, Catholic or Protestant, could afford to treat orthodoxy as a purely ecclesiastical affair. And again, if the State (apart from the personal efforts of some monarchs) was slow to recognize the education of its members as a duty, this was not because one of two conflicting lines of policy was officially preferred, but simply because reflection on the subject was undeveloped. On the other hand, the doctrine that the State is a purely secular organization has never existed, so to speak, by accident, merely because no other view had ever been suggested; it can be only the conscious product of sophisticated theory. Even so it is not unambiguous, but may be advocated for either of two very different reasons. Militant secularism, such as appeared, for instance, at the time of the French Revolution, has nothing to do with any agreed division of province, but is definitely anti-religious and wilfully intolerant. But it is also possible (though hitherto it has been uncommon) for Christians to endorse the opinion that the State, in its proper nature, is secular, and for this very reason to demand full liberty for the exercise of religion. More often, however, one of the many possible intermediate positions has been adopted, with a rather vague assumption that the State, though far from identical with the Church, ought to tolerate and perhaps encourage, religion in "a Christian country". Totalitarianism, of course, is incompatible with any of these compromises, which do at least imply that the life of religion is something more than the behaviour of a good citizen, and that the worship of God is an allegiance of a different order from loyalty to the State. If there is to be any religion at all in a totalitarian country, not only must the State supply it, but the State must contrive to be worshipful.   Some tincture of mysticism must be infused into the essence of citizenship; some terrestrial substitute for the God " who is in heaven " must be enthroned.

With what degree of success this cult of the State has been implanted in the youth of Germany or any other totalitarian country it is difficult to judge.   Probably it is mixed up with fanatical loyalty to dictators, for it will never be easy to venerate an abstraction, and in older experiments like the apotheosis of Roman emperors or " the divine right of kings " there are only doubtful analogies.   The " Leviathan " of Hobbes was a more formidable idol, which did foreshadow some modern inventions, but Hobbes kept up an elaborate pretence of scriptural authority for his doctrines, and, instead of openly professing atheism, he merely transferred to the sovereign all the powers which he denounced so bitterly when they were attributed to the pope.   Now it needs no argument to prove that neither Christianity, nor any other religion that deserves to be so called, can regard deification of the State as anything but blasphemous nonsense; but, since it would be injudicious to suggest that the objections to totalitarianism are exclusively religious, let us pass on to another kind of criticism.

The State, as we have seen, must always be absolute.   Up to a point, indeed, it is no more absolute than the M.C.C. or the Jockey Club, for against the rulings of those august bodies there is no appeal.   You can, however, retire from the Turf, or give up cricket, or possibly start a new association, with a new set of rules for the game.   Or, if you decide to grumble and submit, it will not be your deepest convictions that are outraged, and in the end you may feel that it was scarcely worth while to make a fuss.   Other associations, for the promotion of literature, art, or science, will deal with matters more serious than sport, but in such cases the rules most strictly enforced will not be those that touch the deeper questions of principle.   A member will be obliged to pay his subscription by a certain date, to observe the rules for use of a library, and perhaps, at stated intervals, to make some contribution to the work of the society; but it is unlikely that his views will have to conform to an orthodox standard, or that he will run the risk of expulsion for heresy.   All rules involve a " sanction ", but in many societies rules are of two kinds.   Some are merely administrative regulations, alterable whenever it seems expedient, and in that sense arbitrary: others are declarations of principle, constitutive of the society which enacts them, and essential to its purpose.   Manifestly, then, the latter kind is the more important; but what is not so obvious, until we reflect upon it carefully, is that coercion, which in respect to trifling matters is no affront to liberty, becomes less and less expedient in proportion as rules get nearer to being expressions of doctrine and principle. To be obliged to leave your hat in the hall, or to return a library book at the end of a fortnight, may sometimes be a nuisance, but it is no injury to conscience. On the other hand, if a member of a Conservative Club is forbidden to support a bill proposed by the Labour Party, or if a Wesleyan is denounced for borrowing a collect from the Book of Common Prayer, then indeed there is some point in the cry of intolerance. Any society, in fact, which deals with ideas, doctrines, principles, in any of the higher spheres of mental or spiritual activity, will be well advised to restrict its coercive action to administrative rules which are merely a matter of convenience, with little or no intrinsic relation to the object for which the society exists.

In the case of the State, however, the problem is infinitely more complicated; for, though it may be clear enough that its laws are not all of equal importance, all must stand on the same footing in the sense that all must be obeyed, and that all are backed by force. It is here, too, that we are most likely to fall into confusion. If we compare two historical epochs, in one of which the Government is obliged to spend most of its energy on the making of foreign wars and the suppression of civil disorder, while in the other it can devote itself to all kinds of "social services", nothing, at first sight, is more natural than to judge that only in the first case could the State be defined, with some show of reason, as the organization of force. But this, I submit, is a profound misreading of the facts. The essence of force is not physical; it has nothing to do with the difference between war and peace. Guns and bayonets, soldiers and policemen, are only instruments of ideas; and, if the condition of the world were such that swords could safely be beaten into ploughshares, the risk of violence to liberty by the action of the State would not necessarily be diminished, but might well be increased. When force is open and visible, when it takes the form of military action, or of arrest, imprisonment, and so forth, it is recognized for what it is; and, more often than not (in civilized countries), it is excused as a necessity evoked by some public danger. That the State, and the State alone, should be entitled to put down violence by violence is involved in its nature, and one of its greatest services to liberty is that use of this drastic remedy is thus forbidden to all other associations and to every private citizen. But what we forget, or fail to understand, is that, when we pass from an age of physical force to the more subtle atmosphere of ideas and principles, any authority claimed by the State in the form of law will be just as much an expression of force as the hanging of a traitor or the imprisonment of a thief.   So easily, however, are we deceived by our own inventions that we put all our faith in constitutional government and are content to believe that, so long as laws are passed with the consent of the majority, all legal injunctions must be equitable and no harm to liberty can be done. Coercion, in fact, has assumed a mask, and forthwith the deeper problems are obscured by the protracted struggle for extension of the franchise, which is unlikely to cease until all other qualifications have been swept away and every citizen of full legal age has secured the right to vote.

Many of the controversies incidental to the evolution of democracy lie outside our subject, but this much may be said without trenching, I hope, on party politics, that the more clearly we recognize in practice that public opinion is the ground of public authority, that every citizen has the right to express his opinions in the form of a vote, and that all opinions, as thus measured at the polling booth, are of equal value, the more urgent it becomes to examine the nature and function of the State. As a political expedient, government by majority of votes is (in some parts of the world at least) superior to all others, not only because it is the least likely to excite dangerous opposition, but also because where-ever it is allowed that " the will of the people " is the decisive factor, the only practicable way of discovering that invisible entity is by the counting of votes.   But to convert this sound constitutional principle into the doctrine that the voice of the majority is always (or ever) the exponent of right and truth is to fall into a blind superstition, which would be merely ludicrous if it could not sometimes be tragic.   Our forefathers believed (and some of their descendants, apparently, still believe) that truth can be discovered by the ordeal of battle, but has anyone ever quite succeeded in persuading himself that the ordeal by general elections is equally conclusive ?   In a primitive phase of religion, too, " the Lord is a man of war ", but it scarcely follows that, as we grow more civilized, he should be converted into a democratic politician.   Moreover, the question of truth is quite irrelevant.   The governing force in democracy is not knowledge (which is always aristocratic and oligarchical) but opinion, and, whenever a clear ex-pression of opinion has been given by the electorate, nothing further can be expected or required.   There is no political machinery on earth, nor ever will be, for securing the revelation of truth.   Nor is this the end of the matter.   Still more profoundly deluded shall we be if we assume that, because knowledge is superior to opinion, the ideal of the perfect State must be to translate infallible truth into law.   That assumption, in fact, is what vitiates all ideologies, and what makes the doctrinaire in office the deadly enemy of mankind. Let us suppose, for the sake of argument, that one of the ideologies (whichever you please) is the very gospel of truth. Is that a good reason for its adoption and enforcement by the State? On the contrary, it is the worst of all possible reasons, and the result could only be the destruction of liberty, the reign of persecution, and a mortal injury to truth itself.

As a theme for essayists and debating-societies, " the limits of State interference " has enjoyed a considerable vogue. All attempts, however, to determine those limits *a priori* are doomed to failure, for there is almost no important kind of human activity that may not, in some circumstances, become a public danger, and just when the moment for interference has arrived the State, and the State alone, can decide. The actual decision, of course, on any particular occasion may be wise or foolish, but to argue, for instance, that, because Churches and Trade Unions have a right to exist, neither they nor any other kind of lawful association must ever be restrained, is plainly ridiculous. The chief value, indeed, of the " interference " is that it suggests a rather negative attitude on the part of the State. If, for instance, the police object to football in Trafalgar Square, or to a religious service which blocks the traffic in the Strand, their interference does not imply that football and religion are normally illegal, much less that they are functions of the State improperly usurped by other associations. Or if we take a more thoroughgoing prohibition, like the suppression of gaming-houses, this does not mean that, like the Principality of Monaco, the State will recognize only its own Monte Carlo, but simply that the organization of gambling as a business is forbidden; and, since the same prohibition does not apply to a genuinely private party in a private house, it cannot even be said with accuracy that the State is thus asserting its right to dictate rules of morality. No doubt there are border-line cases not easy to analyse, but clearly we do not reach the deliberate ideology until the State openly declares its intention of obliging all citizens to conform in every respect to a certain pattern of life, with the inevitable corollary that no other pattern can be allowed. Then it is that the term " interference " becomes ambiguous and insufficient, while " suppression " may be equally misleading; for if all voluntary schools, for instance, are suppressed in the totalitarian State, this is not because education is forbidden, but because the State has annexed the function of educating its members, and therefore refuses to tolerate any other method or ideals.

Now there is no kind of State that can avoid " interference " in the sense of prohibition, and in early codes of law (like the Decalogue) the negative aspect is likely to be the most prominent. On the other hand, no society can subsist in pure negation; it must have come into existence for some purpose, however ill-defined; so that, even if the formula of every law were " Thou shalt not ", there would still, presumably, be a reason for prohibiting some kinds of conduct, but not others; and this would imply some reference to a positive ideal. Just as it is impossible to lay it down as an unqualified rule that the State must never " interfere " with commerce, or morality, or religion, so we must freely allow that it is exceedingly difficult to formulate any principle which will assign to the State just so many positive functions, and thus deny its right to exercise any others. On what grounds, for instance, shall we decide that the State may fairly tax its members for the provision of an army, but not for the provision of free dentistry? Or that conscription for military service is right and proper, while conscription of industrial labour is monstrous injustice? And further, it is always possible to maintain that the State, as the supreme society, exists to realize the supreme good; that its concern is not with this or that limited department, but with life as a whole; and that, consequently, it ought to direct and control every kind of activity by which human welfare and happiness can be secured. On some such argument as this the case for totalitarianism must depend.

Nothing is so fallacious as half-truths and, just because none of these propositions about the State can be flatly denied, we may fail to perceive that none of them is true without qualifications which invalidate and destroy the totalitarian conclusion. Is the State the supreme society? In a legal and constitutional sense it certainly is. That the sovereign is " supreme in all causes, ecclesiastical as well as civil ", no one is likely to deny; nor does any other association lay claim to an autonomy which would place it outside or above the law. Yet this scarcely proves that the State, by virtue of its sovereignty, is the supreme authority on art, science, religion—or cricket. But is not the State properly concerned with all these interests which together make up the life of the citizen? In one sense, assuredly, it is; for, as we have observed already, there is no important kind of organized activity that may not be employed to the public detriment. The Royal Society, for instance, could easily contrive a Gunpowder Plot far more effective than the one muddled by Guy Fawkes, while religion, in some of its extravagances, may lead to moral antinomianism or political anarchy. Restraint of disorder, however, is only a negative kind of interest, and it is only when we argue that the State should actively stimulate the development of intellectual, moral, and spiritual ideas that we have to pause and consider. There are, in fact, at least two grades of encouragement which are perfectly distinguishable from the totalitarian principle. The first consists in little more than facilitating a performance which the State allows, and perhaps approves, but does not by any means regard as a manifestation of itself. Just as when the Thames Conservancy clears the course for the Boat Race, or when the police, who smack more strongly of public authority, sweep the spectators off the ground after the luncheon-interval at Lord's or the Oval, we are grateful for the official assistance, but do not infer that these sports are on a level with war and diplomacy, so, too, it is possible for the State to make an analogous contribution to the orderly pursuit of various cultural activities, in schools, museums, or churches, without pretending that they are functions of the sovereign power.

At the second stage we pass beyond friendly co-operation to definite encouragement. When, for instance, a grant in aid of Grand Opera is sanctioned by the Treasury, or when, on a larger scale, public money is allotted to universities for the promotion of science and learning, the State does express a positive intention, and declare its belief that these studies are for the public good. Yet still, as in England we know from experience, it is possible to take official action of this kind without interfering at all with the autonomy of the societies which actually regulate the use of these grants. Hitherto, at least, there has been no Government Department to supervise the programmes and choose the artists at Covent Garden; nor, I think, has there been any official attempt to determine the methods and aims of university teaching. Royal or statutory commissions, to be sure, have drastically ordered the finances of universities and colleges, but, even if this mode of interference could not be justified, the implications of it are not comparable to even the smallest attempt to limit the freedom of the teacher or censure his doctrine. In like manner, the State may undertake the more hazardous task of promoting sound religion, and may think fit (as in Fascist Italy) to make some financial contribution to that end. Yet, even so, it may succeed in abstaining from the regulation of doctrine and the persecution of dissenters.

In determining what kinds of conduct can safely be allowed, what amusements regarded with favour, what professions and occupations authorized, what artistic and intellectual activities encouraged, and what degree of autonomy conceded to various types of organization, the State has a sufficiently complicated task, and occasional errors of judgement must be expected. Yet no display of wisdom or folly in

M

any of these respects need imply the deliberate imposition of an official ideology, any more than the loan of a few policemen to the M.C.C. proves that cricket is a function of the State. Again, every genuine philosophy and every great religion may, if we please, be styled an " ideology ", and every comprehensive system, be it Platonism, or Stoicism, or Catholicism, is " totalitarian ", inasmuch as it offers a complete way of life, a way of " salvation " revealed, as its votaries believe, by knowledge of the truth. Moreover, any society organized for the propagation of its own gospel will tend to develop an orthodoxy, and perhaps to invent some kind of excommunication; while, if it secures, by some evil chance, command of sufficient power, it may end by converting into an insufferable bondage what was meant to be an emancipation of the soul. In the modern world, however, the only society that can push coercion to its uttermost limits is the State, and the tragic fact about the State, as I must repeat, is that its rules—dignified with the name and status of " laws "—not only may be enforced but must be; for to enact a law, and then allow it to be ignored or disobeyed, is to bring the State itself into contempt and almost to ask for a revolution. Hence the formal adoption by the State of any " ideology ", in the current sense of the word, must mean that the whole apparatus of law will be employed for imposing upon all citizens a certain pattern of life, for obliging them to assent in practice to a particular set of intellectual, moral, and spiritual principles, whether they believe in them or not. That is what, according to the totalitarian theory, the State ought to do; and if that is not tyranny, what is?

The impossibility of defining with meticulous accuracy the functions that the State should, or should not, assume has been freely admitted. Necessity and expediency are pleas that every State, at one time or another, will be constrained to admit. In times of war, for instance, much is endurable which in times of peace might well be resented, and there may be other kinds of emergency in which no other remedy but authoritative intervention is likely to succeed. Yet there is all the difference in the world between preferring—in a genuine dilemma—the lesser of two evils and pursuing an evil as though it were a good. The true principle, surely, is that, as we mount from the bare necessities of existence towards the higher manifestations of the human spirit, coercion should steadily diminish until, at the earliest possible moment, it finally disappears. Now this is exactly where the modern State, with its single and undisputed sovereignty, has its golden opportunity. By arrogating to itself the entire authority of law and all coercive power, it has prevented all other societies from converting their principles into instruments of persecution, or at least has made it plain that no other society can deprive a citizen of his fundamental rights. So far, so good; but if, after performing this great service to liberty, the State proceeds, on its own account, to employ all the means at its disposal for imposing on the minds of men a single dogmatic system, embodied, so far as possible, in laws that can be disobeyed only at the cost of rebellion, then indeed the modern world will groan under a despotism more crushing than any known to the confused and disorderly age when popes, emperors, kings, and a host of minor dignitaries fought for their real or imaginary rights. In those days a man had at least some choice of masters: he might serve a king who refused to be dominated by turbulent priests, or, if the king in his turn proved intolerable, he might creep into some sanctuary of the Church. But when "Leviathan" has swallowed all rivals, and is armed with all power and majesty, no refuge is anywhere to be found on the face of the earth. When Hobbes first painted the features of that monster with matchless force and skill, at least he did not flatter or disguise them. He hated liberty, and said so; he hated the Church, and said so; he feared and mistrusted all "corporations", and said so. Least of all did he pretend (though on this point superficial readers have misinterpreted him) that the difference between one form of political constitution and another could affect the absolute character of the sovereign power. The civil war that he witnessed might well be viewed as a contest of rival autocracies, and he had little occasion to anticipate the judgement of Spinoza, that "democracy is the only absolute dominion". Since his day, of course, we have found good reasons for looking askance at despotisms and oligarchies, and that, perhaps, is why we fail to perceive that totalitarianism is most insidious and most deadly when it takes "democracy" for its name.

At the opening of this chapter I expressed my regret that its subject would oblige us to approach the frontiers of controversial politics; but, before concluding it, I can offer at least this much of apology, that the argument entails, as its most important consequence, a decisive objection to any kind of theocracy, and, above all, to the adoption of the Christian faith as the ideology of the State. In view of the actual examples of totalitarianism, and of the general movement of thought at the present time, it is, of course, most unlikely that anything of the kind should happen; but supposing that, by some strange revolution of public sentiment, our own country should be moved to invest a genuine religion (as distinct from the cult of the State) with sovereign authority, I should personally hope that at least it would be a religion in which I did not believe. To a large extent the external acts of men can be standardized and forced to conform to rule; to a large extent, unhappily, their minds can be darkened by propaganda, and their passions inflamed; but the one absolutely impossible thing is to compel them to know the truth, and the one absolutely indefensible thing is to exercise the power of law in that vain attempt. The more one believes, therefore, that the Christian faith is the highest revelation of truth, the less ought one to desire the translation of it into statutory law.

" Render unto Cæsar the things that are Cæsar's, and unto God the things that are God's." The political history of the Christian Church has mainly consisted in a perpetual failure to discover the right interpretation of those words. The first step, however, towards a general understanding of the problem is to remember that in the ancient world there was no such thing as the Church, and in the Middle Ages no such thing as the State. As long as the Roman Empire was a pagan institution, with the pagan religion as one of its functions, the political situation of the Church was comparatively simple, for there was no question of its having to exercise secular power in the kingdom of this world. But when emperors began to call themselves Christians, and as the conception of Christendom gradually took shape, the duality of temporal and spiritual power no longer depended on the antagonism of two religions, one of which had no secular ambition, but came to mean no more than a duality of functions within a single cosmopolitan society, which acknowledged no fundamental principles but those of the Christian religion. The result was discord, confusion, and chaos, compared with which the life of the Church before the close of the pagan era was harmony itself. The story of that strange fantasy, the Holy Roman Empire, is one great chapter, but not the only one; for, besides popes and emperors, there were, on the one side, kings, princes, feudal lords, and more or less independent cities; on the other, archbishops, abbots, and the whole ecclesiastical hierarchy; a medley of powers and privileges, with the " two swords " for ever dangling before the eyes of all aspirants to authority, yet scarcely more easy to clutch and hold than the phantom dagger which haunted the somnambulist queen.

The rights and wrongs of the medieval controversies it is, of course, impossible to examine, but with the break-up of Christendom into national states and the emergence of sovereignty in a sense hitherto unknown or long in abeyance, a reformation of the old dualism was bound, sooner or later, to appear. It was not that the distinction of temporal and spiritual became any easier, but on the horizon could now be discerned two possibilities never plainly acknowledged in earlier times; that the sovereign power, by virtue of its legal supremacy, would claim to be the final authority in spiritual matters; or, on the contrary, that it would discard the religious function altogether and declare itself purely secular. In the latter case there would still be room for two entirely different interpretations; for the implication might be either that the practice of religion, though not the business of the State, was lawful and proper, or that the secularism of the State was binding also on all private persons. Now in England, with our talent for compromise, we have hitherto succeeded pretty well in avoiding both the extreme positions. In spite of many awkward occasions (incidental sometimes to the ill-defined status of " establishment "), it cannot be said that the distinction between spiritual and temporal matters has ever been formally repudiated; much less has the State ever declared itself purely secular, or disavowed religion, even to the extent of discouraging its ministers and officials from going to church. But what we are most likely to overlook is that the adoption by the State of any ideology is not in fact a preference of one of the two most sharply contrasted alternatives, but a fusion of both into one; for any ideology, if taken seriously, must mean a system, a body of doctrine, a way of life, comprehensive enough to affect all the higher activities of the human mind and spirit, and therefore exclusive of all rivals. In other words, it is a religion intolerant of all other religions; and though it sounds, of course, paradoxical to maintain that the evils of theocracy and secularism are thus united, the truth is that militant secularism (as distinct from mere indifference) is not practicable except as based on the conviction that some new creed has destroyed the sanctity of all that hitherto counted as sacred; and even if the official system were to be labelled " atheism ", this would not cease to be true. No effective system can be essentially negative; men must be got to believe in something that destroys or banishes all other beliefs.

All ideologies, then, if adopted by the State and backed by the force of law, are tyrannies; for all involve the attempt to constrain men to accept ideas whether they believe in them or not; or rather, all are rooted in the same deplorable fallacy, that it is possible to compel men to know the truth. To Christians above all others the warning against this ideal of government should be addressed. Of all forms of polity, theocracy, in which the powers of the State are absorbed into the Church, is the most un-Christian. The only conceivable excuse for imposing an ideology by force of law would be that its doctrines were patently false and absurd.

12

The Christian Philosophy or Pursuit of Wisdom

IN some preliminary observations on the meaning of " philosophy "
it was allowed that all the various senses of a term with so long a
history must be taken into account, and that no one of them need be
accepted as exclusively correct. At the same time I expressed the
intention of constantly bearing in mind the etymological suggestion of
this " love of wisdom " which the Greek schools, at least, always
represented as an ideal to be grasped only by the sternest effort of the
mind, yet also to be translated into a " method " or way of life.
Undoubtedly, too, one effect of our rapid survey has been to exhibit
many fluctuations of meaning, with much variety of emphasis on the
respective functions of theory and practice. Neither aspect, however,
has in any age been totally obscured; for even in modern times, when
philosophy is mostly treated as an academic " subject ", and when we
have been invited, for instance, to accept the reduction of its compass
implied in a casual remark of Bradley's (" ' philosophy '—by which I
mean ' metaphysics ' "), a startling reaction has now produced these
formidable " ideologies ", which may be smeared with the colours of
Hegelianism or " dialectical materialism ", but for the most part are
employed as means of bringing about social and political revolutions.
It has therefore been natural to find some corresponding variation in the
form assumed by the Christian challenge to other systems of thought and
life, and thus, perhaps, to run some risk of curtailing its full dimensions.
The problem with which the Church has been immediately confronted in centuries as different in their general conditions as, for
instance, the fourth, the thirteenth, and the nineteenth or twentieth,
could not possibly be identical; but, however true it may be that
doctrinal controversies prominent in one period were unknown in
another, this in itself is a very poor reason for arguing either that there
never was a faith " once delivered to the saints " or that the effect
of perpetual modifications has been entirely to destroy the original.
Without pretending, however, to attack the whole problem of identity
and development, let us attempt a brief review of the Christian position,

so far as it has been revealed by contrast with other philosophies or appreciations of human life.

Religion, as piety and ritual observance, is much older than theology; and European theology, as we have seen, was an invention of philosophers who had come to look with some disfavour on religion. Yet, if either was to survive, their union was inevitable. To worship God, without reflecting upon his nature, is possible only for rather primitive men; to be content with a logical hypothesis or impersonal abstraction, which no one can worship, is to destroy religion. Nothing, therefore, is less surprising than the early appearance of Christian theology, which from the very first was controversial, and which, in many subsequent stages of ecclesiastical history, was bound to be a cause of division. Nevertheless, there is still to be found, floating about in newspapers and ephemeral literature, the opinion that theology is a superfluous obstacle; while in works of another class we get sometimes a plea for doctrinal revision, on the ground that formulas stabilized in patristic or medieval times must now be obsolete in expression, if not also in their deeper intention. Abolition and reformation are, of course, very different policies, but in this case the more drastic proposal deserves, I think, more attention than any scheme for recasting, in the superior style of modern thought, our ancient professions of faith. Those who favour some such critical revision are convinced, presumably, that the authoritative imposition of creeds or doctrines expressed in language appropriate only to transient circumstances was an unfortunate, though possibly an excusable, blunder. But if so, why repeat the blunder, when the lessons of experience have deprived us of the excuse? And in what kind of terminology, pray, or with reference to which brand of modern thought, are we to re-write our doctrinal propositions? We have only to glance at the last hundred, nay, the last fifty years, in the chronicle of philosophy to see that a permanent committee would have to be established in order to keep the Christian religion perpetually up to date. The deeper reasons for preserving forms of words, in creed or liturgy, no longer, perhaps, interpreted in precisely their original sense, may presently come to light, but without delay we may dismiss as frivolous and superficial the suggestion that the Christian faith could be made more reasonable, or more acceptable, by clothing it in a more fashionable dress.

Far more serious is the rather widespread belief that, if only Christian churches and sects would cease wrangling about theology; if doctrinal orthodoxy could be discreetly ignored; we could then return to the original gospel, which was only a sound rule of life that all men of good will might gladly approve. To put the case in another way, it seems to be commonly assumed—by Christians as well as by unbelievers—that the practical side of Christianity is far more easy of interpretation than the speculative; that the perfection of the divine pattern, so to speak, might be freely acknowledged, if only misguided theologians would not insist so much on its being divine. Against this reading of the facts I submit that, on the contrary, the interpretation of the gospel in practice is far more difficult than the theology which seems to carry us into the region of speculation. Suppose, for instance, one had to choose between expounding the doctrine of the triune God and providing a clear application of the Sermon on the Mount to the ordinary business of life, I should personally begin by confessing my incompetence for either task; but if obliged, nevertheless, to make the choice, I should certainly prefer to face what look like intellectual subtleties with little or no reference to practical affairs. But here, of course, it is necessary to make reservations. No human being can hope, or can reasonably be asked, to explain the nature of God, if only for the reason that all philosophical and scientific explanations depend upon comparisons and analogies, and must therefore collapse in the presence of the absolutely unique. But when we set out to discuss the doctrine of the Trinity, we do not pretend to fathom the unfathomable, but only to defend a certain conception of the Divine Being against some other forms of religious monotheism, or perhaps against abstruse philosophical constructions like the One of Plotinus or the Absolute of Bradley. Further, we must observe that the historical question was not so much whether any speculative analysis could be sufficient as whether agreement could be reached upon a creed which would safeguard the Catholic faith against Arianism and other doctrines (quite as " theoretical " as the Catholic) which threatened to destroy it. Now it was in the end, after a protracted struggle, found possible to arrive at forms of expression which have at least passed the test of endurance. This by no means implies that all Christians, or all professional theologians, have really understood the official statements in exactly the same sense, but it does mean that, despite the greater schisms, there has been a creed of Christendom—a theology in fact—from which even " heretics " have not, as a rule, avowedly dissented.

On the other hand, there never has been, nor, I make bold to add, ever will be agreement *de imitatione Christi*; about any one and only way of living which perfectly represents in action the faith proclaimed in the creed of the Church. Observe, too, that this assertion is no mere echo of the opening lines in Browning's *Easter Day*:

> How very hard it is to be
> A Christian! Hard for you and me.

That, indeed, is the greatest of all personal difficulties, but at the moment it is not the point.   What I mean is that, given a firm resolve to be a Christian, a sound intelligence, a sensitive conscience, and a saintly gift of perseverance, it is always possible that the outcome will be a mode of life which many other Christians, well entitled thus to describe themselves, will regard with astonishment, and not improbably with aversion.   Think first of some of the broader distinctions of type recorded in history: the hermit in his cave, the cloistered monk, the wandering friar, the mystic, the crusader, the Jesuit, the Trappist, the prince-bishop, the Richelieus and Mazarins, the Puritan, the country parson in the style of George Herbert, the Cameronian, the Wesleyan, the Quaker.   Or, since fiction (with due allowance for satire and parody) may be no less instructive than history, glance at the long array of portraits in that gallery, and imagine the task of arranging even a few of them according to " schools ".   Compare, for instance, the Vicar of Wakefield with Bishop Blougram or the Bishop who ordered his tomb; set Joshua Geddes side by side with Balfour of Burley; collect from the Barchester district Mr Harding and Archdeacon Grantly, Mr Arabin and Mr Crawley, with Mrs Proudie to keep a sharp eye on them all: or in that remarkable study of seventeenth-century religion, *John Inglesant*, watch the hero as he follows the heavenly light through the mazes of ecclesiastical and political intrigue, and listens to all the conflicting voices that offer to point out the only infallible way.   Or try another line of investigation, and, remembering how different conceptions of the religious life are apt to be symbolized in forms of worship, contrast the gorgeous ceremonies of a Catholic cathedral with the nakedness of some village " Bethel ", or the Masses of Byrd and Palestrina with the succulent hymn-tunes which fill a musician with despair.   Or, once more, examine the Christian attitude at various times towards political and social questions, and not least towards the acquisition and use of wealth.   Which is nearest to the true ideal, the " evangelical poverty " which involves dependence on almsgiving, the decent competence of the beneficed clergyman, or the accumulation of riches almost as a duty, provided they be spent in a Christian way ?   When we gaze with reverence at S. Francis and his barefoot companions, do we promptly infer that the Vatican galleries are a scandal to Christendom ?   Or must we be horrified when a devout and justly honoured philanthropist (one of the Gurneys of Earlham) remarks that, in this respect at least, the Quakers are like the Jews, that they are very fond of making money ?

Neither in history nor in fiction, neither in the larger diversities of type embodied in organized associations nor in the finer shades of individual character, do we find a glimmer of evidence to support the belief that any undogmatic, undenominational, standardized pattern of the Christian life would have the slightest chance of general acceptance by Christians themselves. The only hope of formulating that kind of " Christianity " would be to appoint a committee of unbelievers, who, like Macchiavelli in his advice to princes, might think it politic to encourage religion, but would be quite indifferent to the question of truth. Morality without religion there may always be, and religion without theology there often has been in the past, but to Christians both are unmeaning. The only possible motive of Christian practice is the Christian faith. Remove the faith, and nothing remains but a lifeless code of morals, which might just as well have been borrowed from a Jew or a Stoic, or indeed from any respectable householder in the nobler days of pagan Rome. Meanwhile the fact remains that, whereas in creeds and formulas it has been possible to establish and maintain substantial agreement, in practical interpretations of the common faith there has been a bewildering diversity, almost amounting to chaos. Even when doctrinal schism has been violent, as often as not the true ground of dissension has been the conflict of two apparently incompatible ways of life, accentuated by the inability of partisans to believe that their opponents could be sincere. Yet neither deliberate imposture nor the admitted failure of Christians to live up to their own ideal will serve as an explanation. Idle and lascivious monks, worldly popes, unctuous psalm-singing impostors, there may have been in abundance, but not thus did the ideals of the cloister, of the papal supremacy, or of Cromwell's army, come into existence, and not thus can their peculiarities be explained.

The next step is to understand that, apart from the wilder eccentricities, all this variation of mode in Christian practice is exactly what we ought to expect and approve. The rage for uniformity has two sources, one intellectual, the other political or disciplinary. The aim of science is objective proof, the aim of statesmen, bishops, schoolmasters, and all manner of persons in authority is to frame suitable laws which will be generally obeyed. To think in accordance with rules dictated by the facts, and to live in accordance with rules imposed for the public good, are by no means unworthy ideals. Yet both have their limitations, and one effect of the Christian philosophy is to expose the fallacy of the twofold hypothesis, that truth can be revealed to the understanding in only one objective form and translated into only one unvarying rule or method of action. All scientific investigation of nature, and all philosophy that follows the same general line of thought, is governed by the hypothesis that the multiplicity of phenomena is reducible to, and explicable by, law. The old phrase " uniformity of nature " is, indeed, less favoured now than in the days when John Stuart Mill adopted it as the text of a confused piece of logic; and to some extent, I suppose, the statistical assessment of probabilities has tempered the rigidity of " laws of nature " to which no exception could possibly be allowed. Recent modifications and adjustments of scientific method do not, however, involve any revolution of first principles. The notion of law is still predominant; the constant aim of science is to find unity in plurality, to subordinate the particular to the universal, to discover and emphasize relations, to bring order out of superficial diversity, and ultimately, perhaps, to exhibit the whole vast complex of facts and events as the manifestation of an original " matter " evolving in accordance with a single law.

Now in this great enterprise, with all its wonderful results, there is nothing that Christians should not welcome as enlightenment; nothing that they should not, if so disposed and qualified, enthusiastically promote. The only fatal error is to mistake a perfectly ordered anatomy of the cosmos for the sum total of reality and truth. As an intellectual concept, law is only a half-truth; as a rule imposed by authority, it is only a makeshift, and always, to some extent, a confession of failure. The radical difference between the Christian and the scientific hypothesis is that, for Christians, the supreme fact in the universe is not a law, nor any stupendous concatenation of laws, but a Person; and the knowledge of personality (even at its humblest level) by persons cannot be obtained by the methods upon which the progress of science depends. The clue to such knowledge of God as is possible for man is not absorption of the particular into the universal, but discovery of the individual, and it is by this route, even when it seems to pass through country remote from the precincts of religion, that the whole journey must be made. Let us attempt, then, briefly to indicate the main direction and some of the principal stages.

It is in the realm of the inorganic, where inanimate things are considered generically and in their mutual relations, that individuality is apt to be most completely disregarded. Observation of the " particular " is, of course, the starting-point of most sciences, but the " particular " is not the individual, and anything that looks like singularity is usually taken as a challenge to be met. Suppose, for instance, a geologist comes across a piece of flint in a region where its presence is improbable, he will at once be anxious to know whether it is a genuine relic of an immensely remote epoch or an accidental importation. Even so, it is not the individuality of the object, but its genus, that excites him, and should he presently learn that it was picked up elsewhere by a roving pedestrian, and then carelessly thrown away, this individual fact in its history will put an end to his curiosity. Far from welcoming individuality, the geologist desires only to get rid of it by reducing the unexpected phenomenon to order. The illustration of method, too, is not individual, but typical; for what the geologist does with the fortuitous piece of flint is what natural science is doing perpetually and systematically in every part of its survey of nature.

And what of our ordinary selves, as we make our way, rather amateurishly, through a miscellaneous world? Are we, too, habitually indifferent to all that is properly individual and unique? To a very large extent we are. Inanimate things, at least, we are constantly obliged, and usually content, to estimate and use in their generalized character; to treat them only as specific means to specific ends; and in many cases we are obliged to regard any deviation from standardized pattern and normal behaviour as a positive disadvantage. At the same time, it is easy to detect symptoms of other points of view, of modes of valuation which bring to light something more than abstract qualities of general relations, and point to individuality as a precious fact by no means to be ignored. Thus, for instance, do sentimental associations and cherished memories impart to a landscape, a village, a house, or a single room, a charm that no duplicate or substitute could offer; thus do mere custom and familiarity induce us to feel for the most trifling of our personal possessions an affection that is sensibly injured by their loss or decay. Or, if we ask for evidence more substantial than these private whims and fancies, the whole field of æsthetic appreciation is there to supply it. In all our judgements upon works of art—a poem, a picture, a sonata—we are evidently drawing nearer and nearer to concentration upon the unique. True, there will be much talk still of periods and styles; comparisons of different artists, or of different phases in the development of the same one; but while discussion of that sort is often profitable, it does not annul, but in the end rather serves to emphasize, the individuality of this incomparable portrait or that inimitable ode.

Now the probable reply of any critic who is firmly convinced that objective truth about the nature of things is discoverable only by scientific method will be that all other modes of interpretation are tainted with subjectivity; just matters of taste, about which the familiar adage forbids dispute. It is of vital importance, he will argue, to allow for the personal equation and, as soon as that precept is duly honoured, we shall be forced to confess that all these discoveries and admirations of individuality are merely disclosures of ourselves. We project from within the unique quality, the peculiar charm, the special revelation, and then fondly imagine it was " there " all the time. Or, if he does allow that in what we profess to apprehend there is something rather more substantial than our own image in a mirror, he will still contend that the general attributes and relations disengaged by science from casual accessories are of far deeper import than anything that may strike us as unique. This, of course, is a very old story, and this much of truth there is in it, that emotional bias may disturb the judgement quite as much as ignorance or logical incapacity. On the other hand, the distinction of " subjective " and " objective " is so elusive, and the meaning of those terms so disputable, that one would be hard put to it to name any philosopher of any date whose account of the matter is clear and decisive. Without attempting, however, to reopen the whole question, we may fairly retort our critic's thrust upon himself by a rough *tu quoque.* Nothing, in fact, is more arbitrary than the process by which the objects of any scientific inquiry are constituted and described. In order to justify, for instance, the Newtonian formula for gravitation, we have to tamper with every " instance " of it, to ignore a hundred details in the actual motions of any individual body, to substitute tendency for realization, to play with logical fictions in a system of bodies which, as we define them, are nowhere discoverable in concrete existence. On what grounds, then, is it so confidently asserted that a poet's or a painter's representation of a landscape reveals less of its " objective " reality than a geologist's technical survey or an ordnance map ? The practical advantages of exact measurement are obvious, but, when we are in search of a theoretical principle which is to justify a certain conception of truth, it is not enough to point to the many useful things that you can do with a map and a compass. The " impressionist " painter resolves to present on his canvas exactly what he sees, exactly as he sees it, from a chosen point of view, regardless of everything else that he knows to be " there ": the geologist fastens upon those features of the countryside which are explicable by his science and treats every other kind of fact as totally irrelevant. Deliberate selection and deliberate omission are thus common to both, but in one respect their difference will be remarkable. If another geologist, equally well qualified, presently comes along and examines the same stretch of country, his report (apart from any accidental oversight) will agree precisely with his predecessor's; but if two painters, or ten or fifty, sit down in turn at the same spot and proceed to interpret the " same " scene, the results will not only be distinguishable, but may even be so strongly contrasted, that a mere amateur might be excused for doubting if all the pictures had been painted in the same county.

Now this proves, of course, that painting is not a science in the sense that its results are not calculable or exact. But what else does it prove? That no painter can represent anything but his own subjectivity? That the one whose work agrees most nearly with a careful photograph is the most truthful? That, if we select the two most violently contrasted versions of the scene, they cannot both be true? Every inference of that type is, I submit, entirely fallacious. The painters themselves would give you surprisingly different accounts of their own intentions, and some of them, no doubt, would hotly repudiate the suggestion that they were holding up a mirror to nature; but, as against the assumption that " the facts " can be accurately discerned and reported on by a special science, or by some combination of sciences, they will be unanimous, whether they know it or not. Even at the inanimate level, nature responds only to stimulus, and answers only the questions that are put. To the dispassionate student of laws and abstractions is given a revelation of whatever is generic, standardized, measurable, exact. Investing, as it were, only the least individualized part of his mind, he receives interest on no other, but at least the dividends on his gilt-edged securities are safe. The artist is much more of a gambler, more likely to be disappointed of his ambition, and much less likely to persuade the general public that he has anything of importance to say. Between the two modes of interpretation there is, as a rule, no direct competition; it is only when we happen to be interested in the whole nature of reality, and the whole problem of truth, that the exclusive claim of the scientific method has to be questioned. The whole point of scientific truth is that it has only one face, and that, in order to see it plainly, the observer must standardize his intellect and, so far as possible, depersonalize himself; the whole point, on the other hand, of the richer truth discernible by another kind of vision is that, like a cunningly devised portrait, it always turns its eyes on the spectator, wherever he may take his stand and wherever he may be. Science is impersonal because it is the same for all; art is impersonal because it grants no exclusive right of interpretation, but reveals itself to each man according to his capacity for appreciation. That all appreciations are therefore of equal value by no means follows, and still more fallacious is it to infer from the diversity of judgements that all alike are devoid of " objective " truth.

Works of art may, of course, be classed as inanimate things, but, as products of human genius, they make a useful preface to the more intricate problems connected with our knowledge of the living. New readings of *Hamlet* may be published annually; the *Messiah* may gain or lose by the harmonies of Mozart; *La Gioconda* may continue to smile (if it be a smile) on her admirers, and yet remain inscrutable; but these and all like subjects of artistic controversy will seem comparatively simple when we pass to judgements upon the character and personality of human beings with whom we come into contact, or perhaps have to estimate, without personal acquaintance, from evidence of some other kind. Here again it is clear that much can be learnt, and much accomplished, by attending only to generic attributes and treating mankind as a collection of similar units. In no other way, for example, can a large part of medical science be verified, and in no other way can government be carried on or most of our ordinary business be transacted. Just as in warfare the rank and file may be contemptuously rated as cannon-fodder, so in civil life are they habitually treated as statistics-fodder for all kinds of social and political experiments, on the general assumption that, while the actions of a given individual can rarely be predicted, it is possible to tell with some approach to certainty how a multitude will behave. According to their local habitations, professions, trades, and occupations, men naturally fall into groups; and in every part of our lives we are constantly associated with others by relations often so slender that they barely require us to know the names of our associates, much less to care how they live.

To a large extent this method of dealing with mankind is dictated by necessity, and to a large extent it works very well. Moreover, practical success is good evidence, so far as it goes, of sound theory, or at least implies that there ought to be a theory sufficient to cover the facts. Hence it is not surprising to find a considerable body of sciences explicitly devoted to the study of human behaviour, beginning with anthropology, which, in a well-known dictionary, is defined as " the general science of man ". Closer inspection suggests, indeed, that the definition is rather too ambitious, for in practice the bulk of anthropological literature is occupied either with prehistoric man or with the primitive folk who linger on in a few unfrequented parts of the earth to remind us of the golden age. There is no need, however, to quarrel about a name, and " anthropology " can, if we please, be adopted as a title embracing all the " social sciences ", including economics.   But, although the systematic study of human behaviour, in any of its manifold aspects, may reasonably be called " science ", and though the " laws " discovered in this spacious field of study are less abstract than those exemplified in mathematics or physics, it is still true that their scientific character depends on the elimination of individuality, and their practical applications on the assumption that men are sufficiently alike to be described and handled in the mass.   The " economic man ", for instance, though officially dead, is actually rampant.   Nothing, at least, is more prevalent than an almost exclusively economic interpretation of human life, and nothing, I believe, is more shallow.   Man is governed by motives, and many motives (beginning with hunger) have economic consequences ; but to talk of " the economic motive " is an abuse of language and a confusion of thought.   There is no such thing as the economic motive : it is simply an " idol of the theatre ", which has now reached the market-place with deplorable results.   So again, " there is a real danger ", writes the late Dr Marett, " lest the anthropologist should think that a scientific view of man is to be obtained by leaving out the human nature in him " ; and a no less real danger, we might add, lest those who talk scientifically of human nature should forget that every man is individual.   If we wish to understand how the relation of man to man can best provide a clue to man's knowledge of God, the social sciences will not help us in the least ; we must concentrate upon the fact of personality as something that can neither be apprehended by any effort of the abstract thinking upon which we rely for success in scientific work, nor influenced in its proper character by any of the rough-and-ready methods which serve well enough for the regulation of social life.   " Individualism ", to be sure, has an ugly sound, and it must not be thought that, by emphasizing individuality, we are converting selfishness into a principle of discouraging co-operation.   No matter how much we ally ourselves (as, of course, we must) with other men because they inhabit the same town, collaborate with us in business, vote for the same party, observe the same social conventions, or share at least some of our tastes, no intimacy is so profound or so enduring as that which springs from the perception of something belonging only to this one person, something unanalysable, indefinable, and unique.   And, though this poignant sympathy can never be common, it is the only experience that intensifies our vision of humanity to a degree that raises us above the wisdom of averages, the prudence of business combines and political conspiracies, and gives us a glimpse of the fervent charity which makes no bargains and seeks no advantage. Cosmopolitanism, humanitarianism, philanthropy, are fine-sounding words, but may yet be the most frigid sentiments: it is only by the imaginative realization of personality that *homo sum, humani nihil alienum* becomes more than a formal concession to theory or a rhetorical flourish.

Between our appreciation of the living and our judgements upon the dead there is a plain analogy. Among the figures known to us only through historical evidence there are some, no doubt, that seem to have arrived at a stabilized position which nothing is very likely to disturb. Similarly, among the living, there are many whose reputation would seem to vary but little if we called upon each of their neighbours in turn to furnish a testimonial. We do not quarrel about the mediocrities whose names appear for a moment on the page of history in company with their betters, and in the casual associations of daily life we are bound to meet with many who strike us as inconspicuous, colourless, devoid of individuality, just " average " men. But all this is quite superficial. No sooner do we come upon historical notorieties, no sooner does any man excite our curiosity or affect our feelings, than diversities of judgement begin to appear. About Julius Cæsar, or Cromwell, or Napoleon, historians will wrangle almost as fiercely as the partisans and enemies of living dictators; while, as for that " verdict of history " which some imagine to be final, it is almost as variable as the English climate. Mere paucity of evidence, as there must often be about persons and events of long ago, is not the most interesting cause of divided opinion. It is where documents are plentiful and copious that we seem to get nearest to the position of contemporaries, and for that very reason are least likely to be unanimous. Sheer questions of fact, like the date of a battle or a treaty, we may, indeed, determine with certainty; but about character and motive no testimony can be more than a personal impression, and each fresh witness only duplicates the problem of how to get at the truth about the prisoner at the bar. Autobiography, certainly, is no exception, for no precept is harder of application than " know thyself ", and no literary adventure more hazardous than the attempt to transfer that knowledge to paper. One mistake, however, we must strive to avoid. In our scrutiny of human beings, still more earnestly than in our interpretation of works of art, we must beware of a pseudo-scientific ideal. There is nothing in the core of any human being analogous to the logical universal, the definable essence, the objective fact, distinct from all personal impressions, which an accurate formula can precisely express. Snow is white, we say, and if any observer sees it as yellow, that merely convicts

N

his eye of jaundice. Even in that little piece of philosophy there may soon be doubt, but when we proceed to argue in like manner about the character of a man we are wholly deluded. Every human soul is a chameleon, and in every one of its colours it reveals itself, but to no single observer can it reveal them all. The process, too, is mutual, for it is by the observer's power, or lack of power, to discover the nature of the " object " that his own insight is measured. The revelation of Johnson was, so to speak, the reward of Boswell's faith, and without that faith the greatest and most veracious of all biographical portraits could never have been given to the world. Thus the knowledge of one human being by another undermines the conventional antithesis of subjective impression and objective truth; for only through the medium of our full personality can the reality of another person be apprehended, and if we contribute no more than the dispassionate observation suitable to a chemical laboratory, the result will be the discovery of a clay figure with no more life in it than in a puppet governed by wires.

As a prelude to the supreme application of this principle to the relation of man to God, let us glance at one famous illustration, the case of Socrates. Like some others who have left an ineffaceable impression on human thought, Socrates wrote nothing. We know him only through his disciples and his critics, and had it ever been claimed for him by the faithful that he was divine, there is little doubt that resolute sceptics would even now have protested that his very existence was unproved. Actually, I believe, he has never quite been reduced to a solar myth, but no single portrait of him has ever been universally accepted as authentic and complete. What we have to compare is the very different versions of Xenophon and Plato, supplemented by the brilliant caricature of Aristophanes, the rather jejune commentary of Aristotle, and other evidence less worthy of remark. Now there was a period of criticism, not long ago, when it was thought scientific to detect the real Socrates only in Xenophon, and in Plato to find little more than a creature of imagination, suggested, no doubt, by a genuine model, but chiefly useful as a mouthpiece for the artist's own opinions. Against this view there came in due course a strong reaction, sometimes carried to the point of annexing for Socrates the famous theory of " ideas " traditionally called Platonic; and against this bold hypothesis there has been, as was natural, yet another reaction. Where, then, are we to look for the " historical " Socrates ? The answer is that the " historical " Socrates, as meaning a fixed, objective, invariable being, who really existed just so and not otherwise, is the only Socrates who might properly be described as a myth. The Socrates of Xenophon, the Socrates of Plato, the Socrates of Aristophanes are, one and all, the real Socrates; and, except to those obsessed with a false ideal of truth, there is nothing surprising in the apparently confused result. Even where there is obviously an element of fiction, as in the Aristophanic burlesque or in Plato's verbatim reports of conversations between persons dead, perhaps, before Plato himself was born, it by no means follows that we learn nothing of the real Socrates. Moreover, if we had no other evidence but the Platonic dialogues, we might still object that Socrates could assume a dozen different shapes, and might still draw the extremely bad inference that only one (if any) of them could be genuine. The truth, of course, is that Socrates was all these things. To the Xenophons of this world—honest, brave, intelligent, but a little prosaic —he gave as much of himself as they were capable of receiving; to Plato, much that he could not even verbally express to duller men, and much also that was only latent in his words. Thanks, too, to the art of Plato, we know pretty well how Socrates was seen and judged by those who brought him to his death; for in the masterly sketch of the *Meno* we have a perfect exposure of Anytus (the chief accuser) as the worthy and influential citizen, sincerely convinced that this ugly old critic of everything established and respectable was a danger to the State. On the other side we have not only the *Apology*, but the outrageous tribute of Alcibiades in the *Symposium*, together with many other illuminating sketches of this Protean Socrates, who revealed himself in flashes, but never sat for his portrait in any one rigid pose. Only when we have completely and finally abandoned the ideal of an objective truth discernible by all trained observers, an inflexible personal identity which alone is " historical ", can we begin to understand the influence of a man like Socrates; and only thus shall we find in our personal relations with other human beings a clue to the meaning of " revelation " in the religious sense. It was the Apostle of the Gentiles who declared that he had become " all things to all men ", but of God alone, " in whom is no variableness or shadow of turning ", can that be wholly true, for God alone has infinite ways of revealing himself.

Now Christians believe that in the life and death of Jesus—incidents barely mentioned by Roman historians—and in his resurrection, which writers like Tacitus and Pliny, had they heard of it, would have derided as fable, was given a manifestation of God. But, while in a superficial sense this revelation was open and visible, nothing can be less justifiable than to assume that it must have been easier for those who actually saw and knew Jesus to believe in his divinity than it is for us who cannot have that direct evidence. On the contrary, it must have been enormously more difficult, if only because they had abundance of excellent reasons for believing him to be a human being, in most ordinary respects just like themselves. Which of us, if told that a young man born in the next parish was to be venerated as God would even trouble to make further inquiries? The only question would be whether to be amused or shocked. A modern critic, who sets out to investigate the truths of Christianity, may, of course, reject the Christian interpretation of the evidence, but, whether he realizes it or not, his judgement will be formed in an atmosphere impregnated with ideas of Christian origin, and he will view the whole problem in a perspective which the contemporaries of Jesus inevitably lacked. They were much too close to the facts, and too much hampered by their own religious traditions. In particular, the Jewish anticipation of the Messiah, as one who would " restore the kingdom to Israel ", proved to be one of the greatest obstacles to the acceptance of a Saviour who proclaimed a kingdom of heaven open to all men, and not to be won by force of arms.

That Jesus himself was fully aware of these initial difficulties is evident. It was not only that the prophet had no honour in his own country: still more important was the fact that he could not reveal himself to the multitude, and indeed he never attempted to do so. When he did address a large audience, he made much use of metaphor and parable, leaving it to them to guess the interpretation as best they could. Who and what he was remained a secret, communicable, if at all, to none but the chosen few, and by them, it seems, never more than half understood. Again and again, in the gospel narrative, there is evidence of their failure to grasp either the purport of his actions or the meaning of his words. They stumbled along in the twilight of half-belief, with the result that one of the twelve finally betrayed him, while all the others, in the hour of peril, forsook him and fled. Let us at least, then, avoid the elementary mistake of imagining that the revelation of God in the human life of Jesus could be made in a plain straightforward way to anyone who enjoyed the opportunity; with the further suggestion, perhaps, that a full and faithful record of what Jesus actually said and did would have enabled us to dispense with all later interpretations, theologies, creeds, dogmas, and the whole paraphernalia of an orthodox Church. Not even the baldest historical fact can be wholly divorced from its " meaning ", and when the task of the observer, or at a later stage of the historian, is to read the character of a person, to suppose that a series of gramophone records, or a continuous film, would settle the question is simply childish. In that sense at least, the " Jesus of history " and the " original gospel " are no better than myths. " What manner of man is this ? " " Whom say ye that I am ? " From the very first these have been the crucial questions, and if we are looking for good examples of confused answers, we cannot do better than study the recorded experience of those who saw and knew Jesus, especially of the chosen few to whom he strove daily to reveal himself, but apparently in vain.

The history of the Christian religion is, in fact, the history of an expansion through a series of interpretations, each of which has been a new venture, usually involving the sacrifice of something believed to be essential. In the very first stage, terminated by the crucifixion, when the disciples were called upon to renounce their whole conception of the messianic kingdom, the demand was altogether too much for them, and so complete was their failure that, while Jesus hung on the cross, it is doubtful if a single one of them (unless it were John) retained a spark of faith. At the next stage, when belief in the resurrection (for no other explanation is tenable) had revived their courage and restored their hopes, their mental revolution was still far from complete. Instead of an immediate triumph during the earthly life of their master, they now began to expect this second coming at an early date, but their general outlook was still messianic, and only with great reluctance were they persuaded that the task imposed on them could be more than a special mission to the Jews. The real problem, however, when once the narrow boundaries of Judaism had been overstepped, was not so much racial or geographical as spiritual and intellectual. Within the bounds of the Roman Empire it was possible to travel with fair security, and at Athens or Ephesus it might well be easier than in Palestine to secure an audience for a new gospel. But what manner of audience would it be ? To the Jews, or at least to rabbis expert in the Law, the apostles were unlearned and ignorant men, who might succeed in leading the multitude astray, but would make no serious impression on the educated class. Similarly, when the door was opened to the Gentiles, it must have looked at first as if the teaching of the new sect would appeal to slaves, and perhaps to the humblest sort of freemen, but not to cultivated Roman society or to philosophical Greeks. Now success at that level, and only at that level, would in the end have been equivalent to failure; for it would have meant that the situation produced in the ancient world by the separation of philosophical theology from popular religion was not substantially altered by the new faith. In order to prove its catholicity, the Church had to find a place not only for the slave, but also for the emperor, not only for the uneducated masses, but for those who had turned away from the fables of polytheism to the systematic pursuit of wisdom, and, above all, had grasped the profound truth noted by Plato, that to be virtuous only " by custom, without philosophy " is to dwell in a house built on the shifting sands. Christianity, in fact, had got to be a philosophy, whether Christians liked it or not. Spiritual insight is granted, indeed, to the humblest souls, but it is not their exclusive privilege, in a sense that would debar from " salvation " all whose intellectual conscience, whose very appetite for truth, is the source of difficulties not to be evaded by the stifling of reason or by the facile assumption that all philosophy is arrogant and vain.

There are many gaps in the record, and how soon there was any conscious realization by Christian apologists of the inevitable conflict with other philosophies it is scarcely possible to say. S. Paul, no doubt, was quite ready to face Stoics and Epicureans, but although his Epistles are earlier in date than the Gospels in their present form, it may, of course, be objected that his version of Christianity is not precisely representative of those who saw and heard Jesus in the flesh. From that point of view at least, the Gospels are earlier, but the Gospels, again, cannot be taken indiscriminately. As we all know, three of them are classed as " synoptic ", while the fourth has a character of its own. T. H. Huxley once described it as " a theosophical romance of the first order ", and really, as the book might be judged by one who was frankly an unbeliever, it is not at all a bad description. It is easy, too, to understand how a mystic like Joachim of Flora (*ob.* 1202), when he propounded his curious " heresy " about the kingdom of the Spirit which (as the Son had succeeded the Father) was to succeed the kingdom of the Son, would find his chief support in this work. About its date and authorship I offer no opinion, but even if we ignore the special difficulty of the Prologue, it is clear, from the general quality of the material, that it represents a more advanced stage of reflection on the life and teaching of Christ than anything that we find in the simpler narratives of the other evangelists. Does it follow, then, that the traditional title of the Gospel " according to S. John " is unwarrantable, and that its substance cannot have derived from one of the original disciples? That inference, it seems to me, exemplifies the same egregious fallacy that induced a whole generation of scholars not only to prefer Xenophon's Socrates to Plato's, but also to argue that they could not both be historical. Even in the report of some trivial incident, if **there were three or four truthful eye-witnesses, it will be strange if you** do not get at least two discrepant stories, and not infrequently it is the agreement of witnesses rather than their difference that casts doubt on their testimony. When we turn from mere questions of fact to the appreciation of a personality, unanimity of judgement can mean only one of two things, either that the person under consideration was singularly lacking in what we call individuality, or that the witnesses' knowledge of him was very superficial. By no sound principle of criticism are we obliged to infer from the actual quality of the Fourth Gospel that its material cannot have been drawn from S. John. All we need assume is that one disciple—the one " whom Jesus loved "—had deeper insight than the others into his master's mind, and that when, in later life, he came to meditate more carefully on words and deeds originally, perhaps, only half understood, he was enabled (quite apart from any technical theory of " inspiration ") to offer an interpretation, or fashion a picture, that is in some respects unique. And that, of course, is precisely what we ought to expect. Before we can hope to understand the meaning of " revelation ", we must dismiss without fear or scruple the pseudo-scientific " Jesus of history ", so far as that expression implies that the nature of any personality, human or divine, can be disclosed, like abstract truth, in one and the same form to all methodical inquirers. Like any other human beings, Jesus revealed to each observer as much as he was capable of observing, and no more. That, in fact, is the only possible way of revelation; and just as, in his earthly life, the Saviour dealt variously with the beloved disciple, the half-hearted follower, the curious idler, the complacent Pharisee, the young man with great possessions, the traitor, the High Priest, the Roman Governor, and a host of others, so must it always be in the communication of the Divine Spirit to man.

Whatever, then, may be the exact truth about the date and authorship of the Fourth Gospel, its acceptance by the Church, when the time arrived for fixing the canon, as an authentic portrait was at least justified by a critical principle far superior to the crude assumption that contemporary witnesses are bound to agree. They are bound, on the contrary, to differ, and there is no reason whatever why words and acts of Jesus, unnoticed or forgotten by one member of the inner circle, should not have been regarded by another as supremely important. Analogous illustrations from the biographies of famous men might be quoted by the dozen, and if we prefer a modern example to Socrates, the enigmatic figure of Disraeli will serve very well. How would a sketch of him by Gladstone, or, for that matter, by one of his political allies like Lord Derby or Lord Salisbury, compare with an appreciation by Lady Blessington or Montagu Corry? Was he, as his enemies declared, no more than an adventurer, a sycophant, a charlatan, a picturesque imposter? Or shall we endorse the brief verdict of Bismarck: *Der alte Jude, das ist der Mann*? And even within the smallest circle of devoted admirers, is it certain that anyone quite understood the Disraeli of *Tancred* and *Lothair*? Again and again the " higher critics " have insisted on their right to apply to the New Testament the ordinary principles of historical criticism; but, as it seems to me, it is precisely in respect of those principles that they have so often and so conspicuously failed. " The Disraeli of history ", " the Socrates of history ", " the Jesus of history ": all alike are, in truth, so unhistorical that their only proper place is in what Huxley might have called a pseudo-scientific romance.

And yet, when all the early differences among Christians about the teaching of the Master, and all the early developments provoked by contact with the Gentiles, have been duly recognized and weighed, there is nothing in the New Testament so portentous as its silences, its calm indifference not only to the intellectual problems that exercise philosophers, but to all the complexities and requirements of human life which make up the general content of what we call " civilization ". Consider, for instance, the range of speculation in the *Summa* of S. Thomas, and ask yourself what any of the apostles (even S. Paul) would have made of it. Or pass on to the urgent practical questions of our own time, and seek illumination in the Gospels. Does anyone not blinded by prejudice seriously maintain that in the teaching of Jesus there is even the faintest thought of social reconstruction or political reform? Or again, can we detect any sign of interest in education, literature, the fine arts, natural science, or any other element of the culture which adorns and ennobles human life? Expressions like " Christian art " and " Christian civilization " are, indeed, familiar; but in what sense do we use them, and with what justification by chapter and verse? When Pliny examined the Christians, he was ready to admit (with some surprise) that they were morally respectable, but the rest of their religion he branded as *prava et exitiabilis superstitio*. A modern rationalist might soften the epithets, but should he object that the gospel of Christ, though well adapted to the needs of ignorant peasants and down-trodden slaves, makes no provision for the civilized world, what reply is the Christian to give?

Of the various possible answers, the easiest, and perhaps the commonest, is simply an evasion. The Christian religion, it may be argued, is concerned only with certain basic facts and certain imperative duties.

The sinfulness of man, the need for repentance, faith in redemption by the death of Christ, charity to all men, the hope of everlasting life; such is the essence of the gospel, and nothing else matters; while as for all this " culture ", at its best it is only a harmless diversion, at its worst a snare and delusion.   Now it is perfectly true that the Christian life thus defined and limited does embrace the most vital doctrine and practice of the Church.   Far be it from me to suggest that there are ninety-nine just persons (or even ninety-eight) who need no repentance, or that faith, hope, and charity are less important for the Christian than a taste for poetry or mathematics.   Nevertheless, I call this answer to our critic no solution, but only an evasion of a problem that, in the long run, it is fatal to evade.   To begin with, it is not historically true that the Church has won its victories in the past by thus refusing to meet its adversaries on their own ground.   Platonism was defeated, not because Justinian suppressed the Academy, but because Christianity was in- tellectually, as well as morally, superior; Averroism was defeated, not because Siger of Brabant and his friends were expelled from Paris, but because S. Thomas was a better Aristotelian, as well as a better Christian, than his opponents; and in the same spirit each fresh intellectual crisis must be faced.   It is not, however, of direct conflicts, or of philo- sophical controversy in its restricted sense, that I wish chiefly to speak. The wider question is whether profession of the Christian faith involves a purely negative attitude, a sort of polite indifference, to all those aspects of human culture about which the New Testament, as must freely be admitted, is almost silent.   Is there, in other words, any sense in talking of " Christian art ", " Christian civilization ", and so forth ? And even when it is impossible to pretend that the production of things beautiful and fine owed anything to Christian inspiration (Greek or Chinese art, for instance), does it follow that such things are wholly outside the Christian " philosophy ", or even that they are to be condemned ?

Christian casuistry has proved equal to most emergencies, but in the present case it is not necessary, I think, to have recourse to the dialectical niceties of an apology designed for the refutation of " Gigadibs the literary man ".   What we primarily need is a little reflection on the doctrines of Creation and Incarnation in which we are accustomed to profess our belief.   The Christian rejection of cosmic dualism, of a matter hostile to spirit, of body as the natural antagonist of soul, and of the attempt, common to most other philosophies, to find the origin of moral evil either in the bare fact of the soul's incorporation or in the physical functions common to man and other animals has revolutionized the whole theory of conduct and immensely amplified the field of action in which varieties of life and character may be expressed.   If nothing is originally evil, neither is anything in human nature beyond the reach of sin.   Hence there is no room for the delusive simplifica- tion by which the moral ideal can be represented as the total elimina- tion of the animal and corporeal element, or at least its total subjection to reason.   " Reason ", as we have seen, is a term full of ambiguities, but in so far as it means rationality—the power of reflecting, uni- versalizing, and taking thought for the morrow in a style impossible for animals gifted only with keen perceptions and appetites—there is no reason for counting it morally impeccable, and indeed no reason why a purely and perfectly rational being should not turn out to be Mephis- topheles himself.   On the other hand, when Christians, flying to the other extreme, denounce reason as the enemy of faith, take a pride in obscurantism, or fall into a foolish panic because some new philosophy or some great scientific discovery is advertised, they are in effect denying the doctrines of Creation and Incarnation no less than the pagans who looked upon matter as intrinsically evil, and found the very thought of associating the Son of God with a body degrading and profane.   If God created all things, then all things are " very good " : if Christ took our nature upon him, then all our natural and normal activities are glorified. It does not follow, of course, that all are equal in honour, but the sharp antithesis of reason to all other " faculties " belongs to the tradition of pagan philosophy, and on the whole is not helpful.   By Christians the campaign of life has to be waged in a spiritual country of almost unlimited dimensions.   On every object in the universe, and on every function of man's nature by which enjoyment and understanding of the universe can be obtained, the image of the creative goodness is stamped : yet every- where, too, by the taint of sin, the image may be distorted or obscured. Is it surprising, then, that experiments should be manifold, or that con- ceptions of the Christian life should be not merely diverse, but, to all appearances, conflicting ?

Nothing is evil but sin.   Yet, in view of the constant warnings against " the world " and its vanities, it is quite intelligible that, throughout the history of the Church, there should have been a tradition of austerity, expressed at one time or another in iconoclasm, in denunciations of pagan art and poetry, in the Puritanism which destroyed or mutilated so many exquisite things, in the " evangelical " horror of the theatre, and sometimes in a fanatical conviction that beauty of every kind was a satanic device.   That is one interpretation of the gospel, but against this dark and grim picture of the Christian life we can set the marvels of architecture in our churches, the new revelation of Latin in medieval hymns, the *Divine Comedy*, the mosaics of Ravenna and Monreale, the art of Giotto and Fra Angelico, the many developments of music associated with the liturgy; an endless catalogue, in fact, of beautiful forms which came to life in the Christian atmosphere, and could not, it is safe to add, have been fashioned in any other. Philosophies of art, with their laborious attempts to capture the essence of beauty, to determine the relation of æsthetic to moral judgements, and so forth, have usually been dismal productions, and we may be thankful that none has enjoyed dogmatic authority. Nevertheless, there is a genuine problem for Christians, and from these manifest discrepancies of practice there is an easy transition to perplexing mazes of theory and principle. Let me quote one brief illustration.

Some years ago, the bishop of an African diocese told me the story of one of his many strange experiences. Upon entering a native church which he had not previously visited, he was slightly disgusted to see hanging above the altar a large picture of a ballet-girl executing a high kick. Whether the innocent parishioners took it for a portrait of our Lady, or merely felt that their church was the right place for a beautiful object, he did not inquire; and against this rather touching example of *sancta simplicitas* he was too wise to protest. To our sophisticated minds, however, the story may suggest various reflections. That the picture, in the character of an altarpiece, was inappropriate will, I imagine, be generally agreed; but why? Probably it was a vulgar daub, but suppose it had been a masterpiece of its kind, would that have made any difference? None, surely, unless its artistic worth were an additional reason for removing it to another place. Given, then, that the ballerina had no business in the church, is our objection to her artistic or religious? Here, no doubt, there might be differences of opinion, but my own answer would be that, in a case of this kind, the distinction did not hold. In an obvious sense the picture was irreligious because its subject had nothing to do with the Christian faith, but that was also a conclusive artistic objection to its presence in a church. Suppose next that, in place of the dancer, we hang above the altar an artistically deplorable picture of the Crucifixion, or of the Holy Family, will its wretched quality be sufficiently increased by its subject, by the pious intention of the donor, or perhaps by its edifying effect? That is a more complicated question, which is actually presented in many forms, and most commonly, perhaps, by hymn-tunes and other liturgical music. The subject is too large, in fact, for adequate discussion, and I shall offer for consideration only one elementary principle, that if there is to be any meaning in the expression " Christian art ", the examples of it must be both artistic and Christian.   On the one hand, the suggestion (dear to the " broad-minded ") that all good art is religious is, I believe, empty rhetoric; on the other hand, a bad hymn-tune, though it may be sung with genuine fervour by a devout congregation, does not cease to be a bad hymn-tune, and God forbid that we should accept it as a specimen of " Christian art "!

My object, however, in thus seeking the moral of the bishop's story, is not to introduce a disputable philosophy of art and religion, but simply to point out once more that, while questions of this kind could not possibly be avoided by the Church, there is nothing about them in the New Testament, and least of all in the Gospels.   In a word, the disciples privileged to walk and talk with Jesus can never have received the slightest hint that they were expected to interest themselves in the intellectual or artistic culture of a civilized society.   And here, at the risk of rushing in where angels fear to tread, we are almost obliged to wonder whether Jesus himself, in his character as a man, knew or cared anything about such matters.   The technical doctrine of the *Kenosis* ("emptying") involved in the Incarnation goes back to the New Testament, and we need not dispute the right of theologians to discuss it.   Yet, in order to explain the silence of Jesus, we are not compelled to venture into those deep waters: nothing more is required than a little common sense.   Every teacher must consider the character of his audience and, in some degree, accommodate himself to their needs and capacity.   Now the first disciples belonged to a stratum of society which it might be difficult to compare accurately with any modern " class ", but which was certainly unpretentious and little versed in mental refinements.   Moreover, we have seen already that, far from receiving any sudden and " miraculous " illumination from their Master, they had the greatest difficulty in understanding him, and were frequently at a loss to guess what manner of man he was.   Consider, then, the utter absurdity of supposing that their minds could ever have been ripe for the examination of intellectual and artistic problems, none of them imminent, and some not destined to assume their proper shape for many centuries.

Or suppose, again, that we indulge our fancy, and imagine a Jesus born in other social circumstances, where he would naturally have come into contact with men steeped in the highest culture of the ancient world.   He might then have founded a school, more or less analogous to the Platonists or the Stoics, or perhaps to Hellenized Jews on the intellectual level of Philo.   And with what result?   Apart from

" miracle ", the only probable result would have been that Christianity, like all the ancient schools, would have declined and decayed with the change of intellectual fashions in the upper class, while the masses would never have been touched. As it is, those who affect to despise Christianity, because it was first preached to the vulgar, seem to overlook the fact that in a remarkably short time it began to spread to all classes, and to provide material for philosophical discussion by the acutest minds. Whereas Platonism and all the other recognized philosophies failed to spread downwards, because they had no message for the multitude, Christianity, which began at a modest point in the social scale, without intellectual pretensions, but was founded in the deep places of our common humanity, contained in itself the promise of endless developments, according to the needs and demands of every age. The gospel, in fact, was saved by those very silences that we are apt to find so perplexing. The truths revealed to the Church in its infancy were only those that were then necessary: all the others could await their appointed time.

Fas est ab hoste doceri. Macchiavelli was no friend of the Church, but no one has insisted more earnestly that every commonwealth must perish unless it contains within its own constitution the power of changing with the times: Spinoza was no Christian, but no one has perceived more clearly the tragic risks involved in the translation of eternal truth into positive law. Beyond all other societies the Church has had reason to acknowledge the force of these warnings. Schools of philosophy (after the first unfortunate experiment of the Pythagoreans) have had little to do with political government; the State, though it may dabble unwisely in ideologies, has in its proper nature nothing to do with eternal truth. For the Church, on the other hand, the two tasks, the doctrinal and the practical, are inseparable; on Christian truth depends Christian practice, while conversely, without the practice the truth cannot be discerned. Add to this that for a thousand years or so there was no such thing, in the Latin world, as the State, and at once the troubled course of ecclesiastical history, with all its confusions, blunders, wars, and persecutions, becomes intelligible. Some kind of orthodoxy, some kind of order and discipline there had to be, and thus with every fresh development of the spirit there could hardly fail to be some conflict with the letter of the law. Moreover, there is nothing in the origin and nature of the State analogous to the foundation of the Church upon a gospel believed to be divine, eternal, unchangeable, sufficient for all men and all time. Hence expediency itself is, for the State, no mere expedient, but a principle: *Salus populi suprema lex*, but in that sound maxim of statesmanship there is no room for private interpretation of the law, much less any concern for the salvation of the individual soul. For the Church, on the contrary, the recognition of individuality as a cause of endless variations is as vital as the conservation of principles which do not change. Neither the doctrinal unity affirmed in creeds nor the uniformity of practice enjoined by canon law, embodied in liturgies, or supported by informal custom, can alter the fact that faith and understanding are individual experiences, for which there is no substitute in mere acceptance of a formula or mere obedience to a rule.

Nevertheless, the true defence of ecclesiastical order, whether in doctrine, liturgy, or other matters of common usage, is not public policy, but the liberty of interpretation, entailed by the fact that divine truth can be, or rather, must be, imparted to each individual mind and spirit in accordance with its peculiar ability to receive. Once more, then, let us beware of false analogies and false ideals. Assent to propositions affirming the unity of God or the Incarnation can never mean that an identical significance is understood by the minds of all who repeat the creed. So again, the petitions of the Lord's Prayer are uttered daily by thousands of Christians, but with infinite variety of accent and personal reference. But, while there is nothing in the formal statements of Christian doctrine analogous to the impersonality of science, both in them, and still more in the forms of public worship, the best safeguard of personal religion is something resembling the impersonality of art. The fatal objection to extempore prayer, as a substitute for an ordered liturgy, is that it forces upon an entire congregation expressions and sentiments that may suit the mood of their author, but to many others may be uncongenial or positively offensive. And if even creeds and liturgies, though verbally fixed, can thus leave room for diversities of spirit, how much greater must be the wealth of possibilities revealed to different ages, different types of men, and different individuals by the original pattern of the Christian life. If the anchorite finds the peace of God in his lonely cell, while the missionary ranges far and wide; if one man is composing a *Summa* or decorating a cloister with frescoes, while another is wrestling with kings or emperors or preaching a crusade; if one rejoices in the bland seclusion of a country parish, while another gasps for air in a London slum; on what grounds, and by what authority, do we extol or disparage any one of these conceptions of the Christian life? A Stylites, a Duns Scotus, a Fra Angelico, an Innocent III, a George Herbert—one and all are utterly beyond the horizon of the apostolic age, and so are fifty other characters, lay or clerical, which it would need a brush far bolder than Fra Angelico's to depict.

Alternately, and with about equal frequency, the Church is accused of too much rigidity in its formulas and too little uniformity in its practice.   Both charges, however, should be received with equanimity, for both rest on the utterly false assumption that the truths of religion are, or ought to be, on a par with the scientific truths deduced by logical reasoning or verified by crucial experiment.   A scientific truth, once it is clearly understood, dictates a definite method of application, and any other method is wrong; but that is because it has reference only to abstract qualities and generic modes of behaviour, while individuality— if it cannot be entirely ignored—is merely a disturbing factor for which allowance can be made.   The Christian point of view is wholly different.   Dogmatic propositions had from time to time to be enunciated, and for sufficiently obvious reasons it would have been impossible to dispense with a creed.   Undoubtedly, too, the object of a creed is not to make a display of intellectual subtlety, but to indicate the grounds of Christian worship and the guiding principles of the Christian life.   But, instead of exhausting itself in general applications, instead of resting content with the external obedience exemplified by the good citizen who pays his taxes punctually and conforms to every Act of Parliament, the truth expressed or adumbrated in the language of dogma passes through the crust of formal documents to the manifold needs of individual human beings, and visits all the secret places of the soul.   The scientific universal is realized in " particulars " unlimited in number, but indistinguishable in kind: the Christian gospel discloses its meaning in an endless multitude of individuals, each one of whom, in his heart of hearts, is unique.   The Christian Church is a society united by a single loyalty and a common faith; but, though it declares its allegiance in forms of words and forms of worship consecrated by ancient usage, and not lightly to be varied with each fresh breeze of doctrine, this uniformity of expression no more imposes an inflexible pattern on the spirit of man than the possession of like sense-organs necessitates for all observers the same appreciation of beauty and an identical picture of earth and sky.   " The flight of the alone to the Alone ", said Plotinus in his memorable phrase.   Change it into " the flight of the unique to the Unique ", and it might pass as a true description of the Christian soul on its way to the knowledge and love of God, or rather, as a shadow of the truth.   God, indeed, and God alone, is absolutely unique, sufficient unto himself, related to nothing, resembling nothing, the only one.   Yet God reveals Himself as Love; not only as " *L'amor che muove il sole e l'altre stelle* ", but as the Love which came down from Heaven and died upon the cross. " He who loves God ", wrote Spinoza, " cannot strive to make God love him in return."   That is profoundly true, but only because, when love is freely given, there is no need to strive.

SHORT INDEX OF AUTHORS